Daily Mail

INCOME TAX

1995–96

Daily Mail

INCOME TAX

1995–96

For the year 6 April 1995 to
5 April 1996 in accordance with
the Budget proposals of November 1994

EDITED BY

KENNETH R. TINGLEY

ORION

The right of Kenneth R. Tingley to be identified as the
author of this work has been asserted by him in accordance
with the Copyright, Designs and Patents Act, 1988

While every effort is made to ensure accuracy, the publishers,
the editor, Associated Newspapers Ltd, their assigns,
licensees and printers cannot accept any liability for any
errors or omissions contained herein nor liability for any
person acting or refraining from action as a result of the
information contained in this book. The editor regrets that
he cannot reply to personal tax problems.

First published in Great Britain in 1995 by
Orion
An imprint of the Orion Publishing Group Ltd
Orion House, 5 Upper St Martin's Lane,
London WC2H 9EA

A CIP catalogue record for this book is available
from the British Library

ISBN 1 85797 687 8

Photoset in Monotype Garamond by
Selwood Systems, Midsomer Norton

Printed in Great Britain by
Butler & Tanner Ltd, Frome and London

Contents

Rates and Allowances 1995–96

Income tax is charged on an individual's income at the following rates for 1995–96:

Lower rate	20 per cent on first £3,200
Basic rate	25 per cent on next £21,100
Higher rate	40 per cent on the remainder

Several allowances and deductions may be made from income before calculating the sum chargeable to income tax. However, some allowances and deductions give rise to relief at the reduced rate of 15 per cent or the lower rate of 20 per cent only and are not available for relief at rates exceeding these levels. Modifications are also required where income includes dividends received from companies.

Allowances 1995–96

Additional personal allowance for children	£1,720
Blind person's allowance	£1,200
Married couple's allowance:	
age of elder spouse:	
below 65	£1,720
65 to 74	£2,995
75 and over	£3,035
Personal allowance:	
Taxpayer's age:	
below 65	£3,525
65 to 74	£4,630
75 and over	£4,800
Widow's bereavement allowance	£1,720

The tax system

THE ANNUAL BUDGET

At earlier times successive Chancellors of the Exchequer delivered their main Budget Statements outlining Government proposals for raising revenue during the Spring of each year. A further Statement, 'the Autumn Statement', was presented in the Autumn disclosing plans for future Government spending. The Budget Statement of 16 March 1993 was the last of its kind and has now been replaced by a single 'Unified Budget' delivered in late November, outlining the Government's spending and revenue collection proposals.

Following this tradition, the Chancellor of the Exchequer, Mr Kenneth Clarke, presented his Budget Statement on Tuesday, 29 November 1994. A few days later the Chancellor was compelled to announce a small number of changes following the Government's defeat on a proposal to increase the rate of value added tax on domestic fuel.

These minor changes apart, matters affecting both direct and indirect taxation are subsequently recorded in a Finance Bill. The contents of the Bill are then subjected to lengthy Parliamentary scrutiny, debate and amendment before becoming part of the law of the United Kingdom. The proposed changes announced by Mr Kenneth Clarke are discussed on the following pages and numerous examples illustrate the calculation of liability to taxation. As the proposals must be debated in Parliament it will not be overlooked that further amendments may be introduced at some later time before Royal Assent is eventually forthcoming shortly before 5 May 1995.

THE PERSONAL TAX SYSTEM

The system of personal taxation which applies for 1995–96 is based on taxable income arising, or that which is deemed to arise, during the year of assessment commencing on 6 April 1995, and ending on 5 April 1996. Many allowances and other deductions available to individuals must be set against income chargeable to tax. Where the deductions exceed chargeable income there is unlikely to be any liability. If surplus income remains the first £3,200 will be charged at the lower rate of 20 per cent and the next £21,100 charged at the basic rate of 25 per cent. Should chargeable income exceed £24,300 the excess is taxed at the higher rate of 40 per cent. These rates apply generally to both earned and investment income but some adjustment may be required where a taxpayer's income includes dividends or other distributions from a company. Adjustments will also be necessary for a number of allowances and deductions, notably the married couple's allowance, where relief is confined to the reduced rate of 15 per cent and cannot extend to any rate exceeding this level.

PAYE deductions made from earnings extend to income charged at all three rates, where earnings are sufficiently substantial. Tax at these rates will be collected simultaneously where business and professional profits, rents and other receipts are assessed directly on the taxpayer. Where income is received, or is treated as received, after deduction of income tax, further liability at the higher rate, if any, will be collected by direct assessment on the taxpayer.

Tax relief on many, but not all, payments of

mortgage interest is given under the MIRAS scheme by deducting income tax at the rate of 15 per cent from each payment made in 1995–96. Similar relief may be available on other payments made under deduction of income tax although some deductions are made at the basic rate of 25 per cent and others at the reduced rate of 12.5 per cent. This deduction procedure is merely a method of providing relief and has little effect on the net income tax liability eventually borne.

The unified personal tax system incorporating tax payable at all three rates is administered by Inspectors of Taxes and their staff.

INDEPENDENT TAXATION

Before the introduction of independent taxation on 6 April 1990, the income of a married woman 'living with' her husband was usually assessable to tax in the husband's name. However, with the inception of independent taxation this system was abandoned. It is now a well established feature of taxation in the United Kingdom that all individuals, whether married or single, are independently assessed to income tax. In the case of a married couple 'living together' each spouse is responsible for submitting his or her own tax returns, satisfying compliance requirements and discharging the amount of income tax due.

All individuals receive a basic income tax personal allowance, which may be increased for those aged 65 or over and further increased for those who have celebrated their 75th birthday. The amount of the increased personal allowance may be reduced where the individual's income exceeds stated limits. With the exception of severely limited transitional reliefs, any unused personal allowance of one spouse cannot be transferred to the other.

A married man whose wife is 'living with' him qualifies for a married couple's allowance. This allowance may be retained by the husband, shared in equal proportions with his wife or made entirely available to the wife. If the spouse to whom a married couple's allowance, or share of that allowance, has been allocated cannot fully absorb the allowance against income, the excess may be transferred for the benefit of the other spouse.

Apart from the personal allowance and the married couple's allowance, the only remaining allowances comprise:

a An additional personal allowance for children.
b A widow's bereavement allowance.
c A blind person's allowance.

Of these three allowances, only the blind person's allowance can be transferred from one spouse to the other where it cannot be fully absorbed by the qualifying spouse.

A number of special transitional allowances have been made available to ensure that the level of aggregate allowances granted after 5 April 1990 does not fall by reason only of the introduction of independent taxation.

Capital gains tax is also subject to independent taxation, with individuals being separately assessed. It is unnecessary to restrict the annual exemption to the combined gains of a husband and his wife as each may obtain his or her separate exemption. However, it remains possible for assets to be transferred between husband and wife 'living together' without incurring any capital gains tax commitments.

THE APPROACH TO INDEPENDENT TAXATION

When approaching the independent taxation of husband and wife the following steps are of great importance:

a The allowances which are available to each individual must be identified.
b The reliefs which each individual may obtain for outgoings must be established.
c The income of each individual must be accurately determined.
d The capital gains and capital losses realised by each individual must be separately calculated.

Where a husband and wife are 'living together' there may be an opportunity for allocating income and outgoings between the spouses to obtain the most beneficial result. These and other matters affecting the taxation liabilities of a husband and wife are reviewed on page 144.

SELF ASSESSMENT

For many individuals the existing system used to calculate profits, gains and income liable to income tax and that used to discharge liability is on the verge of a massive change. This change is explained by the impending introduction of self-assessment. A feature of self-assessment is that an individual will calculate the amount of income tax due and remit that amount to the Inland Revenue without awaiting a formal assessment. Those wishing to avoid this step may provide the Inland Revenue with details and require a calculation to be made on their behalf. Self-assessment will affect the discharge of income tax liabilities for 1996–97 with the first income tax returns being submitted by 31 January 1998 or, where the Inland Revenue are required to provide calculations, by 30 September 1997. The discharge of any capital gains tax liability will also be brought within self-assessment.

The system of self-assessment, which is outlined in greater detail in a chapter commencing on page 140, will not affect those whose only source of income is from an employment to which the PAYE deduction procedure applies.

If an individual is to calculate his or her own tax commitments some simplification in the existing tax system is required. In an endeavour to achieve a measure of simplification several significant changes are being introduced. For example, the complex 'preceding year' basis of assessment has for many years been used to measure profits arising from a trade or profession carried on by an individual. This is being abandoned and replaced by a new 'current year' basis. The new basis will apply generally for 1997–98 and future years with special transitional arrangements for 1996–97. However, new businesses commenced after 5 April 1994 are brought within the current year basis from their inception. Significant changes are also being introduced for the assessment of profits accruing to members of a partnership. A new current year basis will replace the long established preceding year basis where profits, gains or income arising overseas become chargeable to United Kingdom taxation. Finally, considerable changes are being introduced from 6 April 1995 governing the calculation of rental and other income arising from property in the United Kingdom.

Although the present work is primarily concerned with liability to taxation for the year ending on 5 April 1996, comments have been inserted to review the future effect of these most significant changes.

Liability to income tax

PERSONS LIABLE TO PAY TAX

All individuals whose incomes exceed £3,525 may be liable to income tax for 1995–96, but there are increased exemption limits for persons aged 65 or over. Most forms of income are assessable to income tax, although there are a number of exceptions. The following lists illustrate income which is, and that which is not, liable to tax. The lists are not intended to be exhaustive but provide an indication of the approach applied to many items of income experienced by a large number of taxpayers.

INCOME ASSESSABLE TO INCOME TAX

Annuities excluding the 'capital' portion of certain purchased life annuities.

Bank interest arising on deposits.

Benefits in kind made available to most directors of companies, and to employees earning £8,500 per annum or more. Certain benefits enjoyed by employees earning less than this sum may also be assessable.

Building society interest on deposits.

Christmas boxes to employees.

Dividends from companies.

Foster care contributions, should these exceed the cost of providing care.

Furnished letting receipts.

Interest on Government securities.

Interest on National Savings Income Bonds, Capital Bonds and First Option Bonds.

Pensions, whether voluntary or received under the terms of employment and whether received in respect of the recipient's services or those of another person.

Premiums from letting premises for periods which do not exceed fifty years (part only may be assessable).

Profits from businesses and professions.

Rents and other income from land and property.

Rent-free accommodation occupied by certain employees (income assessed by reference to a notional value).

Salaries, wages, bonuses, commission, and all other earnings from offices and employments. Voluntary payments made at the end of an employment and payments of compensation for loss of office are usually taxable, but liability may be limited to the excess of the aggregate sum received over £30,000.

Social security benefits. A list of those benefits which are taxable appears on page 158.

Tips received in connection with a business or employment.

INCOME NOT ASSESSABLE

Annuities paid to holders of the Victoria Cross, George Cross, Albert Medal, Edward Medal and certain other gallantry awards.

Bounty payments to members of the armed forces who voluntarily extend their service.

Compensation for loss of office and redundancy payments for loss of office, but where the aggregate receipts exceed £30,000 the excess is taxable.

Covenanted payments made under a voluntary non-charitable deed of covenant.

Dividends arising under Personal Equity Plans.

Dividends from Venture Capital Trusts.

Interest on contractual savings under the Save As You Earn scheme.

Interest on National Savings Certificates, Children's Bonus Bonds and Yearly Plans.

Interest arising under TESSA deposit schemes.

Maintenance payments under most Court Orders or agreements, although liability remains for payments under older arrangements.

National Lottery winnings.

National Savings Bank Interest. The first £70 of interest received on ordinary deposits with the National Savings Bank is exempt, but the excess will be taxable. This exemption does not extend to interest on investment deposits.

Payments in kind (where not convertible into cash or money's worth), except where received by most directors or by an employee earning £8,500 per annum or more. Certain benefits, received by employees earning less than this sum may also be taxable.

Premium Bond prizes.

Rent received under the 'rent a room' scheme where gross receipts do not exceed £3,250 or perhaps some lower figure.

Scholarship income.

Social security benefits. A list of those benefits which are not taxable appears on page 158.

Travel vouchers, warrants and allowances for members of the armed forces when travelling on leave.

3

Allowances

APPLICATION OF ALLOWANCES

Individuals may be entitled to a range of allowances and reliefs, depending on individual circumstances. Some reliefs, dealt with in later chapters, are based on the amount of qualifying expenditure which an individual has incurred. Other allowances are made available as of right and will apply to reduce or eliminate the amount of income tax payable. The availability of these allowances is reviewed in the present chapter. However, the method of providing relief for allowances must be carefully distinguished.

Firstly, some allowances, notably the personal allowance, are subtracted from the taxpayer's income and these reduce the amount of that income on which income tax must be paid. It follows that relief will be effectively obtained at the top rate of income tax suffered by the individual.

Secondly, and in complete contrast, other allowances, including the married couple's allowance, are given as a deduction in tax payable, usually at the rate of 15 per cent of the allowance. Therefore all taxpayers only obtain relief at this restricted rate whatever their maximum income tax commitment. Clearly, where income is small and there is little or no liability the application of relief at 15 per cent will only reduce tax payable to nil. The benefit of any excess allowance will then be lost.

HUSBAND AND WIFE LIVING TOGETHER

The nature and amount of the allowances which a married couple can claim may be affected by whether a husband and wife are 'living together'. This relationship of 'living together' will be treated as satisfied unless the couple are:

a separated under an order of a court of competent jurisdiction;
b separated by deed of separation; or
c in fact separated in such circumstances that the separation is likely to be permanent.

PERSONAL ALLOWANCE

For 1995–96 all individuals receive a personal allowance. The amount of this allowance is governed by the individual's age and in some cases by the level of income received.

Individuals below the age of 65 years receive a basic personal allowance of £3,525. The allowance

---

1
BASIC PERSONAL ALLOWANCE

Sue is 42 years of age and divorced. Her only income for 1995–96 is a salary of £13,750.

	£
Total income	13,750
Less Personal allowance . . .	3,525
	£10,225

Tax payable:	
On first £3,200 at 20 per cent . .	640.00
On balance of £7,025 at 25 per cent	1,756.25
	£2,396.25

2
INCREASED PERSONAL ALLOWANCE

George is a widower aged 78. He receives a social security retirement pension of £3,060 and taxable income from letting properties of £7,400.

Total income:

			£
Retirement pension	.	.	3,060
Letting income	.	.	7,400
			10,460
Less Personal allowance	.	.	4,800
			£5,660

Tax payable:

On first £3,200 at 20 per cent	.	640.00
On balance of £2,460 at 25 per cent		615.00
		£1,255.00

The maximum personal allowance can be allowed as the taxpayer is over the age of 74 years and his income does not exceed £14,600.

3
MARGINAL PERSONAL ALLOWANCE

Ethel is a widow aged 69. In 1995–96 she receives aggregate income of £11,500 from a social security retirement pension and a company occupational pension scheme administered by her late husband's employers. Interest of £4,000 (gross) is received from a number of deposits.

Total income:

			£
Pensions	.	.	11,500
Interest	.	.	4,000
			15,500

	£	
Less Personal allowance .	4,630	
Deduct one-half of excess over £14,600		
(£15,500 less £14,600)	450	4,180
		£11,320

Tax payable:

On first £3,200 at 20 per cent	.	640.00
On balance of £8,120 at 25 per cent		2,030.00
		£2,670.00

Part, or all, of the tax payable will be offset by tax deducted from interest received and PAYE deducted from payments made by the previous employer's pension scheme.

4
LOSS OF MARGINAL PERSONAL ALLOWANCE

Applying the facts in Example 3, let it be assumed that the investment income was increased to, say, £6,000, thereby increasing total income to £17,500.

The marginal personal allowance would then be calculated as follows:

		£
Maximum allowance	.	4,630
Deduct one-half of excess over £14,600		
(£17,500 less £14,600)	.	1,450
		£3,180

However, as the figure of £3,180 is less than the basic personal allowance of £3,525, no marginal personal allowance will be granted and the basic allowance will be obtained. The calculation continues:

Total income:

			£
Pensions	.	.	11,500
Investment income	.	.	6,000
			17,500
Less personal allowance	.	.	3,525
			£13,975

Tax payable:

On first £3,200 at 20 per cent	.	640.00
On balance of £10,775 at 25 per cent		2,693.75
		£3,333.75

is not affected by the amount of the individual's income.

For those who were 65 years of age or more at any time in the year ended 5 April 1996, the allowance will be increased to £4,630. A further increase to £4,800 is available to those who are 75 or over in the same year. In both cases the increased allowance will be forthcoming for an individual who died before reaching his or her 65th or 75th birthday if that age would otherwise have been achieved before 6 April 1996.

The amount of the increased allowance available to older taxpayers will be reduced if the total income of the individual exceeds £14,600 for 1995–96. Where this level is exceeded the increased personal allowance is reduced by one-half of the excess. This process continues until the personal allowance is reduced to the level of the basic allowance of £3,525 when no further reduction will be made. Where the taxpayer is a married man entitled to the married couple's allowance, the personal allowance will firstly be reduced, before reducing the married couple's allowance. When establishing the total income of an individual the income of that individual's spouse, if any, is ignored.

All individuals receive a personal allowance. Therefore both a husband and his wife will independently receive a personal allowance of £3,525, or some increased amount based on age, for 1995–96. Subject to an exception designed to smooth the introduction of independent taxation (see page 13), any unused personal allowance of one spouse cannot be transferred to the other.

Unlike some other allowances, relief for the personal allowance is not restricted to the reduced rate of 15 per cent, but is deducted when calculating the individual's top rate of tax.

The personal allowance is not confined to adults but can also be obtained by children of any age. There are, however, complex rules which prevent tax advantages being obtained by parents who transfer income-producing assets to their young children.

MARRIED COUPLE'S ALLOWANCE

Where a married man is 'living with' his wife throughout, or during any part of, the year ending on 5 April 1996, a married couple's allowance will be available. The amount of this allowance is also governed by the age of the parties to a marriage and perhaps by the level of the husband's income.

The basic married couple's allowance is £1,720. This may be increased to £2,995 if either the husband or the wife is 65 years or over at any time in the year ending on 5 April 1996. A further increase to £3,035 will be forthcoming if either spouse is 75 or over at any time in the year. In the case of a spouse who died during the year but would otherwise have reached the age of 65 or 75 respectively before 6 April 1996, the appropriate increase will be available.

It has been shown above that the increased personal allowance due to an single individual over the age of 64 may be reduced where that individual's total income exceeds £14,600 for 1995–96. A similar restriction may apply when calculating the increased married couple's allowance. To prevent the same restriction being applied twice over the order to be adopted for 1995–96 is as follows:

a Calculate one-half of the husband's total income (not including any income for the wife) in excess of £14,600.

b Reduce the personal allowance of the husband by the product of **a** but not beyond the basic allowance of £3,525.

5
BASIC MARRIED COUPLE'S ALLOWANCE

Peter and his wife Katherine are both below the age of 65 and 'living together'. Peter has earnings of £18,000 in 1995–96. Katherine receives a salary of £9,200 and interest of £250 (gross). No election has been made to transfer any part of the married couple's allowance.

Peter	£
Total income – earnings	18,000
Less Personal allowance . . .	3,525
	£14,475

Tax payable:	
On first £3,200 at 20 per cent . .	640.00
On balance of £11,275 at 25 per cent	2,818.75
	£3,458.75
Less Married couple's allowance – £1,720	
at 15 per cent	258.00
	£3,200.75

Katherine	
Total income:	£
Salary	9,200
Interest	250
	9,450
Less Personal allowance . . .	3,525
	£5,925

Tax payable:	
On the first £3,200 at 20 per cent . .	640.00
On the balance of £2,725 at 25 per cent	681.25
	£1,321.25

c Reduce the married couple's allowance by the product of **a**, less the amount of the reduction in **b**, but not beyond the basic married couple's allowance of £1,720.

The limitation under **c** is necessary to ensure that two different allowances are not both reduced by reference to the same amount of excess income. Subject to this, the reduction process continues until the married couple's allowance has been reduced to the basic allowance of £1,720 when no further reduction will take place.

A man may qualify for only one married couple's allowance for the year 1995–96, notwithstanding that one marriage terminates and a second marriage takes place in the same year.

There is a limitation in the amount of the married

6
MARGINAL MARRIED COUPLE'S ALLOWANCE

Joe and his wife Eileen are both 72 years of age and 'living together'. Joe's total income for 1995–96 is £17,400. Eileen has a total income of £4,450. No election has been made to transfer any part of the married couple's allowance.

Joe has an income of £17,400 which exceeds £14,600 by £2,800. Allowances must therefore be reduced by:

One-half × £2,800 =	.	.	.	.	£1,400

The personal allowance must be reduced as follows:

Full allowance	.	.	.	.	4,630
Less restriction	.	.	.	.	1,105
Revised allowance	.	.	.	.	£3,525

A restriction is necessary to ensure that the allowance is not reduced below the basic allowance of £3,525:

The married couple's allowance becomes:

	£	£
Full allowance		2,995
Less restriction . .	1,400	
Deduction applied to personal allowance .	1,105	295
Revised allowance . .		£2,700

Joe

	£
Total income	17,400
Less Personal allowance . .	3,525
	£13,875

Tax payable:

On first £3,200 at 20 per cent . .	640.00
On balance of £10,675 at 25 per cent	2,668.75
	3,308.75

Less Married couple's allowance – £2,700 at 15 per cent	405.00
	£2,903.75

Eileen

	£
Total income	4,450
Less Personal allowance . .	4,630
Tax chargeable on	NIL

7
MARRIED COUPLE'S ALLOWANCE – TRANSFER

For 1995–96 the business profits of Roy were only £4,650. He was 'living with' his wife Jane throughout the year and her income comprised a salary of £11,200. Neither spouse had any other income and both were under the age of 65. No election has yet been made to transfer any part of the married couple's allowance.

Roy is entitled to a personal allowance of £3,525 and a married couple's allowance of £1,720. The aggregate of these allowances exceeds his total income of £4,650 and there will be no liability to income tax. Roy may transfer the unused married couple's allowance to his wife. If he agrees, the amount to be transferred is calculated as follows:

	£	£
Married couple's allowance . .		1,720
Less Total income . . .	4,650	
Deduct personal allowance	3,525	1,125
To be transferred		£595

If total income was reduced to, say, £3,000 the maximum married couple's allowance capable of being transferred could not exceed £1,720, the amount of the allowance. The unused personal allowance cannot be transferred unless the special transitional reliefs discussed on page 13 apply.

Jane

	£
Total income	11,200
Less Personal allowance . . .	3,525
	£7,675

Tax payable:

On first £3,200 at 20 per cent . .	640.00
On balance of £4,475 at 25 per cent	1,118.75
	1,758.75

Less Married couple's allowance – £595 at 15 per cent	89.25
	£1,669.50

couple's allowance for 1995–96 where the marriage takes place after 5 May 1995. This limitation is discussed on page 103.

As a transitional measure, the married couple's allowance may occasionally be available to a husband who separated from his wife before 6 April 1990 (see page 15). Further transitional relief may be obtained by elderly persons who would otherwise suffer a disadvantage from the introduction of independent taxation (see page 14).

8

MARRIED COUPLE'S ALLOWANCE – ELECTION

Adapting the facts in Example 5, on page 8, let it be assumed that an election was made by Katherine to take one-half of the married couple's allowance.

Peter

		£
Total income – earnings	. . . .	18,000
Less Personal allowance	. . .	3,525
		£14,475

Tax payable:

On first £3,200 at 20 per cent	. .	640.00
On balance of £11,275 at 25 per cent		2,818.75
		3,458.75
Less Married couple's allowance – £860 at 15 per cent	. . . .	129.00
		£3,329.75

Katherine

		£
Total income:		
Salary	. . . . .	9,200
Interest	. . . . .	250
		9,450
Less Personal allowance	. . .	3,525
		£5,925

Tax payable:

On first £3,200 at 20 per cent	. .	640.00
On balance of £2,725 at 25 per cent		681.25
		1,321.25
Less Married couple's allowance – £860 at 15 per cent	. . . .	129.00
		£1,192.25

Married couples are provided with the following alternatives where a married couple's allowance is available for 1995–96. These alternatives were also available for the previous years, 1993–94 and 1994–95.

a To take no action with the allowance being allocated to the husband only.

b For the wife to elect, as of right, to take one half of the basic allowance of £1,720, leaving the remaining one-half allocated to the husband.

c For the couple to elect jointly that the entire basic married couple's allowance should be given to the wife, with no part of that allowance being absorbed by the husband.

The elections available under **b** and **c** must be restricted to the basic married couple's allowance of £1,720. It is not possible for individuals over the age of 64 years and receiving an increased allowance to include the amount of the increase in any election.

Subject to two exceptions, an election will only be effective for a year of assessment if it is made before the commencement of that year on 6 April. The first exception enables the election to be made not later than 5 May, if HM Inspector of Taxes was notified before the previous 6 April that an election would be forthcoming. The second exception deals with the year of marriage and enables an election to be made at any time in that year.

Once made, an election continues indefinitely for each succeeding year until it is withdrawn. The time limits for withdrawal are similar to those which govern the ability to make an election.

Where a joint election has been submitted under **c** for the wife to take the entire basic married couple's allowance, the husband can subsequently elect to retrieve one-half of that allowance. This election also must be made within the normal time limits.

It is possible that the husband or wife to whom all or part of the basic married couple's allowance has been allocated cannot utilise the entire allowance due to an absence of income. The spouse involved may then give written notice transferring the unabsorbed part to the other spouse. This option is also available to a husband who obtains that part of the married couple's allowance in excess of the basic allowance.

Rate of relief

For 1993–94 and earlier years the married couple's allowance was deducted from total income and therefore achieved relief at the individual's top rate of income tax. However, for 1994–95 relief was restricted to the reduced rate of 20 per cent and further restricted to 15 per cent for 1995–96. This restriction is achieved by subtracting relief, at 15 per cent for 1995–1996, from the amount of tax otherwise payable. Relief for the married couple's allowance is not given by deducting that allowance from the taxpayers' total income.

ADDITIONAL PERSONAL ALLOWANCE

An additional personal allowance of £1,720 may be available to:

a A woman who is not, throughout the year ended 5 April 1996, married and living with her husband.

9
ADDITIONAL PERSONAL ALLOWANCE

Peggy is a divorced mother aged 43, with an eleven-year-old daughter and a nine-year-old son living at home. She has not remarried and earns a salary of £12,500 for 1995–96.

		£
Total income	.	12,500
Less Personal allowance . .	.	3,525
		£8,975
Tax payable:		
On first £3,200 at 20 per cent .	.	640.00
On balance of £5,775 at 25 per cent	.	1,443.75
		2,083.75
Less Additional personal allowance –		
£1,720 at 15 per cent .	.	258.00
		£1,825.75

b A man who is neither married nor living with his wife for the whole or any part of the year. A man separated from his wife but who may claim the special transitional married couple's allowance discussed on page 15 must be excluded.

c A man who, for the whole or any part of the year, is a married man living with his wife, if the wife is totally incapacitated by physical or mental infirmity throughout the entire year.

To obtain the additional personal allowance the claimant must show that a qualifying child is resident with him or her for the whole or part of the year. Only one allowance of £1,720 is available, notwithstanding the number of qualifying children.

The expression 'qualifying child' means a child:

a born during the year ending on 5 April 1996, or

b under the age of 16 years on 6 April 1995, or

c over the age of 16 on 6 April 1995, and either receiving full-time instruction at a university, college, school or other educational establishment or undergoing training for a trade, profession or vocation throughout a minimum two-year period.

It is also necessary to demonstrate that the qualifying child:

a is a child of the claimant, or

b not being a child of the claimant, was either born during the year ended 5 April 1996, or under the age of 18 years on 6 April 1995, and maintained

for the whole or part of the succeeding twelve-month period by the claimant at his own expense.

'Child' includes a stepchild, an illegitimate child if the parents have subsequently married, and an adopted child under the age of 18 years at the time of the adoption.

A woman may be married and living with her husband during part of the year of assessment. She will only qualify for the additional personal allowance if the qualifying child is resident with her during that part of the year when she was not living with her husband, i.e. following separation.

A man who marries during the year may elect to forgo the married couple's allowance and obtain the additional personal allowance for that year should that allowance otherwise be available; a course of action which would usually be advantageous.

Where a man and woman are unmarried but living together as husband and wife it is not possible for both to obtain the full additional personal allowance for different children. In this situation the claim must be limited to the youngest of the qualifying children only. In those cases where two or more individuals can each claim the allowance for the same child, the allowance can be divided between them in whatever proportions may be agreed.

The additional personal allowance will often be claimed by a separated spouse or divorced former spouse, having custody of a child or children. It will also be available to other single persons, including widows, and a married man with an incapacitated wife, if of course there is at least one qualifying child.

An individual who qualifies for the additional personal allowance of £1,720 also receives the lower personal allowance of £3,525 (or perhaps more if the individual is over 64). These two allowances aggregate £5,245, which is identical to the aggregate of the personal allowance and the married couple's allowance available to a married man. It will therefore be apparent that a single parent family is effectively taxed on a basis similar to that of a married man 'living with' his wife.

The additional personal allowance cannot be transferred and is available only to the claimant.

Rate of relief

The additional personal allowance was deducted from total income and therefore obtained relief at the individual's top rate of income tax for 1993–94 and earlier years. For 1994–95, however, relief was restricted to the reduced rate of 20 per cent and further restricted to 15 per cent for 1995–96. Like the married couple's allowance, relief for the additional personal allowance is given by subtracting an amount from tax otherwise payable.

WIDOW'S BEREAVEMENT ALLOWANCE

Where a husband and wife are 'living together' and the husband dies the widow is entitled to a widow's bereavement allowance. The allowance is available for the year in which death occurs. It will also be available for the following year only, unless the widow remarries in the year of her late husband's death. For 1995–96 the amount of the allowance is £1,720.

A widow entitled to the widow's bereavement allowance of £1,720 for 1995–96 also receives a personal allowance of £3,525 (or perhaps some greater amount if the widow is over 64). The aggregate of these two allowances is £5,245, which is identical to the aggregate of the personal allowance and married couple's allowance available to a married man 'living with' his wife. In addition, a widow with a qualifying child or children may also obtain the additional personal allowance of £1,720.

10
WIDOW'S BEREAVEMENT ALLOWANCE

John and Margaret were 'living together' until 15 October 1995, when John died. The two children of the marriage, aged fourteen and eleven, continued to reside with their mother. Margaret's total income for 1995–96, comprising a salary, a pension and taxable social security benefits, amounted to £10,600. No part of the married couple's allowance was transferred. The tax payable by Margaret will be calculated as follows:

	£
Total income	10,600
Less Personal allowance . . .	3,525
	£7,075
Tax payable:	
On first £3,200 at 20 per cent . .	640.00
On balance of £3,875 at 25 per cent .	968.75
	1,608.75
Less Widow's bereavement allowance – £1,720 at 15 per cent	258.00
Additional personal allowance – £1,720 at 15 per cent	258.00
	516.00
	£1092.75

It is a necessary requirement that immediately before the time of his death the husband and wife were 'living together'. The widow's bereavement allowance will not usually be available if the parties were separated at that time.

The widow's bereavement allowance is available only for the year of assessment in which the husband dies and for the immediately following year and cannot be obtained for future years. The allowance is confined to widows and there is no similar allowance for widowers.

Further information governing the liability of parties to a marriage where one spouse dies will be found on page 104.

The widow's bereavement allowance is available to the widow only and cannot be transferred to any other person.

Rate of relief

In earlier years the widow's bereavement allowance was deducted from total income and achieved relief at the individual's top rate of income tax. However, in line with the changes affecting the married couple's allowance, relief is restricted to the reduced rate of 20 per cent for 1994–95 and further restricted to 15 per cent for 1995–96. It is given as a deduction from income tax payable.

BLIND PERSON'S ALLOWANCE

An individual who, at any time in the year ending on 5 April 1996, is registered as blind on a register maintained by a local authority may obtain a blind person's allowance of £1,200. Although the allowance is only available for a year of assessment during which registration has been made, it may also be granted in the year before initial registration, if proof of blindness was available in that earlier year.

The blind person's allowance available to a husband may exceed the balance of total income remaining after making deductions for other allowances and reliefs. If the husband is a married man living with his wife any unused excess of the blind person's allowance may be transferred to the wife.

It is possible that the wife cannot use her own blind person's allowance. She may then transfer the unused blind person's allowance to her husband.

A transfer from either spouse to the other will only be effective if it is evidenced by written notice given by the transferor within a period of six years following 5 April 1996.

Unlike some other allowances, relief for the blind person's allowance is not restricted to 20 or 15 per cent.

11
BLIND PERSON'S RELIEF

Eric is a single man aged 35 and registered as blind. His only income for 1995–96 is a salary of £6,400.

	£	£
Total income		6,400
Less Personal allowance . .	3,525	
Blind person's allowance	1,200	4,725
Tax chargeable on		£1,675
Tax payable:		
On £1,675 at 20 per cent . . .		£335.00

TRANSITIONAL RELIEFS

When changing from the old pre April 1990 system of taxing husbands and wives to the present system of independent taxation it was the intention that the change should not result in any increased income tax liability due to the reduction or loss of allowances. There were, however, three situations where a fall in allowances could occur, and special transitional reliefs have been introduced to prevent this. These situations concern:

a Husbands with insufficient income to absorb the personal allowance.
b Husbands with older wives.
c Separated couples.

The transitional reliefs affect only couples who were married before 6 April 1990, and can have no application to those who marry subsequently.

It must be emphasised that the great majority of taxpayers will not be affected by these special transitional reliefs, which are discussed below.

TRANSITIONAL RELIEF – HUSBANDS WITH LOW INCOMES

Where the income of a husband is insufficient to absorb the personal allowance it is not normally possible to transfer any unused allowance to his wife. However, it may be possible for the wife to obtain the benefit of the unused allowance where the parties were married before 6 April 1990. The first step is to establish the amount of the husband's unused personal allowance transferred to the wife in 1990–91. For this purpose a distinction must be made between marriages taking place before 6 April 1989, and those taking place on or after that date but before 6 April 1990.

Marriage before 6 April 1989
To obtain the transitional allowance for 1990–91 in the case of marriages taking place before 6 April 1989, it must be shown that:

a a husband and wife were living together for the whole or part of both 1989–90 and 1990–91;
b no wife's earnings election was in operation for 1989–90; and
c the allowances available to the husband for 1989–90 (including married man's allowance, wife's earned income allowance and blind person's allowance) exceeded the aggregate of:

  i the husband's total income for 1990–91, and
  ii the allowances available to the wife for 1990–91 (including married couple's allowance and blind person's allowance).

Where these requirements are satisfied and there is such an excess the wife may obtain a special transitional allowance for 1990–91 equal to that excess.

Marriage after 5 April 1989
To obtain the transitional allowance for 1990–91 in the case of marriages taking place during the year 1989–90 it must be shown that:

a a husband and wife were 'living together' for the whole or part of 1990–91; and
b the allowances available to the husband for 1989–90 (disregarding any wife's earned income relief) exceeded his total income for 1990–91.

Where these requirements are satisfied and such an excess arises the wife may obtain a special transitional allowance equal to the amount of that excess. However, if the allowances available to the wife for 1990–91 (including married couple's allowance and blind person's allowance) exceed the lower of:

a the wife's total income for 1989–90, and
b the allowances available to the wife for 1989–90 (excluding any additional personal allowance, widow's bereavement allowance or allowances transferred from the husband),

the transitional allowance must be reduced by the excess, or perhaps eliminated.

The transitional allowance will not be available for 1990–91 unless the husband provides written consent on Form 575 within a period of six years after 5 April 1991. It will also be necessary for the husband to transfer the married couple's allowance and any blind person's allowance to his wife.

The allowance for 1995–96

If the special transitional allowance is to be obtained for 1995–96 it must be shown that:

a the transitional allowance was made to the wife for 1990–91;

b the transitional allowance was also made to the wife for each of the years 1991–92, 1992–93, 1993–94 and 1994–95; and

c the couple are 'living together' throughout or during some part of 1995–96.

Where these requirements are satisfied, the transitional allowance capable of being transferred to the wife for 1995–96 will comprise the smaller of:

i the transitional allowance given to the wife in 1994–95, less any increase in the personal allowance and married couple's allowance given to the wife for 1995–96 over that for the previous year;

ii the husband's personal allowance for 1995–96 which he cannot use.

This calculation ensures that once there is a year in which the transitional allowance is not available, or not claimed, no allowance will be forthcoming in any future year.

TRANSITIONAL RELIEF – HUSBANDS WITH OLDER WIVES

For 1989–90, before the introduction of independent taxation, a married man 'living with' his wife was entitled to an increased married man's allowance (often referred to as an age allowance) where the older of the two was above the age of 64 years, or perhaps 74 years if relevant. Whilst the age of the older spouse governs the married couple's allowance for 1990–91 and future years, it is only the age of the husband which determines the amount of his personal allowance for those years. The possibility therefore arises that where a husband falls in a lower age group than his wife there could be a loss of allowances as between the old basis and the new. This possibility is removed by providing the husband with a special transitional personal allowance for 1990–91 and future years in place of the personal allowance which would otherwise be available.

To obtain the special personal allowance the husband must show that he qualified for an increased age allowance in 1989–90 because his wife's age fell into a higher age group (over 64 or over 74 years). It must also be demonstrated that the amount of the 1989–90 allowance exceeded the aggregate of the personal allowance and married couple's allowance available to the husband for 1990–91 or a future

12

TRANSITIONAL ALLOWANCE – HUSBAND WITH LOW INCOME

Brian and Mary, both under the age of 65, had been married for many years. In 1990–91 Brian was unable to use any part of his married couple's allowance and the entire allowance of £1,720 was transferred to Mary. A claim was also made under the special transitional provisions for part of Brian's personal allowance to be transferred to his wife. As a result, £435 was transferred. Similar claims were made in 1991–92, 1992–93, 1993–94 and 1994–95 which resulted in a transfer of £100 in the later year. The entire married couple's allowance was transferred in each year.

The following information was obtained for 1995–96:

a Brian's total income was £3,225

b Mary's income was £16,500

c The married couple's allowance of £1,720 was transferred by Brian to Mary

The special transitional allowance representing part of Brian's personal allowance which can be transferred to Mary will be the lower figure produced by the following calculations:

	£	£
i Transitional allowance for 1994–95	.	100
Less Increase in allowances to Mary:		
1995–96 £3,525 + £1,720	5,245	
1994–95 £3,445 + £1,720	5,165	80
		£20
		£
ii Brian's personal allowance 1995–96		3,525
Less income 1995–96 . .		3,225
		£300

The smaller figure is £20 and this will comprise the special transitional allowance available to Mary for 1995–96.

Brian has no income tax liability for 1995–96 and the tax payable by Mary becomes:

	£	£
Total income		16,500
Less Personal allowance . .	3,525	
Special transitional allowance . .	20	3,545
		£12,955

Tax payable:		
On first £3,200 at 20 per cent . .		640.00
On balance of £9,755 at 25 per cent		2,438.75
		3,078.75
Less Married couple's allowance – £1,720 at 15 per cent		258.00
		£2,820.75

Transitional relief will continue for future years until it is overtaken by increases in allowances or Brian's ability to use his personal allowance in full.

year. In this situation the husband's personal allowance will be:

a £3,400 if the wife was over 64 but not over 74 in 1989–90, or

b £3,540 if the wife was over 74 in that year.

The amounts of £3,400 and £3,540 comprise the single personal allowance (or age allowance) available for 1989–90 for those in the appropriate age group and replace the personal allowance which otherwise applies based on the husband's age. The special personal allowance for 1995–96 may be reduced if the husband's income exceeds £14,600.

The special personal allowance will continue for future years until the parties cease living together or the allowances exceed the level of the age allowance for 1989–90. The basic personal allowance has been increased beyond £3,400 for several years. It follows that relief under **a** can no longer apply. Nor will relief be available under **b** once the husband reaches the age of 65 and can obtain a personal allowance of £4,630. This transitional relief must therefore be confined for 1995–96 to a husband below the age of 65 and entitled to a personal allowance of £3,525 whose wife is 75 years or more.

The special allowance cannot be obtained if a wife's earnings election was in force for 1989–90.

The special personal allowance can also be obtained by a separated husband maintaining his wife if the requirements outlined below are discharged.

TRANSITIONAL RELIEF – SEPARATED COUPLES

For 1989–90 and earlier years an increased married man's personal allowance was available to a husband 'living with' his wife, unless a wife's earnings election was in force. Exceptionally, the married man's allowance could be obtained by a husband separated from his wife if she was wholly maintained by him and the husband obtained no tax relief for the cost of providing maintenance. As no married couple's allowance can be obtained for 1990–91 and future years in this situation the separated husband could be at a disadvantage from the introduction of independent taxation. To remove this possibility a special transitional married couple's allowance may be available. This allowance can only be obtained if:

a The couple ceased to live together before 6 April 1990;

b The couple have remained husband and wife;

c The wife has been wholly maintained by her husband;

13
SPECIAL PERSONAL ALLOWANCE

William will celebrate his 65th birthday on 4 July 1996. His wife, Anne, was 65 on 18 October 1989. This enabled William to obtain a married man's age allowance of £5,385 for 1989–90, as there was no restriction due to income exceeding the, then, income limit of £11,400.

The allowances available to William for 1995–96 were:

	£
Personal allowance (below 65) . . .	3,525
Married couple's allowance (wife over 64)	2,995
	£6,520

The aggregate allowances of £6,520 exceed the age allowance of £5,385 for 1989–90. As a result no special transitional allowance will be available.

d The husband cannot obtain any tax relief for sums paid to his wife as maintenance; and

e The husband was entitled to the married man's personal allowance for 1989–90.

Where these several requirements are satisfied the husband can obtain a special transitional married couple's allowance, based on the age of the older party, for 1995–96. The husband cannot transfer any part of an unused married couple's allowance to his separated wife, the wife cannot claim a special transitional personal allowance where the husband's income is small, and any blind person's allowance cannot be transferred between the parties.

The special transitional married couple's allowance continues for later years until the conditions shown above cease to be satisfied. Once this stage has been reached no further transitional relief will be available.

Rate of relief

In line with restrictions which apply to the married couple's allowance, the special married couple's allowance produces relief at the reduced rate of 20 per cent for 1994–95 and 15 per cent for 1995–96.

INDEXATION

The tax legislation contains provisions for index-linking the allowances discussed above, with the exception of the blind person's allowance. This is achieved by increasing the allowances in line with changes in the retail prices index. Similar index-linking may be applied to income tax rate bands. However, Parliament may disregard changes in the retail prices index and impose some increased or smaller adjustment, or no adjustment at all.

The basic personal allowance, the income limit for age related allowances and the tax rate bonds were increased by reference to increases in the retail price index for the year to 30 September 1994. Greater increases were made in the personal allowance for individuals over the age of 64 to offset the fall in relief to 15 per cent for the married couple's allowance. However, no increase was made in those allowances giving rise ro relief at the reduced rate of 15 per cent.

How to obtain allowances

IN NORMAL CASES the allowances, shown on the previous pages, are given in arriving at the tax payable, or in fixing the code number used for PAYE purposes. The allowances cannot be granted unless the Inland Revenue are informed of the taxpayer's personal circumstances and for this purpose a proper claim must be made. A suitable form, namely an Income Tax Return, may be obtained from the local office of HM Inspector of Taxes, if one has not been received without request. The completion of the claim portion of the form is simple but the information *must* be inserted as follows:

Personal allowance
All individuals receive a basic personal allowance. Those aged over 64 years should indicate their date of birth in the space provided. This will enable any increased personal allowance to be calculated. There is a further space for those wishing to claim the special transitional personal allowance.

Married couple's allowance
A man must insert the full Christian or other forenames of his wife and should indicate the date of marriage, if during the previous income tax year, in order that the allowance may be claimed for that year also. Special boxes require the insertion of an 'X' if the increased married couple's allowance is being claimed for older taxpayers or the special transitional allowance is being claimed for those separated before 6 April 1990. It must be stated whether the couple are 'living together'. A further box is available for the insertion of an 'X' if a transfer notice form is required.

Additional personal allowance
It is necessary to indicate whether the qualifying child for whom an allowance is claimed resides with the claimant. Details of the child's age and other information should be given, together with a note of any other person claiming for the same child. If the claim is being made by a married man on the grounds that his wife is incapacitated, the nature of the incapacity and whether it is likely to continue throughout the year of claim should be stated.

Blind person's allowance
The date of registration and the name of the local authority with whom registration was made should be recorded.

Death and superannuation benefits
The name of the friendly society, union or scheme concerned, the full year's contribution and the part attributable to death benefits.

Note
Many taxpayers arrange to have these matters handled by qualified accountants who are expert in tax affairs and can ensure that allowances are properly claimed and that no more tax is paid than the law requires.

Pension contributions

PENSIONS FROM THE STATE

The provision of a pension or lump sum payment arising on retirement, disablement or some other event is of considerable importance. Most individuals will qualify for pensions or other social security benefits provided by the State. These may arise in several differing forms but there are two main headings. Firstly, there is a general entitlement to the basic social security retirement pension. Secondly, an additional pension may be due under the State Earnings-Related Pension Scheme (SERPS) which is available to those who have been in employment. The level of the basic retirement pension is determined annually, with increases becoming payable from the beginning of April. In contrast, the additional pension provided by SERPS is governed by the amount of Class 1 national insurance contributions paid within upper and lower limits. The volume of additional pension payments is growing as contributors reach retirement age and in an attempt to reduce the escalating cost the value of this pension (but not the retirement pension) will fall from a future date.

It has long been possible to 'contract out' from the SERPS scheme, where a satisfactory alternative pension arrangement was made under a scheme linked with an individual's employment. Previously contracting out implied a reduction in both primary and secondary Class 1 contributions to eliminate the SERPS element of those contributions. With the introduction of personal pension schemes on 1 July 1988, the ability to contract out has been increased without directly reducing the level of con-

tributions. Contracting out may also be achieved by employees contributing additional voluntary contributions.

There are no particular taxation reliefs or advantages which can be obtained when securing title to the basic retirement pension or the additional pension, or indeed other social security benefits, with the exception of relief for Class 4 contributions paid by the self-employed (see page 33).

However, many individuals will increase the future level of retirement and other benefits by involvement in an employer's occupational pension scheme, a retirement annuity scheme or a personal pension scheme during their working lives.

OCCUPATIONAL PENSION SCHEMES

Many directors and employees pay contributions to an approved occupational pension scheme or superannuation fund. Individual arrangements differ but are designed to provide pensions or other benefits in the event of an individual's death or retirement. The rules of the scheme or fund must be approved by the Inland Revenue before tax relief can be obtained, both by the contributors and by trustees or other persons administering the arrangements.

Maximum annual contributions paid by a director or employee must generally be limited to 15 per cent of earnings. Contributions payable under most occupational pension schemes usually fall below, perhaps substantially below, this limit but it is possible for individuals to make additional voluntary contributions (AVC's) provided the limit of 15 per cent is not exceeded. AVC's may be paid to trustees or others administering an occupational pension scheme. Alternatively, it is possible to make 'free standing' AVC's to an insurance company or other qualifying institution of the employee's choice.

Any contributions paid to trustees or others administering an approved occupational pension scheme qualify for tax relief when calculating the liability of the payer. Relief is usually given by deducting the approved contributions from earnings arising from the office or employment. This ensures that the earnings chargeable to income tax are reduced by the amount of the approved contributions and PAYE deductions limited to the net sum. However, where 'free standing' AVC's are paid these are usually discharged after deducting income tax at the basic rate of 25 per cent. This provides full relief at that rate but where the contributor is liable to the higher rate of 40 per cent further relief will be forthcoming. The introduction of a 20 per cent income tax band does not affect the ability of a contributor to deduct, and to retain tax at the basic rate from payments of 'free standing' AVC's.

Difficulties may sometimes arise in determining whether the amount of contributions to be paid on 'free standing' AVC's will exceed the permissible limit. This can only be verified if detailed information is forthcoming on the amount of contributions made to the employer's scheme. However, unless the AVC's exceed £2,400 in any year a check will only be applied when the contributor retires. Any excess contributions will then be returned, subject to a tax charge.

The primary purpose of paying contributions is to provide a pension to the contributor on retirement, or to the spouse or dependants of the contributor following death. For older contributors the pension will usually be limited to two-thirds of final salary. Whilst the two-thirds approach is retained, an initial earnings cap of £60,000 was placed on the maximum amount of final salary for new schemes introduced after 13 March 1989, and for individuals joining existing schemes after 31 May in the same year. This supported a maximum pension of £40,000 per annum for those joining after these dates, although increased amounts applied for earlier entrants.

The ceiling of £60,000 not only applied to determine an individual's final salary but also governed the maximum amount of earnings which could be recognised when calculating contributions capable of being paid. However, the initial ceiling may be index-linked to changes in the retail prices index. Approached on this basis the earnings cap has been increased on several occasions to the following levels:

Year of assessment					Amount £
1990–91.	.	.	.	.	64,800
1991–92.	.	.	.	.	71,400
1992–93.	.	.	.	.	75,000
1993–94.	.	.	.	.	75,000
1994–95.	.	.	.	.	76,800
1995–96.	.	.	.	.	78,600

It is often possible to take a tax-free lump sum at retirement and a reduced pension subsequently. For those joining after the dates mentioned above the maximum lump sum will be limited to one and a half times the earnings cap.

The maximum pension and other benefits which can be provided by an approved occupational pension scheme may be considered insufficient by the prospective pensioner. However, it is possible for an employer to set up an unapproved 'top-up' scheme providing additional pension rights. Contributions to this scheme will not secure tax reliefs and there are other taxation disadvantages, but the existence of an unapproved scheme will not, of itself, affect recognition of a qualifying scheme.

Occupational pension schemes remain unaffected by the introduction of personal pension schemes, but it is no longer mandatory for an employee to remain, or indeed to become, a member of an employer's scheme.

RETIREMENT ANNUITIES
Self-employed individuals, together with directors and employees not in pensionable employment, cannot retain membership of an occupational pension scheme. For many years it has been possible for these individuals to secure annuities or lump sums payable on retirement or death under retirement annuity arrangements. Premiums paid to obtain an annuity or lump sum may entitle the payer to tax relief if, but only if, a number of conditions are satisfied. Both the conditions governing relief and the application of that relief are briefly discussed below, but it is not possible to conclude *new* retirement annuity arrangements after 1 July 1988. Contributions paid after this date in respect of arrangements concluded previously will, however, continue to obtain relief. The inability to conclude new retirement annuity arrangements is explained

by the introduction of personal pension schemes, discussed later, which retain most but not all of the features to be found in retirement annuity arrangements.

It is a necessary requirement that the retirement annuity contract or other document is drafted in a form approved by the Inland Revenue but in general the contract will:

a provide the taxpayer with a life annuity in retirement;

b provide an annuity for the spouse of the taxpayer or for one or more dependants of that individual; or

c provide a lump sum on the death of the individual before he or she attains the age of 75.

Where these requirements are satisfied, any premiums paid qualify for relief in calculating liability to income tax. Premiums paid in a year of assessment are primarily allocated to that year. However, the taxpayer may elect to treat the payments as having been made in the previous year, or in a year falling two years before the year of payment if there were no net relevant earnings in the previous year. Individuals deriving relevant earnings from Lloyd's underwriting activities may relate premiums paid back to even earlier years.

Relief for premiums paid, or treated as paid, in a year of assessment is not to exceed 17.5 per cent of the contributor's net relevant earnings for that year. This percentage may be increased to the levels shown by the following table for 1995–96 for those over the age of 50 on 6 April 1995:

Age on 6 April 1995	Percentage
51 to 55.	20
56 to 60.	22.5
61 and above	27.5

'Net relevant earnings' comprise the taxpayer's earned income, after subtracting capital allowances and losses. Personal outgoings, such as mortgage interest, may be ignored. The earnings cap of £78,600 which applies to restrict the amount of earnings on which personal pension scheme contributions can be based has no direct application to retirement annuity premiums.

Where the premiums relate to a contract falling under b or c above, the allowable premiums are limited to 5 per cent of the individual's net relevant earnings for the year of assessment. However, the figure of 17.5 per cent, suitably increased for older taxpayers, represents the maximum relief which can be obtained for all premiums falling under a, b and

c paid by the claimant. This maximum figure cannot be further increased by the addition of premiums falling within the 5 per cent restriction.

It is possible that the full potential relief for a year of assessment has not been obtained, due to an absence of sufficient premiums paid. This unused relief may be carried forward for a maximum period of 6 years and applied to relieve premiums paid which exceed the 17.5 per cent (or higher) limitation in future years. The relief is given for the year of assessment in which premiums are paid, or treated as having been paid, and not for the year in which the unused relief arose. Once the six-year period has expired the unused relief can no longer be carried forward and will be lost.

Unused retirement annuity relief can be carried forward in this manner and set against future excess contributions paid under personal pension schemes.

PERSONAL PENSION SCHEMES

On 1 July 1988, personal pension schemes were introduced in place of retirement annuity contracts. Personal pension schemes do not replace occupational pension schemes, which continue largely undisturbed. Overlapping is avoided by ensuring that earnings from a pensionable employment carrying membership of an occupational pension scheme cannot be taken into account when calculating relief under personal pension scheme arrangements. Thus an individual whose sole source of income arises from an employment, and who is a member of the employer's occupational pension scheme, cannot contribute to a personal pension scheme unless he ceases membership of the employer's scheme. An individual who receives earnings supporting membership of an occupational pension scheme and who also receives non-pensionable earnings from a different source may incorporate the latter earnings in a personal pension scheme. Any shortfall in benefits arising under an occupational pension scheme can be overcome by contemplating the payment of AVC's, either to trustees administering the scheme or under 'free standing' contracts.

With the exception of retirement annuity arrangements commenced before 1 July 1988, and which continue subsequently, personal pension schemes entirely replace those arrangements. This is achieved by precluding the introduction of any new retirement annuity arrangements on and after 1 July 1988.

As the name implies, personal pension schemes are 'personal' to the individual concerned. A scheme is retained when an individual changes jobs or becomes self-employed, although arrangements may be made to transfer from a personal pension scheme to an occupational pension scheme where an individual becomes a member of such a scheme.

Scheme requirements

Contracts for personal pension schemes are made between the individual and an approved institution including assurance companies, banks, building societies and friendly societies, among others. Each contract must be approved by the Inland Revenue and provide one or more of the following benefits:

a an annuity payable to the contributor and commencing on reaching an age between 50 and 75 years. A reduced age may apply by reason of early retirement on the grounds of ill-health, or perhaps engagement in an occupation where it is customary to retire before reaching 50;

b a lump sum not exceeding 25 per cent of the value of the annuity when it first becomes payable, with a correspondingly reduced future annuity;

c an annuity payable to the surviving spouse or dependants on the death of the contributor;

d a lump sum payable on the death of the contributor before reaching the age of 75;

e the return of contributions with interest and bonuses on the death of the contributor.

Allocation of contributions

Contributions paid under a qualifying personal pension scheme entitle the contributor to tax relief. It is possible for an individual to contemplate involvement in two or more schemes simultaneously, but a limit is placed on the aggregate relief which will be forthcoming for contributions paid.

Any contributions paid in a year of assessment ending on 5 April will be primarily allocated to that

------------------------------- 14 -------------------------------
ALLOCATION OF CONTRIBUTIONS

On 29 September 1995 Harry paid a qualifying contribution of £6,000 (gross). In the absence of an election the contribution will be treated as paid in the actual year of payment, namely 1995–96.

However, not later than 5 July 1996 Harry may elect to treat the contribution as having been paid in 1994–95 (or perhaps in 1993–94 if there were no net relevant earnings for 1994–95).

By re-allocating the contribution in this manner it may be possible to obtain relief for an earlier year which would otherwise be lost.

year. However, within a period of three months following the end of the year of assessment in which payment is made the taxpayer can elect for contributions to be treated as paid in the previous year, or perhaps earlier if there were no net relevant earnings in the previous year or earnings arose from Lloyd's underwriting activities.

Limitations on relief

The maximum contributions paid, or deemed to be paid, in a year of assessment and which qualify for relief in that year are not to exceed 17.5 per cent of net relevant earnings. This percentage may be increased to the following levels for 1995–96 for those over the age of 35 on 6 April 1995:

Age on 6 April 1995	Percentage
36 to 45.	20
46 to 50.	25
51 to 55.	30
56 to 60.	35
61 and above	40

Where the personal pension scheme produces entitlement to a lump sum falling under **d** above the maximum contributions qualifying for relief and attributable to that scheme are not to exceed 5 per cent of net relevant earnings. This limitation of 5 per cent is not to increase the total relief above the 17.5 per cent (or higher amount for older taxpayers) level.

When applying the appropriate percentage to net relevant earnings for 1989–90, any excess of those earnings above £60,000 must be disregarded. This is in line with the earnings cap which applies to members of an occupational pension scheme, but the limit may be increased annually as the retail prices index increases.

Such increases have occurred subsequently to the following levels:

Year of assessment	Maximum £
1990–91.	64,800
1991–92.	71,400
1992–93.	75,000
1993–94.	75,000
1994–95.	76,800
1995–96.	78,600

Occasionally, both an employee and his or her employer may pay contributions under a personal pension scheme taken out by the employee. Any contributions discharged by the employer will be subtracted from the maximum amount on which the employee can otherwise obtain relief.

'Net relevant earnings' will comprise most items of income arising from an employment, office, trade or profession, after subtracting capital allowances and losses, among other items. There must be excluded earnings from an office or employment which entitles the employee to membership of an occupational pension scheme.

15
CALCULATION OF RELIEF

Sandra, a single woman aged 34, had profits of £39,000 assessable for 1995–96. On 24 November 1995, she paid a contribution of £6,000 under an approved personal pension scheme. The contribution remained allocated to the year of payment.

			£
Total income .	. . .	. .	39,000
Less contribution .	. .	.	6,000
			33,000
Less Personal allowance	. .	.	3,525
			£29,475

Tax payable:	
Lower rate:	£
On first £3,200 at 20 per cent . .	640.00
Basic rate:	
On next £21,100 at 25 per cent . .	5,275.00
Higher rate:	
On balance of £5,175 at 40 per cent .	2,070.00
	£7,985.00

Unused relief
Contributions attributable to a year of assessment may fall below the maximum relief calculated by applying the 17.5 per cent, or some other increased, level. The unused relief may then be carried forward for a maximum period of 6 years and applied to relieve contributions paid in a future year which exceed the 17.5 per cent (or other) limit for that year. Relief is given for the year in which contributions are paid, or treated as paid, and not in the year during which unused relief arose.

Transitional relief
The method of providing relief for contributions paid under approved personal pension schemes is similar to that which applies to premiums paid under the 'old' retirement annuity arrangements. This close

relationship is recognised by transitional provisions which effectively preserve aggregate relief. For example, unused relief arising before 1 July 1988 under the retirement annuity regime could be carried forward within the six-year period and absorbed by excess personal pension scheme contributions. In addition, personal pension scheme contributions paid after 1 July 1988 could be carried back within the normal time limits and used against income for earlier years as if those payments were made under retirement annuity arrangements.

It is possible for an individual to pay both retirement annuity contributions and personal pension scheme contributions in the same year of assessment. Where relief is available for both, retirement annuity contributions are afforded priority. Before contemplating payments under both headings in the same year expert advice may well be required. This will recognise that whilst the earnings cap does not apply to retirement annuity arrangements, those arrangements may attract a reduced percentage of earnings supporting relief.

Deductions of tax
Personal pension scheme contributions will be discharged net, after deducting income tax at the basic rate of 25 per cent where the relevant earnings are assessable under Schedule E. Deduction and retention of tax in this manner provides the contributor with relief at the basic rate. This remains unaffected by the lower rate band of 20 per cent. Other contributions, namely those discharged by self-employed individuals, are paid gross and relieved when assessing relevant income. Relief at the higher rate will be given separately.

Contracting out
As an inducement to invest in a personal pension scheme employees are provided with a 'contracting out' option. This is limited to those paying Class 1 national insurance contributions and can have no application to the self-employed. The purpose of contracting out is to remove the SERPS contribution element from Class 1 contributions. Unlike contracting out for members of an occupational pension scheme, the full Class 1 contributions are paid both by the employer and by the employee. The Department of Social Security will then contribute towards the employee's own personal pension scheme a sum representing:

a the employer's contribution to the SERPS element, grossed up at 25 per cent; and

16
CARRYING FORWARD UNUSED RELIEF

In the absence of sufficient premiums paid, Andrew had the following amounts of unused relief for earlier years:

	£
1989–90	740
1990–91	1,620
1991–92	5,800
1992–93	2,900
1993–94	3,250
1994–95	1,760

Andrew's net relevant earnings for 1995–96 were £40,000. He paid contributions of £17,000 on a qualifying personal pension scheme policy which were allocated to 1995–96. Assuming Andrew was 40 years of age on 6 April 1995, and therefore qualified for the increased relief calculated at the rate of 20 per cent, these contributions will be absorbed as follows:

	£
Maximum relief for 1995–96 20 per cent of £40,000	8,000
Unused relief brought forward (earlier year first)	
1989–90	740
1990–91	1,620
1991–92	5,800
1992–93	840
Total relief available for 1995–96	£17,000

Unused relief available for future years (subject to six-year time limit)

	£
1992–93	2,060
1993–94	3,250
1994–95	1,760
1995–96	NIL

If Andrew is a married man with no other income, and entitled to the full married couple's allowance, the tax payable for 1995–96 becomes:

	£
Total income:	
Business profits	40,000
Deduct personal pension contributions	17,000
	23,000
Less Personal allowance	3,525
	£19,475

Tax payable:	
On first £3,200 at 20 per cent	640.00
On balance of £16,275 at 25 per cent	4,068.75
	4,708.75
Less Married couple's allowance – £1,720 at 15 per cent	258.00
	£4,450.75

b the employee's contribution to the SERPS element not grossed up.

In addition, for a period of years ending on 5 April 1993, the payment was increased by a bonus representing 2 per cent of the employee's earnings used to calculate the SERPS element, or £1 per week, whichever is the greater. A further bonus of 1 per cent applies from 6 April 1993, for employees who have reached the age of 30.

Contracting out will only be permitted where the personal pension scheme provides a pension equal to that otherwise due under SERPS. Thus before electing to contract out individuals must recognise the loss of a future SERPS additional pension. Contracting out may also be possible for employees who contribute towards 'free standing' AVC's which provide a sufficiently substantial alternative pension.

Husband and wife
Independent taxation requires that the relevant earnings of a husband and his wife are calculated separately and relief given to each individual without regard to the affairs of the other.

Taking an annuity
When a benefit is first taken from a personal pension scheme and an annuity becomes payable, a suitable annuity must be purchased with proceeds from the scheme. If annuity rates are low this purchase will provide a lower annuity in contrast to that which could be obtained if annuity rates were high. Previously it has not been possible for the scheme member to postpone the purchase of an annuity once a benefit is first taken from the scheme. However, from the Spring of 1995 a scheme member may exercise his or her right to defer taking an annuity. This will enable the purchase of an annuity to be deferred until, hopefully, annuity rates improve and an increased annuity will be forthcoming. Pending such a purchase the member may withdraw from the scheme sums of an amount not exceeding that which would have become payable if the annuity had actually been purchased on the initial date.

Also from the Spring of 1995, an annuity need not necessarily be purchased from a financial institution in the United Kingdom. It is now possible for the annuity to be obtained from a limited range of approved insurance companies operating in a Member State of the European Community. However, the overseas body must have a representative in the United Kingdom. The existence of United Kingdom representation is required to ensure that the PAYE scheme of tax deduction will apply to future payments of any annuity. This scheme now applies generally to all annuities paid under personal pension scheme arrangements.

5

Interest paid

MANY INDIVIDUALS make payments of interest, particularly on mortgages or loans obtained to acquire their own homes. These individuals are entitled to income tax relief for interest paid if, but only if, a number of conditions are satisfied. When approaching this matter there are two quite separate problems to be resolved, namely the identity of the interest which qualifies for relief and also the manner in which that relief can be granted. For many payments of mortgage interest made after 5 April 1995, relief is restricted to the reduced rate of 15 per cent. This restriction does not extend to other qualifying interest payments.

No relief will be forthcoming for payments of interest on a bank overdraft or similar facility, unless those payments can be included in the calculation of business profits. Relief for other payments which do not comprise a business outlay will only be available if interest is payable on a debt incurred to finance expenditure falling under one of the headings discussed below. If the requirements of these headings are not satisfied the interest cannot qualify for relief when calculating the payer's liability to income tax.

PRIVATE RESIDENCES – MORTGAGE INTEREST

Occupation by borrower

Interest paid on a loan applied to acquire land or buildings in the United Kingdom or the Republic of Ireland will qualify for relief, if at the time the interest is paid the property is used as the borrower's only or main residence. Relief also extends to interest paid on a loan to purchase caravans and houseboats used for a similar purpose.

For interest paid within a period of twelve months, or perhaps longer at the discretion of the Inland Revenue, from the date of borrowing, relief will also be available should the property be used for a qualifying purpose at any time within the twelve-month period. In such cases it is immaterial whether the property was actually used at the time interest was paid.

The recent fall in property values has created many situations, known as 'negative equity', where the value of a property is less than the outstanding mortgage. This may prevent the owner of that property finding a purchaser and acquiring a new home as the sale proceeds may not be sufficient to discharge the outstanding mortgage. However, it may be possible to overcome this difficulty and retain an entitlement to interest relief if:

a interest is being paid on a qualifying loan used to acquire the old property; and

b the lender agrees to substitute the new home for the old as security for the loan.

Although this arrangement will not result in the old loan being applied to acquire the new home, relief for interest paid will be forthcoming if the new home is a qualifying residence. Before agreeing to this 'substitute' arrangement, lenders will be anxious to ensure that the value of security is not reduced.

Occupation by dependent relatives and others

Relief may also be available for interest paid on a loan applied before 6 April 1988 to purchase land, buildings, caravans and houseboats used as the only or main residence of:

a a dependent relative of the borrower; or
b a former or separated spouse of the borrower.

Occupation by a dependent relative will only be recognised if the property is provided rent-free and without other consideration. The expression 'dependent relative' when applied to an individual identifies a relative of that individual, or his spouse, who is incapacitated by old age or infirmity from maintaining himself. It also includes the mother or mother-in-law of the individual if she is widowed, living apart from her husband or divorced.

This relief for property occupied by a dependent relative, a former spouse or a separated spouse is only available where the loan was applied before 6 April 1988. No relief will be forthcoming for interest on loans applied on or after that date. It also remains a condition for obtaining relief that the individual occupying property before 6 April 1988 continues to occupy the same property when future payments of interest are made on 'old' loans. Should the 'old' loan be replaced by a new loan, no relief can be allowed for interest on the replacement loan.

Improvement loans

The relief mentioned above was previously available for interest paid on a loan applied to improve property occupied by the borrower, a dependent relative or a former or separated spouse, as a qualifying residence. However, relief cannot apply to interest on any home improvement loan granted after 5 April 1988, unless the loan is used to finance the construction of a new building for occupation by the borrower and otherwise satisfying the remaining requirements governing relief. Interest on loans obtained before 6 April 1988 continues to obtain relief. Should an older loan be replaced by a new loan on or after this date, no relief will be available for interest on the replacement loan.

Limitations of relief

A limitation is placed on the maximum amount of interest paid by an individual in the year ending on 5 April 1996 which can qualify for relief. This limitation is imposed by restricting relief to interest on loans of £30,000. It is the amount of the qualifying loan, or loans, which establishes relief and not the amount of interest paid. £30,000 is an overriding maximum, incorporating all qualifying

loans falling under this heading. Any loans applied after 5 April 1988 which fail to qualify for relief may be disregarded when calculating the limit.

Notwithstanding independent taxation, a husband and wife 'living together' cannot each obtain the benefit of the £30,000 limit. This limit applies to the aggregate amount of qualifying loans made to a husband and his wife. As will be seen later (page 30) there is considerable flexibility in selecting the spouse who can be treated as having paid interest qualifying for relief. Unfortunately, this flexibility has lost a great deal of its former attraction with relief being restricted to 15 per cent for interest payments made after 5 April 1995.

A problem may sometimes arise where a man and a woman were each obtaining relief for interest paid on loans of £30,000. If the couple subsequently marry, the limit of £30,000 will apply to the aggregate loans of both. This will result in a substantial reduction in the amount of future interest qualifying for relief.

Joint owners

The ceiling of £30,000 was previously applied to loans made to an individual, with an aggregate limitation of £30,000 for husband and wife 'living together'. This approach continues for loans applied for a qualifying purpose before 1 August 1988. It was, however, considered unfair that two or more unmarried persons occupying a single property could each obtain relief for interest paid on maximum loans of £30,000, in contrast to a husband and wife who were limited to relief for interest on aggregate loans of £30,000 only. In the case of loans applied on and after 1 August 1988, this anomaly is removed by restricting relief to £30,000 for all loans, or joint loans, affecting a single property. The maximum relief for interest on £30,000 will be shared equally between the several individuals involved. However, where there are unequal contributions, with the result that the interest paid by one individual is less than his or her share of interest on £30,000, the balance may be transferred to other joint borrowers.

If the joint contributors include a husband and wife, each spouse counts as a separate share. These persons retain the ability to vary each other's shares, providing that the aggregate shares allocated to husband and wife are not altered (see page 30).

Bridging loans

It has previously been pointed out that a property must be used for a qualifying purpose at the time interest is paid, or be so used within a period of

17
JOINT OWNERS

On 15 October 1989, three unmarried friends, Peter, Paul and Mary borrowed £90,000 to purchase a house which they subsequently occupied as their only residence. Peter borrowed £40,000, Paul £30,000 and Mary £20,000. Interest of £8,100 (gross) paid in 1995–96 was shared in these proportions.

Although each individual has borrowed a different amount, the limit of £30,000 must be shared equally, namely £10,000 each. Therefore the relief available to each joint owner will be calculated as follows:

Interest attributable to £30,000:

$$\frac{30,000}{90,000} \times £8,100 = \underline{£2,700}$$

Each individual will obtain relief on:

$$1/3rd \times £2,700 = \underline{£900}$$

18
JOINT OWNERS – RESTRICTION

Adjusting the facts in Example 17, let it be assumed that Mary contributed a loan of £5,000, with Peter contributing £50,000 and Paul £35,000. Mary has been allocated interest relief on a loan of £10,000 but this must be limited to her actual contribution of £5,000. The balance of £5,000 will be re-allocated between Peter and Paul on the basis of their otherwise disallowed loans. This produces the following shares of the qualifying loan:

	£	£
Peter		
Basic allocation . . .	10,000	
Add		
$\frac{40,000}{65,000} \times £5,000$ . .	3,077	13,077
Paul		
Basic allocation . . .	10,000	
Add		
$\frac{25,000}{65,000} \times £5,000$ . . .	1,923	11,923
Mary		5,000
		£30,000

Relief for aggregate interest of £2,700 will be allocated on this basis also.

twelve months following the acquisition date, before relief for interest will be forthcoming. This may give rise to difficulty where an individual moves from one property to another and delay is experienced in selling the old asset. To reduce hardship, interest paid on the old loan will usually continue to qualify for relief for a period of twelve months, and perhaps longer, following the cessation of use. In such cases the upper limit of £30,000 will apply separately to both the old and the new loan. This provides the exception to the general rule that relief will be limited to interest on qualifying loans not exceeding £30,000.

It was previously a condition of the extended relief that the individual obtained a fresh loan to acquire the new home. The relief was not available for individuals who moved into rented accommodation or acquired a new home without the assistance of mortgage facilities. This restriction no longer applies and relief is now available to all those moving from their homes, provided the 'old' property is placed on the market for sale.

Other matters

Subject to the exception which applies on leaving property, and the withdrawal or restriction of relief for new loans applied after 5 April or 31 July 1988, relief can only be obtained for interest paid in relation to the only or main residence. Where an individual retains two or more residences, for example a town house used on weekdays and a country cottage occupied at weekends, it is not possible to choose the qualifying dwelling, as it only remains to determine which is 'the' main residence.

This selection may prove troublesome where husband and wife are 'living together' and each owns a separate property. The selection must be made, but where a husband uses, or intends to use, a property as his only or main residence and the wife uses, or intends to use, some other property for a similar purpose, the property first acquired must be taken as the qualifying residence.

Employees earning £8,500 or more and directors who receive loans either interest-free or at a rate of interest falling below a commercial rate may be assessed to income tax on the benefit arising. However, where the notional interest creating the taxable benefit would produce relief by applying the above rules, if actually paid, a reduced liability to tax may arise (see page 56).

JOB-RELATED ACCOMMODATION

Some employees may be required to reside in living accommodation provided by their employer for the purpose of carrying out the obligations of employment. This accommodation will normally comprise the employee's only or main residence and prevent relief being obtained for interest paid on a loan applied to acquire some other property. However, relief will be forthcoming for interest paid on a loan applied to purchase land, a building, a caravan or a houseboat which is also used as a residence by such an employee, or is intended to be used as the only or main residence on some future occasion, perhaps following retirement, where a number of conditions are satisfied. Included in these conditions is the requirement that living accommodation provided by the employer must be job-related. Living accommodation will only be job-related:

a where it is *necessary* for the proper performance of the duties of the employment that the employee should reside in that accommodation; or

b where the accommodation is provided for the *better performance* of the duties of the employment, and it is one of the kinds of employment in the case of which it is *customary* for employers to provide living accommodation for employees; or

c where, there being a special threat to the employee's security, special security arrangements are in force and the employee resides in the accommodation as part of those arrangements.

Most company directors are precluded from satisfying requirements a and b.

The availability of relief for interest paid by an employee occupying job-related accommodation is extended to certain self-employed individuals. These individuals must be carrying on a trade, profession or vocation and in this capacity be contractually bound to occupy living accommodation. This requirement will be satisfied if the taxpayer's spouse is similarly bound. Examples will include the proprietor of licensed premises required to reside in those premises under arrangements with brewers. The requirement cannot be satisfied where accommodation is supplied by certain persons closely associated with the self-employed individual.

In the case of both employed and self-employed individuals, relief for interest paid remains governed by the ceiling of £30,000. In addition, payments made after 5 April 1995 give rise to relief at the reduced rate of 15 per cent only.

LOANS TO PURCHASE LIFE ANNUITY

Where at least 90 per cent of monies borrowed are applied to purchase an annuity ending on death, and the borrower is at least 65 years of age, interest on the borrowings may qualify for limited relief. It is a condition that the loan is secured on land in the United Kingdom or the Republic of Ireland, and that either the borrower or the annuitant uses the land as his or her only or main residence. This requirement is relaxed where the individual leaves the property as relief will remain available for interest paid in the succeeding 12 month period, and perhaps longer. Should the borrowing exceed £30,000, only interest calculated on this figure will be allowable. Higher rate income tax relief cannot be obtained for payments made after 5 April 1991, but relief continues to remain available at the basic rate of 25 per cent and is not limited to the reduced rate of 15 per cent.

PARTNERSHIPS

Interest paid to finance the purchase of an interest in a trading or professional partnership will qualify for relief without limitation. This relief will also extend to interest paid on monies borrowed which are applied as a contribution towards capital or loans and made to the partnership for use in the business. Relief is confined to persons who are members of the partnership at the time any interest is paid.

Where a loan is taken out after 30 March 1994 as part of an arrangement to refinance borrowings by the partnership, there may be some restriction in the amount of relief which can be obtained.

INDUSTRIAL CO-OPERATIVES

Interest on a loan obtained by an individual for the purpose of contributing capital to an industrial co-operative may be relieved in full.

EMPLOYEE CONTROLLED COMPANIES

Interest paid on a loan used to acquire ordinary shares in an employee controlled company will usually qualify for relief where paid by an employee of that company. The company's shares must not be quoted on a stock exchange, and several further conditions require satisfaction before relief will be forthcoming.

CLOSE COMPANIES

Interest paid to finance the purchase of ordinary shares issued by a company retaining 'close company' status may often be relieved in full. This relief extends also to interest paid on monies which are reapplied in loaning funds to such a close company for use in its business. If the individual paying interest does not retain a significant shareholding, he or she must devote the greater part of their time to the company's affairs. Broadly, a company retains 'close company' status if it is under the control of five or fewer shareholders, or is controlled by its directors. No relief can be obtained under this heading if the cost of shares qualifies for enterprise investment scheme or business expansion scheme relief.

PLANT AND MACHINERY FOR USE IN AN EMPLOYMENT

Interest paid by an employee on a loan obtained to finance the acquisition of plant or machinery for use in his or her employment will qualify for relief in full.

PERSONAL REPRESENTATIVES

Relief is available for interest paid on a loan used by personal representatives of a deceased person to satisfy inheritance tax becoming payable on death. This relief is limited to interest on money borrowed for the payment of tax before the grant of representation, or the delivery of an account, and applies only to tax on personal property. In addition, relief is restricted to interest paid in a period of one year from the making of the loan.

Where at the time of death a person could claim relief for interest paid on a loan applied to acquire land, buildings, a caravan or a houseboat used, or to be used, as an only or main residence, the obligation to satisfy future interest payments may be assumed by the personal representatives, or by trustees administering a settlement created by the deceased's will. These persons may continue to obtain relief for interest paid if the asset is used, or is intended to be used, by a surviving spouse of the deceased. Relief may also be available if the deceased died before 6 April 1988 and a dependent relative was in occupation of the property at that time.

COMMERCIAL PROPERTY

Previously any interest paid on a loan to finance the purchase of land, a building, a caravan or houseboat which was not used as a qualifying residence, as outlined on page 24, could only obtain relief if the property was let at a commercial rent. The property had to be so let for at least 26 weeks in a 52-week period and throughout the remainder of the time the property must have been either available for letting or undergoing repair or improvement. Any interest attributable to the acquisition of commercial property satisfying these requirements was set against rent received and not against income generally. If the interest paid exceeded the rent any surplus could be carried forward and set against rental income for future years.

As explained on page 81, a new system applies for calculating income arising from property located in the United Kingdom. The new system operates from 6 April 1995 and enables interest paid to be treated as an expense when calculating Schedule A profits or losses. With the introduction of this new system it is now unnecessary to consider separately the availability of relief for interest paid to acquire commercial property.

BUILDING SOCIETY INTEREST

Mortgage interest paid to a building society will usually relate to a loan made for the acquisition of property. If the requirements outlined on the previous pages are satisfied, relief for the interest paid will be forthcoming, although after 5 April 1995 this will usually be limited to the reduced rate of 15 per cent.

OVERDRAFT INTEREST

Interest paid on a bank overdraft, or that which may be charged on the account of a person as the holder of a credit card cannot obtain relief in the manner outlined on the previous pages. If any interest of this nature is to be relieved it must be included in the calculation of profits or gains of a business.

OVERSEAS INTEREST

Interest paid to a person residing overseas may now entitle the payer to relief where the interest is paid on a loan applied for a qualifying purpose. Relief of this nature was not usually available for payments made before 6 April 1994.

In general, where land or buildings are situated outside the United Kingdom or the Republic of Ireland, for example, in the Channel Islands, the Isle of Man, France, Spain or Portugal, no relief for interest paid on a loan obtained to acquire the property will be forthcoming. This previously gave rise to an anomaly where the overseas property produced rental income as that income, less expenses, could be chargeable to United Kingdom taxation without relief being obtained for interest paid on a loan applied to acquire the property. However, the anomaly has been removed for payments made after 5 April 1995 and it is now possible to subtract interest paid from rental income arising when calculating the net sum chargeable to United Kingdom taxation.

HIRE-PURCHASE INTEREST

The so-called 'interest' payable under a hire-purchase agreement is not really interest but a 'hire charge'. No relief can be obtained for such a payment, unless the payer may treat it as a business expense in computing profits.

BUSINESS EXPENSES

The requirements outlined above, which must be satisfied before payments of interest made by an individual can qualify for tax relief, have no application to 'business' interest. An individual carrying on a trade, profession or vocation may include in the calculation of business profits or losses sums laid out 'wholly and exclusively' for the purposes of the business. For example, interest paid by a sole trader on a loan applied to acquire assets used in the business, or to provide working capital, may usually be relieved in this manner without regard to the requirements outlined on the previous pages. However, relief for an interest payment cannot be obtained both as a deduction from business profits and also by reducing the amount of income tax payable. In some situations it may be advisable to consider which form of relief is to be preferred, if indeed any choice is available.

COMPANIES

The above rules governing relief for interest paid have little application to companies, as special provisions apply for the purpose of determining liability to corporation tax.

How to obtain relief for interest paid

MORTGAGE INTEREST – RESTRICTIONS ON RELIEF

Payments of interest made on a loan applied to acquire an only or main residence may obtain relief where the requirements outlined earlier are satisfied. For payments made before 6 April 1991, the payer could obtain relief at the basic rate and at the higher rate also where income was sufficiently substantial. Subject to rare exceptions which have long ceased to be available, no higher rate relief can be obtained

for interest payments made on and after 6 April 1991. The preservation of relief at the basic rate was relatively short-lived. Interest payments made after 5 April 1994 give rise to relief at the reduced rate of 20 per cent only, with a further reduction to 15 per cent for payments after 5 April 1995.

Relief at these rates extends to interest paid on a loan used to acquire an only or main residence of a dependent relative or other persons or to finance the improvement of property where the loan was obtained before 6 April 1988. However, relief remains available at the basic rate of 25 per cent for interest paid on loans applied by an individual over 65 to acquire an annuity secured on land.

The removal of relief at the higher rate and the introduction of restrictions to the reduced rates of 20 and 15 per cent does not extend to other payments of qualifying interest. These payments continue to support relief at the higher or basic rate, where of course the income of the payer is sufficiently substantial.

MORTGAGE INTEREST —
THE MIRAS DEDUCTION SCHEME

Relief for payments of qualifying mortgage interest could be given either by adjusting the PAYE tax deductions made from earnings paid to employed persons or by deducting the interest from income on which tax is payable by direct assessment. This would give rise to considerable administrative difficulties, particularly in the case of PAYE, when changes are made in the rate of mortgage interest payable.

To avoid these and other problems a mortgage interest relief at source scheme (MIRAS) is used. It must be emphasised that the purpose of the scheme is to provide a more efficient method of granting relief and it does not affect the net income tax liability of most individuals, although occasionally increased relief will be available to those having little or no liability to income tax. Not all payments of mortgage interest are brought within the scheme and any excluded qualifying interest will be relieved in the manner outlined later.

Reduced rate relief – 1995–96

The substance of the MIRAS scheme is that when payments of interest are made to a qualifying lender during 1995–96 the payer will deduct and retain income tax at the reduced rate of 15 per cent. There is a lengthy list of qualifying lenders, including building societies, banks, insurance companies, local

19

RELIEF FOR INTEREST PAID – MIRAS

In 1982 David obtained a mortgage loan of £35,000 from a building society to purchase his own home. The loan was repayable by monthly instalments, including interest. The interest element in monthly instalments paid during 1995–96 aggregated £2,860, before deducting income tax at the reduced rate of 15 per cent.

The total amount of interest actually paid in the year will be:

	£
Gross interest	2,860
Less income tax deducted at 15 per cent	429
Payments actually made . . .	£2,431

The only income of David for 1995–96 comprised a salary of £26,000. The income tax payable on this salary, assuming the taxpayer is a married man entitled to the full basic married couple's allowance, will be:

	£
Total income	26,000
Less Personal allowance . .	3,525
	£22,475
Tax payable:	
On first £3,200 at 20 per cent . .	640.00
On balance of £19,275 at 25 per cent .	4,818.75
	5,458.75
Less Married couple's allowance – £1,720	
at 15 per cent	258.00
	£5,200.75

The net income tax burden is:

	£
Tax payable	5,200.75
Deduct tax retained by deduction . .	429.00
Net tax suffered	£4,771.75

authorities and others. The qualifying lender is obliged to allow the deduction of income tax and will recover the sums deducted from the Inland Revenue.

The MIRAS deduction scheme applies to mortgage interest payable on a loan made to acquire an only or main residence in the United Kingdom which satisfies the requirements shown on page 24. It also extends to interest on a loan used to purchase other property by a person compelled to reside in job-related accommodation. Although MIRAS extends to interest on a loan used to purchase an annuity secured on land (see page 27), tax is deducted from such interest at the basic rate of 25 per cent and not the reduced rate of 15 per cent. Where the amount of any loan exceeds the £30,000 limit

governing relief for interest paid, qualifying lenders will operate MIRAS on that part of the loan which does not exceed £30,000.

It is important that borrowers fully advise lenders of any other qualifying loans existing at the time of new borrowings as these other loans may affect the availability of relief under the MIRAS scheme. Notification must also be made where interest on a loan ceases to qualify for relief. This is a most significant matter as the Inland Revenue have often expressed concern that the MIRAS deduction scheme is being heavily abused. Responsibility for its operation rests primarily between the lender and the borrower. Once errors or maladministration have been detected, serious financial consequences will arise.

The MIRAS deduction scheme is limited to income tax at the reduced rate of 15 per cent for 1995–96. As the amount of tax deducted can be retained, it is not also possible to subtract interest when calculating income chargeable to income tax. If the taxpayer has insufficient income to produce tax liability, for example where income is exceeded by allowances, income tax deducted can still be retained.

MORTGAGE INTEREST – RELIEF OUTSIDE THE MIRAS SCHEME

Not all payments of mortgage interest are brought within the MIRAS scheme; for example, where interest is paid to a person whose name does not appear on the list of qualifying lenders. In these circumstances interest will be paid gross, leaving the taxpayer to obtain relief either in the PAYE notice of coding or by deduction from direct assessment.

One disadvantage of this approach is that full relief will only be forthcoming where net income chargeable to tax, calculated by disregarding interest, equals or exceeds the amount of interest paid.

MORTGAGE INTEREST – HUSBAND AND WIFE

Where a husband and wife are 'living together' there can be only one qualifying residence between the parties. Interest paid on a loan applied to acquire that residence will qualify for tax relief in the normal manner. This requires that where a husband and his wife jointly acquire a property the maximum ceiling of £30,000 will be divided equally, with each able to obtain relief for interest on £15,000. If the loan is made to one spouse only that individual will obtain relief for interest paid on a loan up to the maximum of £30,000.

20
RELIEF FOR INTEREST PAID GROSS

Mark obtained a loan from a person who was not a qualifying lender within the MIRAS scheme. The loan was applied to acquire Mark's home. Interest amounting to £2,860 was paid gross in 1995–96 and qualified for relief. The only income of Mark, a married man, was a salary of £26,000. No election had been made to apportion the married couple's allowance.

Income tax payable for 1995–96 becomes:

		£
Total income		26,000
Less Personal allowance . . .		3,525
		22,475
Tax payable:		
On first £3,200 at 20 per cent . .		640.00
On balance of £19,275 at 25 per cent .		4,818.75
		5,458.75
	£	
Less		
Married couple's allowance –		
£1,720 at 15 per cent	258.00	
Interest – £2,860 at 15 per cent	429.00	687.00
		£4,771.75

It will be seen that the tax payable of £4,771.75 is identical to the net tax suffered by David in Example 19 above who paid interest falling within MIRAS. This illustrates that the purpose of MIRAS is to provide income tax relief by deduction at source, rather than when calculating the liability of the payer.

21
RELIEF FOR INTEREST PAID – HIGHER RATE

In 1984 Michael borrowed a substantial sum of money which he applied to acquire shares in a close company. Interest of £4,500 was paid gross on the borrowings in 1995–96 and qualified for relief. Michael was a married man entitled to the full basic married couple's allowance. His only income for the year comprised a salary of £45,000 from the company. Income tax payable will be:

		£	£
Total income			45,000
Less			
Personal allowance . . .		3,525	
Gross interest		4,500	8,025
			£36,975
Tax payable:			
Lower rate:			£
On first £3,200 at 20 per cent . .			640.00
Basic rate:			
On next £21,100 at 25 per cent .			5,275.00
Higher rate:			
On balance of £12,675 at 40 per cent .			5,070.00
			10,985.00
Less Married couple's allowance – £1,720 at 15 per cent			258.00
			£10,727.00

The gross interest of £4,500 has reduced taxable income by the same amount and therefore obtained relief at the full higher rate of 40 per cent. As the interest is not payable on a loan to acquire an only or main residence no restriction to 15 per cent is necessary.

However, it is possible to submit an 'allocation of interest' election. Where the election applies the interest paid by either, or both, parties to the marriage can be allocated between them in whatever proportions they consider appropriate. The election may also allocate the collective interests held by husband and wife between the parties where there are two, or perhaps more, individuals retaining interests in a single property and the £30,000 limit must be apportioned.

The election must be made jointly by husband and wife before a period of 12 months has elapsed following the end of the year of assessment to which the election relates. The election will then apply not only for the year of assessment concerned but for all following years. However, either husband or wife may withdraw the election by giving notice within a period of 12 months following the end of the year of assessment to which the withdrawal relates. Once a valid withdrawal has been submitted the normal

rules will apply, unless of course the parties submit a revised election.

At earlier times the election was widely used where one spouse incurred liability to income tax at the higher rate but the other spouse did not. There would usually be an advantage in all interest being treated as paid by the spouse with the higher income. With the removal of higher rate relief and the introduction of relief at reduced rates the 'allocation of interest' election has lost much of its former attraction. In limited situations it may still be beneficial; for example, where:

a interest is paid outside the MIRAS scheme and there is insufficient taxable income of one spouse to absorb the relief; or,

b increased personal allowances and married couple's allowances are available to individuals over the age of 64.

OTHER INTEREST

Although most items of interest qualifying for relief and paid by an individual will comprise mortgage interest falling to be relieved in the manner outlined above there are other classes of interest which may also obtain relief for income tax purposes. This other interest will be paid gross without deduction of income tax unless, exceptionally, it is paid to a lender residing overseas. The payment will qualify for relief at the lower rate, the basic rate and the higher rate of tax where these rates are suffered by the payer.

6

Other reliefs

National insurance contributions

NATIONAL INSURANCE contributions are payable by many employed and self-employed individuals. There are numerous exceptions and the level of contributions due will frequently be governed both by the amount of earnings and also by upper and lower thresholds. In summary form, the scope of the four contribution Classes is as follows:

Class 1 An employee pays primary contributions based on a percentage of earnings. A secondary contribution, also based on a percentage of employee's earnings, is payable by the employer.

Class 2 Self-employed individuals pay a flat rate contribution.

Class 3 Some individuals may pay voluntary flat rate contributions for the purpose of securing social security benefits.

Class 4 In addition to Class 2 flat rate contributions, self-employed individuals suffer a percentage rate Class 4 contribution based on taxable profits.

Secondary Class 1 contributions paid by an employer may usually be deducted when calculating taxable profits of the employer's business, if the contributions are satisfied for an employee engaged in such a business. Subject to this, no relief is

---

22

NATIONAL INSURANCE CONTRIBUTIONS

John is a married man deriving his sole livelihood from a business. Profits of the business assessable for 1995–96 amounted to £28,200 and John paid maximum Class 4 national insurance contributions of £1,186 for the year. No election had been made to apportion the married couple's allowance.

Income tax payable for 1995–96 becomes:

	£	£
Total income . . .		28,200
Less		
Personal allowance . .	3,525	
Class 4 contributions 1/2 × £1,186	593	4,118
		24,082
Tax payable:		
On first £3,200 at 20 per cent . .		640.00
On balance of £20,882 at 25 per cent .		5,220.50
		5,860.50
Less Married couple's allowance – £1,720		
at 15 per cent		258.00
		£5,602.50

---

generally available in respect of national insurance contributions paid when calculating the contributor's liability to income tax.

An exception applies to Class 4 contributions paid by a self-employed individual. One-half of these contributions attributable to a year of assessment may be deducted from total income when arriving at liability to income tax for that year. No similar deduction is available for Class 2 flat rate contributions. It must be emphasised that the one-half deduction is not made when calculating the *amount* of profits assessable to income tax, as relief is given in *charging* liability to that tax.

Business expansion scheme

THE AMOUNT of income tax payable by an individual may be reduced by a range of allowances and outgoings. Comments on the previous pages have examined such matters as personal and other allowances, together with deductions made for pension contributions, interest and Class 4 national insurance contributions. A further deduction which was previously of considerable interest to some taxpayers involved relief for subscriptions made under the business expansion scheme. This scheme ceased to apply for transactions taking place after 31 December 1993, but as future events may lead to the retrospective withdrawal of relief a brief description of the scheme's main features may be helpful.

Business expansion scheme relief applied to the cost of subscribing for eligible shares issued by a company. Most shares were eligible unless they carried unusual or preferential rights. At the time of any share issue it was a requirement that the individual subscriber should be resident and ordinarily resident in the United Kingdom. Throughout a period commencing two years before the issue date and ending five years after that date the individual could not become a paid director or an employee of the company without losing relief.

The company issuing shares had to be incorporated in the United Kingdom. Throughout a period of three years following the issue of shares or the commencement of trading, if later, it was a requirement that the company's shares should not have a share quotation on the Stock Exchange or be dealt with on the Unlisted Securities Market, the company should exist wholly or mainly for the purposes of carrying on a qualifying trade and not be under the control of a second company. Most trades carried on by a company were 'qualifying' but there were a number of exceptions. Of particular significance to the business expansion scheme was the ability of a company to acquire or construct buildings to be let on assured tenancies. Indeed, it was activities of this nature which formed the function of most companies in the latter years of the scheme.

Maximum relief for each individual was limited to £40,000 for share subscriptions made in a year of assessment ending on 5 April. Where investment was made not later than 5 October, one-half of the subscription could, at the taxpayer's option, be treated as taking place in the previous year of assessment ending on 5 April. The maximum subscription capable of being carried back in this manner was limited to £5,000.

Business expansion scheme relief once granted could be withdrawn retrospectively if the individual or company ceased to satisfy numerous requirements at any time in the five-year or three-year period. There could also be the complete or partial withdrawal of relief should the individual dispose of his or her holding within a period of time, usually five years from the issue date. It is the possibility of this withdrawal which must not be overlooked for events taking place after 31 December 1993.

No liability to capital gains tax arises on the subsequent disposal of shares issued after 18 March 1986, if business expansion scheme relief has been obtained and not withdrawn.

Enterprise investment scheme

FOLLOWING THE DEMISE of the business expansion scheme on 31 December 1993, a new enterprise investment scheme was launched on the following day, 1 January 1994. This scheme retains many features similar to those used by its predecessor but there are significant differences. It remains a common feature that enterprise investment scheme relief will be confined to the cost of subscribing for eligible shares issued by a qualifying company. Most shares remain eligible, for this purpose, unless they carry preferential or unusual rights.

INDIVIDUALS WHO QUALIFY
At the time of the share issue the individual subscriber must be either resident in the United Kingdom or, if not so resident, be liable to United Kingdom income tax. This will enable a non-resident individual to claim relief against liability to United

Kingdom taxation. An individual who is an employee or director of a company is usually precluded from obtaining relief when subscribing for shares issued by that company. However, this prohibition does not prevent an individual becoming a paid director if he or she was neither connected with the company or with the company's trade at any time before eligible shares were issued.

QUALIFYING COMPANIES

The company must be carrying on a qualifying trade in the United Kingdom. It is unnecessary for the company to be resident here as the only requirement is that there must be a trade in the United Kingdom.

Most trades carried on by a company qualify under the enterprise investment scheme. However, unlike the former business expansion scheme, relief is not be available for investment in a company providing private rented housing.

Previously a company was disqualified if it retained interests in land having a substantial value, but this ceased to apply after 28 November 1994.

The company must not have shares quoted on the Stock Exchange or dealt in on the Unlisted Securities Market. The maximum sum which a company can raise under the scheme in a twelve-month period is limited to £1 million. This ceiling may be increased to £5 million for companies engaged in shipping activities.

RELIEF FOR THE INVESTMENT

Where the several requirements are satisfied an investment in shares under the enterprise investment scheme will qualify for income tax relief. This relief must be limited to the reduced rate of 20 per cent. It is not possible to obtain relief at the basic rate of 25 per cent or the higher rate of 40 per cent.

The maximum investment, or aggregate investments, which an individual can make during a year of assessment ending on 5 April is £100,000. This remains subject to a special restriction which applied to the year of assessment 1993–94 only. For this year aggregate investments qualifying for business expansion scheme relief or enterprise investment scheme relief were limited to £40,000.

The calculation of relief for a year of assessment will be primarily governed by subscriptions actually made in that year. However, where a qualifying investment is made not later than 5 October an amount not exceeding one-half of that investment may, at the taxpayer's option, be treated as made in the previous year of assessment ending on 5 April. The maximum subscription which can be related

23
ENTERPRISE INVESTMENT SCHEME – RELIEF

In 1995–96 Roger received a salary of £125,000. He was married and entitled to the entire married couple's allowance. During the year Roger subscribed £75,000 to acquire shares in an unquoted trading company. It was agreed that the investment qualified for enterprise investment scheme relief.

The tax payable for 1995–96 will be calculated as follows:

		£
Total income	. . . . .	125,000
Less Personal allowance	. . .	3,525
		£121,475

Tax payable:		£
Lower rate:		
On first £3,200 at 20 per cent	. .	640.00
Basic rate:		
On next £21,100 at 25 per cent	.	5,275.00
Higher rate:		
On balance of £97,175 at 40 per cent	.	38,870.00
		44,785.00
Less	£	
Married couple's allowance – £1,720 at 15 per cent . .	258.00	
Enterprise investment scheme relief – £75,000 at 20 per cent . .	15,000.00	15,258.00
		£29,527.00

back to an earlier year is not to exceed £15,000. Any amount related back in this manner cannot increase relief beyond the £100,000 ceiling in the previous year.

Enterprise investment scheme relief may be withdrawn retrospectively should the individual subscriber or the company cease to satisfy a range of requirements throughout a period of years.

Gains arising from the eventual disposal of qualifying shares will be exempt from capital gains tax if income tax relief once granted has not been withdrawn. However, should losses arise these may be relieved against capital gains on other assets, or perhaps relieved against income chargeable to income tax.

An additional attraction is the ability to "roll-over" gains on the disposal of other assets against the cost of subscribing for shares under the enterprise investment scheme – see page 119 for further details.

HUSBAND AND WIFE

The annual threshold of £100,000 applies separately to a husband and wife, whether or not the couple are 'living together'.

Venture capital trusts

A new form of tax efficient investment, namely the venture capital trust, became available on 6 April 1995. It is a requirement that shares issued by such a trust must be quoted on the Stock Exchange. The trust's main function is to invest in unquoted trading companies. At least 70 per cent of all investments made must be in these unquoted companies, with not more than 15 per cent of trust funds being invested in any one company. The investment may be in the form of shares or loans with a minimum of five years to maturity but at least 50 per cent of the investment must be made in new ordinary shares. Trusts will initially have five years to satisfy the 70

24
VENTURE CAPITAL TRUST RELIEF

James earned profits of £85,000 from a business which were assessable for 1995–96. He is married and entitled to the entire married couple's allowance. James invested £50,000 when subscribing for shares in a venture capital trust during 1995–96. The tax payable for 1995–96 will be calculated as follows:

		£
Total income		85,000
Less Personal allowance . .		3,525
		£81,475
Tax payable:		
Lower rate:		£
On first £3,200 at 20 per cent .	.	640.00
Basic rate:		
On next £21,100 at 25 per cent .	.	5,275.00
Higher rate:		
On balance of £57,175 .	.	22,870.00
		28,785.00
Less		
Married couple's allowance –	£	
£1,720 at 15 per cent .	258.00	
Venture capital trust relief –		
£50,000 at 20 per cent .	10,000.00	10,258.00
		£18,527.00

---

per cent and 50 per cent requirements. Should an unquoted company become quoted, investments in that company may continue to be held for a further five years without breaching the requirements.

Investments in most unquoted trading companies will qualify but there are a number of excluded trades.

Individuals may subscribe for ordinary shares in a venture capital trust and obtain income tax relief on the investment. Relief is limited to investments up to a maximum of £100,000 in any year of assessment ending on 5 April. Subject to this upper limit, relief is given at the reduced rate of 20 per cent and may be withdrawn if the shares are sold or otherwise disposed of within a five-year period.

Dividends arising on qualifying shares in a venture capital trust will be exempt from income tax and gains from the disposal of the shares will not be chargeable to capital gains tax if the holding is retained for the required period.

Like investments under the enterprise investment scheme, it will be possible to "roll over" gains on the disposal of other assets against the cost of acquiring shares in a venture capital trust. Further details are available on page 120.

Life assurance premiums

TAX RELIEF may be available where premiums are paid on older qualifying life assurance and other policies. This relief applies only to premiums on policies made before 15 March 1984, and cannot be obtained for new policies entered into on or after that date. Changes to a pre-1984 policy which secure increased benefits may result in relief being withdrawn from the date of the change. Where relief is available this has no effect whatsoever on the policyholder's liability to income tax but merely reduces the amount of the premium.

When paying premiums on an approved pre-1984 policy the policyholder will deduct and retain income tax at the rate of 12.5 per cent. It is immaterial whether the individual is liable to income tax, or exempt on the grounds that his or her income is insufficient to justify liability. In all cases the deduction can be made. A restriction arises, however, where the premiums paid in any one year exceed £1,500, as relief will be limited to deductions of £1,500 or one-sixth of the individual's total income, whichever is the greater. If the amount deducted at the rate of 12.5 per cent exceeds these limits the policyholder will be required to refund the excess.

Separate calculations of total income must be prepared to establish whether premiums paid by a husband or his wife exceed the one-sixth limit.

Medical insurance premiums

PREMIUMS paid under a private medical insurance contract may qualify for income tax relief. This relief is limited to premiums paid on a policy for the benefit of an individual aged 60 years or over. In the case of husband and wife, only one spouse need have achieved this age. Where a contract provides cover for a married couple it is possible that on the death of the older spouse the survivor would be below the age of 60. This previously disqualified future premiums until the survivor achieved the age of 60 years, but the disqualification no longer applies.

To qualify for relief the policy must be in a form approved by the Inland Revenue, be limited to a period not exceeding twelve months and provide medical cover. The provision of cash benefits must usually be excluded. Subject to this the contract may cover charges for medical and surgical procedures, including diagnosis, the purpose of which is the relief of illness or injury. It is a general requirement that the procedures must be given or controlled by a registered medical or dental practitioner in the United Kingdom, but physiotherapy, following consultation with a general practitioner, is also included.

Relief will not be confined to premiums paid by the person insured but may extend to premiums paid by some other person, perhaps a son or daughter, providing the insured has reached the required age.

Qualifying premiums paid before 6 April 1994 were discharged after deduction of income tax at the basic rate under a scheme similar to MIRAS, which applies to payments of mortgage interest. In common with the MIRAS scheme, tax deducted at the basic rate could be retained whether or not the payer was liable to income tax at that rate. Unlike MIRAS, however, contributors liable to tax at the higher rate could obtain relief on the excess over the basic rate, either through the PAYE notice of coding or against direct assessment.

25
MEDICAL INSURANCE PREMIUMS

William is a single man aged 48 earning £26,000. During 1995–96 he paid a premium of £700 on an approved medical insurance policy providing cover for his elderly mother. The actual premium paid will be:

					£
Gross payment	.	.	.	.	700.00
Less tax at 25 per cent		.	.	.	175.00
Actual payment	.	.	.	.	£525.00

Liability to income tax becomes

					£
Total income	.	.	.	.	26,000
Less Personal allowance		.	.	.	3,525
					£22,475

Tax payable:

On first £3,200 at 20 per cent	.	.	640.00
On balance of £19,275 at 25 per cent		.	4,818.75
			£5,458.75

The tax of £175 deducted on payment of the premium can be retained, which effectively reduces the cost of insurance.

Premiums paid on and after 6 April 1994 continue to be discharged after deducting income tax at the basic rate of 25 per cent. However, no relief is now available at the higher rate on those premiums. Indeed, the payments virtually fall outside the tax system and will not affect other allowances or reliefs. The reduced rate of 15 per cent which applies when obtaining relief for payments of interest under MIRAS has no application whatsoever to medical insurance premiums.

A new insurance premiums tax was introduced in the Autumn of 1994. The amount of this tax is be added to the qualifying premium and relief obtained at the rate of 25 per cent on the aggregate sum.

Vocational training

A TAX RELIEF designed to encourage vocational training came into operation on 6 April 1992. This relief is available for study and examination fees paid by an individual resident in the United Kingdom who undertakes qualifying training. Detailed arrangements have to be observed but to qualify for relief the training must lead to National Vocational Qualifications or Scottish Vocational Qualifications at levels 1 to 4, with level 5 added from 1 January 1994. These are qualifications accredited by the National Council for Vocational Qualifications which covers England, Wales and Northern Ireland, or by the Scottish Vocational Education Council. Levels 1 to 4 incorporate training up to middle management and supervisory skills. Level 5 extends to senior managerial and professional skills including degree level qualifications. However, children under the age of 16 together with 16 to 18 year-olds in full-time education at a school must be excluded. In addition training undertaken wholly or mainly for recreational purposes or as a leisure activity does not qualify.

When making qualifying payments of study and examination fees the payer will deduct income tax at the basic rate. The tax deducted may be retained whether or not the payer is liable to income tax at that rate. Any payers who are liable to income tax at the higher rate may deduct their outgoings when calculating liability at this rate. Relief for payments made after 5 April 1995 is not restricted to the lower rate of 15 per cent which applies to MIRAS from that date.

Persons providing training and who receive fees after deduction of income tax at the basic rate can obtain repayment of the tax deducted from the Inland Revenue.

7

Employments

Pay As You Earn

PAYE is *not* a separate tax but a scheme whereby income tax on wages, salaries and other earnings is collected by deduction as and when the wages and salaries are paid. A 'receipts basis' governs the year of assessment into which earnings fall. The rules which determine the time of 'receipt' are discussed on page 44. Identical rules apply to establish the date of 'payment' for the purposes of PAYE.

Although all wages and salaries are subject to assessment under Schedule E, circumstances occur where it is impractical to operate a PAYE scheme of tax deduction. For example, an individual employed abroad by a foreign employer may be liable to tax on his earnings but the employer could not operate PAYE, and in such a case the employee will be assessed direct. However, this approach cannot be used as a device to avoid the PAYE scheme where an employee is paid abroad, perhaps on secondment to a United Kingdom employer. PAYE extends to all income tax payable on earnings to which the scheme relates, including tax at the lower rate, the basic rate and the higher rate.

In most situations it will be apparent whether an individual rendering services holds an office or employment to which the PAYE deduction scheme applies. There are, however, inevitably borderline cases where the distinction between employment and self-employment is not easy to resolve. Some employers choose to disregard this distinction and

discharge earnings without deducting PAYE. This is a most dangerous practice, as subsequent detection by the Inland Revenue may have serious financial and other consequences.

Many individuals whose services are supplied through agencies and who do not technically become employees of the person to whom services are supplied are regarded as 'employees' for income tax purposes. PAYE will be applied to any remuneration paid by the employer of such persons. However, certain individuals engaged in diving operations who could be correctly treated as employees may be regarded as self-employed and outside the PAYE scheme.

The collection of tax on most unemployment benefits paid to the unemployed is brought within the PAYE deduction scheme. The scheme also applies to the collection of tax on social security maternity pay, payments of short term incapacity benefit made by an employer, to many pensions paid under occupational schemes and to annuities paid under personal pension scheme arrangements.

CODE NUMBERS

Each employee should have a code number and this is arrived at by the tax office from the income tax return or other information disclosing details of allowances claimed. All the allowances are added together and if the employee has no other income the total of his allowances, less the last figure, could fix his code number. However, some allowances, including the married couple's allowance, are given at the reduced rate of 15 per cent for 1995–96. The code number will then be adjusted to ensure that relief is only given at that rate when applying PAYE.

If the taxpayer has other income, e.g. a retirement pension, untaxed interest or income from property, the estimated amount of this income may be deducted from the total allowances to calculate the code number. Whilst this will increase the amount of tax deducted under PAYE, it will avoid the need to raise assessments directly on the taxpayer to recover tax on the other income. Tax on car and car fuel benefits enjoyed by directors and higher paid employees is also collected through the PAYE system. This was previously achieved by deducting the estimated benefits from total allowances when fixing the code number. However a new 'K' code procedure was introduced to replace the previous practice (see page 41). PAYE may also be used to tax other notional earnings (see page 41).

No adjustment is usually made on the coding notice for contributions to an occupational pension scheme or superannuation fund as these will be deducted from earnings in arriving at the net earnings chargeable to tax. A number of special adjustments will be required to the code number where tax has been underpaid for earlier years, tax is being deducted from annual payments made, or liability arises at the higher rate.

The letters 'L', 'H', or 'T' will often appear at the end of the code number, e.g. Code Number 352L. The letter 'L' indicates that the individual concerned is entitled to the basic personal allowance and the letter 'H' that the married couple's allowance, or the additional personal allowance available for single parent families, is available. The use of these letters enables the code to be adjusted quickly where there is any change in the rate at which relief is given.

The letters 'L' and 'H' do not indicate the remaining allowances or reliefs to which an employee may be entitled, but if the employee does not wish his employer to know which allowance is available he may request the Tax Office to replace the letter 'L' or 'H' with the letter 'T'. The letter 'T' will also be used where no personal allowance is available, e.g. where an individual has two employments and the personal allowance and any other allowances have been applied in calculating the code number for the main employment only. Code numbers issued to elderly taxpayers entitled to claim the increased personal allowance or increased married couple's allowance have the letter 'P' to denote a single person and 'V' for a married man.

Although these are the main letters used, others apply in special circumstances. For example, BR indicates that tax is to be deducted at the basic rate and NT shows that no tax is to be deducted. D implies that tax will be deducted at the higher rate and F requires that tax due on a social security pension or benefit is being collected from earnings or a pension from a previous employment. Social security retirement pensions and widows' benefits are paid gross, without deduction of income tax. This requires that where tax is due, recovery of that tax must be made by adjusting the PAYE code number of an employment or by direct assessment.

CHANGES IN THE CODE NUMBER

Should any change in the available allowances occur during the year the Tax Office must be notified immediately as this will enable the code number to be quickly altered. The need for an alteration may arise, for example, where a taxpayer marries and qualifies for the married couple's allowance, becomes entitled to the additional personal allowance for children or qualifies for the widow's bereavement allowance.

DEDUCTIONS WORKING SHEETS

Tax tables are supplied to all employers so that the actual tax deductions can be calculated. The amount of the deduction in any particular case depends upon the code number, and the employer is advised of this number so that the correct amount of tax to be deducted can be ascertained by him from the tax tables. Employers are provided with official Deductions Working Sheets for each employee, unless the employer chooses to use a similar record of his own design. Details of payments made to employees are entered on these sheets together with information extracted from the tax tables. This enables the employer to calculate the amount of PAYE deductions which should be made. At the end of the income tax year the employer completes End of Year Returns, or similar documents, and forwards these to the Tax Office.

The Inland Revenue then knows the total earnings for the year and the total amount of tax suffered by deduction by each employee. The exact amount of tax which should be paid on the total earnings of the year can then be calculated. If any tax has been under- or over-paid, this adjustment will usually be carried forward to the following year; but the taxpayer has the right to require any tax overpaid to be refunded instead of having it carried forward. Should the amount under-deducted be substantial, the employee may be required to pay this amount to the Inland Revenue by direct assessment.

Class 1 national insurance contributions are also entered on the Deductions Working Sheets. However, these contributions do not represent the payment of income tax and are only dealt with under the PAYE scheme for administrative reasons.

Failure on the part of an employer to submit End of Year Returns and other documents for 1995–96 in good time may result in a demand for penalties.

REPAYMENT OF TAX

If current earnings are smaller than those for earlier weeks or months falling in the same tax year, it is possible that some tax will be repaid to the employee. This may happen if the tax paid for previous weeks or months is greater than the tax due up to the end of the week or month in respect of which the earnings are small. It may also occur where entitlement to some further allowance or relief arises. In these circumstances the employer will refund to the employee part of the tax deducted on earlier occasions.

UNEMPLOYMENT

Most unemployment benefits are now taxable. However, no deduction of tax will be made until the period of unemployment has ended.

On becoming unemployed an individual will be handed a leaving certificate, Form P45. If he or she claims unemployment benefit the form must be handed to the benefit office. On subsequently finding a new employment the individual will deliver a completed card UB40 to the benefit office. This office then issues the individual with an updated Form P45, including the amount of taxable benefit, and will make any repayment of PAYE deductions which may be due. The new employer uses the information shown on the P45 to make future deductions from earnings. If the period of unemployment extends to the following 5 April, the benefit office will make any repayment of PAYE which may be due.

It follows that where an individual becomes unemployed, no repayment of PAYE deductions can be obtained until the end of the tax year, or the end of the period of unemployment, whichever occurs first. Persons becoming unemployed by reason of strike action cannot obtain repayment of PAYE until the strike ends.

The purpose of withholding refunds during a period of unemployment, and refraining from deducting PAYE on benefits paid, is one of administrative convenience. In many cases the amount due to be refunded will be similar to the tax due on taxable social security benefits.

Unemployment benefit is due to be replaced by a job seeker's allowance in April, 1996. It seems unlikely that this will affect the above procedure but details will be forthcoming at a later date.

THE 'K' CODE

The PAYE scheme is used to collect income tax by deduction when earnings are paid. Not all rewards chargeable to income tax are received in the form of cash payments. Examples include a large number of benefits in kind enjoyed by directors and employees (see page 51). It was previously the practice to collect tax indirectly on these non-cash sums by subtracting the estimated taxable benefits from allowances when arriving at the code number used to operate PAYE. However, this approach was not fully effective where the total non-cash items exceeded the amount of the allowances, as it was not possible to use a negative code number. Where excessive benefits arose, the Inland Revenue were required to raise an assessment on the taxpayer with the inevitable delay in collecting tax due.

To resolve this problem a new 'K' code procedure was introduced. This procedure does not require any amendment to code numbers. Instead, additions are made to the amount of taxable pay from which PAYE deductions must be subtracted. The additions, to be made at agreed rates, reflect the value of taxable benefits and enable income tax to be collected on those benefits through the PAYE system.

The new 'K' codes also replace the special 'F' codes given to pensioners whose social security retirement pensions exceed their personal tax allowances.

It may be found that by adding notional earnings, reflecting taxable benefits, to actual earnings the amount of PAYE to be deducted from payments made is excessively high, or may even exceed the amount of the actual payment. To avoid distortions of this nature a restriction is placed on the maximum deduction, which will not usually exceed 50 per cent of the actual pay. Subject to this modification, the existing PAYE procedure will apply generally to those taxpayers allocated 'K' codes.

NOTIONAL PAYMENTS

The insertion of notional earnings where 'K' code arrangements are in operation does not exhaust the list of special additions which must be made when accounting for PAYE deductions. Further adjustments were inserted in recognition of the increasing number of employers avoiding the PAYE deduction procedure by rewarding employees in gold bullion, coffee beans, or other commodities or assets. As rewards of this nature were not 'payments' the PAYE deduction scheme could not apply. It was unlikely that this achieved any permanent tax avoidance as the employee was directly assessed on the value of assets received. However, a considerable interval of time could elapse before tax was assessed and paid in this manner, in contrast to the immediate liability where the PAYE deduction procedure applied.

To counter this form of avoidance employers are now required to account for PAYE when directors or employees are rewarded with a wide range of 'tradeable assets'. Notional earnings, representing the cost of assets supplied, must be entered on the deductions working sheets for the month in which the supply of assets is made. Where earnings are sufficiently substantial to absorb the additional amount of PAYE this will be deducted. However, where earnings are not sufficient the employer must still account for the proper amount of PAYE deductions which ought to be made. Any tax accounted for in this manner will be treated as borne by the director or employee.

CHANGING JOBS AND NEW EMPLOYMENTS
If an individual changes his job he will receive from his old employer a leaving certificate (Form P45) which sets out the code number, the total pay to date and the total tax that has been deducted in the tax year. This certificate should be handed to the new employer, if any, who will then continue the deductions from the later earnings of the same tax year. It is often found that delay occurs in obtaining a Form P45, and some individuals may fail to take proper care of the form handed to them. This causes considerable work, both for the new employer and also the Inland Revenue, as laborious steps must be taken to trace details relating to the tax affairs of the employee. Individuals should take great care of a Form P45 and hand it to the new employer at the earliest opportunity. If they do not, excessive PAYE deductions may be made by the new employer until a revised notice of coding is issued. To avoid problems of this nature a special procedure is used. This procedure, which applies where a Form P45 is not handed to the new employer promptly, requires the issue of a short questionnaire. The questionnaire

urges the new employee to contact his old employer for the speedy production of Form P45 and also requires the provision of sufficient information for the Tax Office to compute a provisional code if there is further delay.

School leavers and others commencing employment for the first time should be placed on an emergency code until they have completed an income tax return which enables an accurate code to be issued. However, such persons will, after signing a simple declaration, be given a code number for a single person and no income tax return will be issued, unless requested by the taxpayer.

Taxpayers starting an additional job are placed on an emergency code, if their earnings are sufficiently substantial, or may have no tax deducted until the Tax Office issues a code number. Tax deductions made from earnings arising from the additional job are imposed at the basic rate of 25 per cent.

Where the 'K' code procedure outlined above applied to the old employment, this will be reviewed by the Inland Revenue to establish whether it should be continued by the new employer, if any.

ACCOUNTING FOR DEDUCTIONS
Most employers are required to pay over to the Collector of Taxes, not later than fourteen days after the end of each tax month, deductions made in the previous month. A tax month ends on the fifth day with the result that the employer's liability to account for deductions arises on the nineteenth of each month. A similar procedure applies to the discharge of Class 1 national insurance contributions.

However, a change in the accounting procedure is available for small employers. If the average aggregate monthly payments of PAYE deductions and national insurance contributions fall below £600 the employer may adopt a quarterly, rather than a monthly, accounting basis. Payments will then fall due fourteen days after the end of each quarter terminating on 5 July, 5 October, 5 January and 5 April.

Contractors in the construction industry may also adopt a quarterly basis when accounting for deductions from payments to sub-contractors (see page 70) where the average aggregate monthly payments of PAYE, national insurance contributions and sub-contractors' deductions fall below £600.

OMISSION TO DEDUCT TAX
The purpose of the PAYE deduction scheme is to collect tax on earnings when emoluments are paid to an employee. However, the employer's obligation

is not limited to the satisfaction of sums actually deducted but extends to the amount of deductions which ought to have been made, less repayments properly due to employees. Failure on the part of the employer to make the full deductions may therefore have serious consequences, as the Inland Revenue may demand payment of the full sums due. This situation often arises following an investigation of an employer's affairs and the allegation that the deduction procedure has not been properly applied.

In two situations the employer may be relieved of his or her obligation to account for deductions which have not been made. First, where the Collector of Taxes can be satisfied that the employer took reasonable care to comply with the PAYE regulations, and the under-deduction was due to an error made in good faith, he may direct that the outstanding sum should be recovered from the employee or employees concerned. The effect of such a direction is to absolve the employer from further liability.

The second exception arises where the Commissioners of Inland Revenue (and not the Collector of Taxes) are of the opinion that an employee has received his emoluments knowing that the employer has wilfully failed to make the deductions required by the PAYE regulations. In these circumstances also the Commissioners may absolve the employer from liability to account for under-deductions and recover the proper amount of tax from the employee or employees.

The application of either approach is very much a matter for the discretion of the Inland Revenue, and no employer should anticipate that an appropriate direction will be issued. This merely serves to emphasise the obligation placed on employers to ensure that the proper PAYE deductions are made when paying emoluments to employees.

There are similar provisions which enable underpayments of national insurance contributions to be recovered.

RECOVERY OF TAX AND INTEREST

Some employers fail to account for PAYE deductions made, or indeed to operate properly the statutory requirements. HM Inspector of Taxes may then determine the amount thought to be due and raise an assessment. If the amount of such an assessment, known as a Regulation 49 determination, is to be disputed the employer must provide notice of appeal within a period of thirty days from the issue date. Failure to provide the required notice of appeal will result in the tax shown by the assessment falling

due for payment. Frequently the amount of tax shown by a disputed assessment which is under appeal will be settled by agreement between the parties, but where it is not, the appeal will be heard by a body of Commissioners. A liability to satisfy interest will usually arise where action is taken under Regulation 49 and an amount of tax falls due.

On many earlier occasions the Inland Revenue were unable to impose an interest charge where there had been delay in accounting for PAYE deductions. However, this no longer applies and where PAYE deductions have not been paid over to the Collector of Taxes within 14 days after the end of a year of assessment (namely, by 19 April) a general interest charge may be imposed. The change first applied to deductions made in 1992–93 where the amount deducted was not paid over by the employer by 19 April 1993. The rate of interest imposed will vary in line with changes in the money market generally but is applied at rates identical to those which are used for late payments of tax (see page 113). It will not be overlooked that any interest commitment discharged in this manner cannot form an ingredient in the calculation of profits chargeable to tax.

The interest charge is limited to sums remaining outstanding 14 days following the end of the year of assessment. It does not apply to late monthly or quarterly payments made during the year.

Similar interest procedures also apply to deductions made under the sub-contractors' scheme (see page 70) and to late payments of Class 1 national insurance contributions.

ASSESSMENTS

After 5 April 1996, when the Tax Office receives all 1995–96 returns from employers, the tax deducted is checked. If the amount deducted correctly represents the tax payable for 1995–96 and the code number does not require adjustment due to any alteration in the taxpayer's allowances, no formal notice of assessment will be sent to the taxpayer. But the latter has the right to give written notice to the Tax Office within five years from 5 April 1996 requiring an assessment to be made upon him showing the manner in which the tax paid is to be calculated.

ASSESSING TOLERANCE

It is apparent that the administrative cost of raising assessments to collect small amounts of tax may substantially exceed the tax eventually collected. This is recognised by the Inland Revenue who apply an 'assessing tolerance' of £30 below which the tax is not assessed or collected. However, if an assessment is raised, particularly where the taxpayer has requested such an assessment, steps will be taken to collect the entire tax, notwithstanding that the amount involved is small. Where the tax payable exceeds the assessing tolerance by a small amount, all tax will be collected and not only the excess.

Widows and single women pensioners under the age of 65 may receive social security pensions on which any tax due must be recovered by direct assessment. No assessments will be raised on such persons to recover small amounts falling within the assessing tolerance.

ALLOCATION OF EARNINGS

All earnings of directors and employees must be allocated to, and treated as income of, the year of assessment in which they are 'received'. There is no need to apportion bonuses and other lump sum payments between one year of assessment and another or to make an adjustment where earnings are received late. In all cases the date of 'receipt' will determine the year of assessment into which earnings fall.

DATE EARNINGS RECEIVED

For most employees, earnings will be treated as 'received':

a on the date emoluments are paid; or
b on the date an employee becomes entitled to those emoluments,

whichever event first occurs.

These rules apply also to company directors but for such individuals there are three further possible dates, namely:

c the date emoluments are *credited* in the accounts or records of the company;
d if emoluments for a period are *determined* before the end of that period – the last day of the period; or
e if emoluments for a period are *determined* after the end of that period – the date of determination.

In all cases it is the earliest of the possible dates which establishes the time of receipt. Particular caution must be exercised when dealing with remuneration payable to directors of family companies for the purpose of ensuring that the date of 'receipt' is not unduly advanced or delayed.

The 'receipt' date will also establish that on which earnings are treated as 'paid' for PAYE purposes. In addition, it may apply to determine the accounting period in which a deduction for earnings paid can be made.

OVERSEAS EMPLOYMENTS

Earnings from an office or employment are only capable of being assessed to income tax under Schedule E and cannot be dealt with under any other Schedule. For this purpose it is immaterial whether duties are performed in the United Kingdom or in some territory overseas. However, the liability to United Kingdom taxation in respect of earnings from employments undertaken wholly or partly outside the United Kingdom will largely depend on whether the employee is resident here or abroad and also the place where duties are actually carried out.

Employees resident and ordinarily resident

If an employee is both resident and ordinarily resident in the United Kingdom, all earnings, whether from duties carried out at home or overseas, are initially liable to tax. It may be possible to reduce the amount of taxable earnings by applying a 'foreign earnings deduction' where duties are performed overseas, but the application of this deduction is severely limited.

Where an employee works full-time overseas for a qualifying period of 365 days or more, he may deduct 100 per cent of his overseas earnings when calculating liability to United Kingdom taxation, and therefore avoid any liability in respect of those earnings. A period is treated as a 'qualifying period' for this purpose unless during that period the employee was present in the United Kingdom:

a on more than 62 consecutive days; or
b for more than one-sixth of the total number of days in that period.

The 'foreign earnings deduction' is limited to earnings for duties carried out overseas and cannot extend to duties performed in the United Kingdom, unless those duties are merely incidental to the overseas activities.

For seafarers the number of days in **a** is increased to 183 days and the factor in **b** to one-half.

Other employees

An individual who is either not resident or not ordinarily resident in the United Kingdom will be charged to tax on his earnings for work undertaken in the United Kingdom. This charge does not extend to earnings for work performed overseas.

Special rules apply to employees domiciled outside the United Kingdom and employed by non-resident employers. If these individuals perform the whole of their duties overseas only sums remitted to the United Kingdom will be chargeable to tax.

PROFIT-RELATED PAY

The calculation of earnings received by employees will sometimes be influenced by the level of profits achieved by the employer. Earnings of this nature are fully chargeable to income tax unless they comprise profit-related pay.

To achieve relief from taxation, profit-related pay must arise under a scheme approved by the Inland Revenue. The scheme enables employees to receive profit-related pay based on the employer's profits for a profit period, in addition to the employees' normal earnings. A profit-related pay scheme is applied to an 'employment unit' and need not necessarily extend to all business activities of the employer. At least 80 per cent of employees working in that employment unit must be members of the scheme, although part-time staff working less than 20 hours weekly and new employees having less than three years of service may be excluded. Controlling directors must not be permitted to participate and the scheme is limited to employees in the private sector. A profit-related pay scheme can be introduced for a single accounting period of twelve months in duration or extend throughout a longer period.

A participating employee will receive both normal earnings and profit-related pay. However, the profit-related pay may be wholly or partly exempt from income tax. The level of exemption has changed from time to time but, for profit periods com-

26
PROFIT-RELATED PAY

Charles was a member of an approved profit-related pay scheme throughout the twelve-month profit period to 30 September 1995. On 15 January 1996, he received profit-related pay of £3,500 for that period. Normal pay received by Charles in the year ended 30 September 1995 was £12,000.

The profit-related pay of £3,500 comprises income for 1995–96. However, the exempt amount will be the smaller of:

							£
a	Profit-related pay	.	.	.	.	.	3,500
b	1/5 × (£3,500 + £12,000)	.	.	.	.	3,100
c	maximum	.	.	.	.	.	4,000

Calculation **b** produces the smaller figure and £3,100 will be exempt from income tax. The taxable part of profit-related pay therefore becomes £400 (£3,500 less £3,100).

mencing after 31 March 1991 the exemption will comprise the lower of:

a the actual profit-related pay;

b one-fifth of normal pay plus profit-related pay; and

c £4,000.

When applying the PAYE deduction scheme the employer will disregard the exempt profit-related pay and confine deductions to net earnings remaining. The exclusion of pay in this manner has no application to the calculation of national insurance contributions, which extends to the full earnings.

Applications to register a profit-related pay scheme may be submitted at any time, but the scheme must be registered before the commencement of the employer's first profit period used to measure profit-related pay if the tax exemption is to be obtained.

PENSIONS

Any pension from an office or employment in the United Kingdom is assessable to income tax under Schedule E. In most cases the pension will be subject to deduction of tax under the PAYE scheme outlined above. By concession, any additional pension awarded due to injury, work related illness or war wounds is not charged to tax.

An exception arises where the pension is paid by an overseas employer to a former employee resident in the United Kingdom, as in such a case PAYE will not usually apply. Overseas pensions are chargeable to tax under Schedule D but assessment is limited to 90 per cent of the pension, whether it is remitted to the United Kingdom or not. The remaining 10 per cent will escape liability.

EXPENSES

Any expenses which the holder of an office or employment is *necessarily obliged* to expend *wholly, exclusively and necessarily* in the *performance of the duties of the office*, including expenses of travelling, may be deducted from the earnings to be assessed. Before an expenses claim is admitted by the Inland Revenue the items of expenditure are closely scrutinised to establish whether the requirements have been satisfied. For example, the cost of travelling from home to the place of employment cannot be allowed, as travelling is not undertaken whilst performing the duties of the office but to place the individual in a position from which to carry out those duties. On the other hand, once the place of employment has been reached the cost of any further business journeys will usually qualify for relief. When determining those expenses which may obtain relief, a distinction must be drawn between expenses which are personal to an employee and those which would be incurred by any holder of the office. For example, an incapacitated employee may have to incur expenses by reason of his incapacity, e.g. the maintenance of a guide dog by a blind person, but this expense would not be incurred by *any* holder of the office and it must be disallowed. From 6 April 1995 some expenditure relating to insurance and insurable risks may confer an entitlement to relief as shown below.

An expenses claim should show, where possible, each individual item making up the total sum claimed. Vouchers and receipts must always be obtained when making payments and subsequently submitted in support of the claim. Unless these details are tendered they will usually be asked for and in the absence of sufficient information the claim may well be rejected. Many trade unions have negotiated round sum allowances on behalf of their members. These allowances should be granted without further enquiry, although individual employees may attempt to establish increased relief if supporting evidence can be supplied.

Employees performing services wholly outside the United Kingdom under the terms of a separate contract may usually deduct the cost of travelling from, and returning to, the United Kingdom.

Fees and subscriptions paid to a large number of professional bodies and learned societies may be deducted from earnings. The Inland Revenue retains a list of approved bodies and only subscriptions paid to a body or society whose name appears on the list can be deducted.

Examples of expenditure which can be included in an expenses claim:

a **Hotel Expenses** for sales representatives and others who have to go from place to place in the performance of their duties. No restriction will normally be necessary for any 'home saving' effected by the employee while away on business trips.

b **Office Accommodation**, clerical assistance, stationery, and similar expenses where necessary to the employment.

c **Overalls, Clothing and Tools** where the employee must supply these items specially for his employment. Many trade unions have negotiated round sum allowances for these items on behalf of their members.

d **Travelling Expenses** actually incurred in performing the duties.

e **Professional Fees and Subscriptions** paid to Societies with activities related to an employee's work.

f **Rent** and other outgoings incurred by clergymen and ministers of religion.

Examples of expenditure which cannot be included in an expenses claim:

a **Travelling Expenses** in travelling to and from the taxpayer's place of employment, unless the employment is carried out overseas.

b **Instruction Fees and Cost of Books** where incurred by the employee to enable him to qualify in his appointment or to put him in a position to carry out his employment. There may be some relief for expenditure incurred on approved vocational training (see page 37).

INSURABLE RISKS
Some directors and employees must increasingly contemplate taking out personal insurance cover against work-related risks. Others who have no or insufficient cover may be compelled to personally discharge uninsured liabilities. Neither the cost of obtaining cover nor the cost of discharging insurable liabilities could previously be relieved when calculating liability to income tax.

However, this approach has been relaxed for expenditure incurred after 5 April 1995. From that date the cost of obtaining insurance cover against work-related risks can be subtracted from income chargeable to tax. In addition, the cost of meeting uninsured work-related liabilities can also be relieved. This latter relief is limited to risks capable of being insured against and will not apply to other risks, for example, liabilities associated with criminal convictions.

Similar relief for both the cost of obtaining insurance cover and meeting uninsured liabilities will be available to a former director or employee. It is a condition that the expenditure is incurred within a period of six years following the end of the year of assessment in which the employment ended.

Where the employer discharges the cost of personal insurance cover or the cost of satisfying uninsured risks this previously created a benefit on which the director or employee was required to suffer income tax. However, tax commitments of this nature may now be avoided (see page 49).

MOTOR MILEAGE ALLOWANCES
Where an employee uses his or her own motor car for business purposes the employer will usually pay a motor mileage allowance. This allowance may be

27
FIXED PROFIT CAR SCHEME

Throughout the year of assessment 1995–96 Sam used his own motor car when travelling on his employer's business. The vehicle was of 1,600 cylinder capacity and 6,200 miles of business motoring were involved in the year. The employer paid a mileage allowance at the rate of 45p per mile and the Fixed Profit Car Scheme applied.

The tax-free mileage allowance for 1995–96 will be calculated as follows:

		£
First 4,000 miles at 43p		1,720.00
Next 2,200 miles at 23p		506.00
		£2,226.00

Total mileage allowances paid		
6,200 at 45p		£2,790.00

Sam will suffer income tax on £564 (£2,790 less £2,226). This tax should be imposed through the PAYE system. There can be no expenses claim, or claim for capital allowances on the cost of the motor car.

generous or austere, but any sum paid is strictly income chargeable to income tax with PAYE deductions being imposed. It then remains for the employee to submit an expenses claim in an endeavour to obtain relief from income tax suffered.

This is a cumbersome and time-consuming exercise and considerable administrative savings may be achieved by adopting the 'Fixed Profit Car Scheme', with the approval of the Inland Revenue. The broad effect of this scheme is that the Inland Revenue announce the maximum amount of mileage allowances which will not result in the employee becoming chargeable to income tax. Motor cars are graded into a number of bands for this purpose.

To the extent that mileage allowances exceed the approved levels, the excess will be treated as income chargeable to income tax without the benefit of any expenses claim.

The Fixed Profit Car Scheme is limited to mileage allowances paid for business motoring and has no application to other matters. Employees are not obliged to adopt the scheme and may choose to apply the statutory basis. Whilst consideration must be applied to individual circumstances, it is unlikely that the statutory basis will result in any increased exemption from taxation.

The mileage rates used for the Fixed Profit Car Scheme take account of depreciation, insurance, road tax, fuel, services and repairs attributable to the business miles travelled. They do not include interest. It follows that any interest paid on a loan applied to acquire a motor car may enable the employee to obtain relief for the business proportion of that interest.

The rates used for the purposes of the Fixed Profit Car Scheme for both 1994–95 and 1995–96 are shown below.

FIXED PROFIT CAR SCHEME TAX-FREE LIMITS 1994–95		
Cylinder capacity	Up to 4,000 miles per mile (p)	Over 4,000 miles per mile (p)
Up to 1,000	27	15
1,001–1,500	33	19
1,501–2,000	41	23
2,001 and above	56	31

FIXED PROFIT CAR SCHEME TAX-FREE LIMITS 1995–96		
Cylinder capacity	Up to 4,000 miles per mile (p)	Over 4,000 miles per mile (p)
Up to 1,000	27	15
1,001–1,500	34	19
1,501–2,000	43	23
2,001 and above	60	32

8

Benefits in kind

ALL EMPLOYEES

Assessment under Schedule E extends to 'emoluments' arising from an office or employment. The expression 'emoluments' is defined to include all salaries, fees, wages, perquisites and profits whatsoever. This definition will embrace most 'rewards' received by an employee but some advantages may be enjoyed which are not necessarily subject to tax, including earnings arising under a profit-related pay scheme. As a general rule, any advantages which can be turned into money will be taxed but those which cannot may escape liability. For example, an employee may enjoy the use of a company car but as such an advantage cannot be converted into money no liability will arise. This remains subject to the special rules, discussed on page 52, which apply to directors and many employees.

In those cases where an employee receives 'money's worth' which is chargeable to tax, liability will arise on the market value of the benefit and not necessarily on the cost to the employer of providing that benefit, but there are many exceptions. An employee who is provided with a voucher, by reason of his office or employment, will be taxed on the cost to the employer in providing the voucher and not on the value of goods for which that voucher can be exchanged. Advantages which arise from the provision of season tickets financed by an employer, or the use of an employer's credit card, incur liability to income tax. Payments made to an employee during a period of sickness or disability are taxable, except to the extent that the payments are funded from contributions made by the employee. This is in addition to the tax imposed on statutory short term sickness benefit paid by an employer. The first 15p in value of a luncheon voucher is exempt but the excess is not. Travel vouchers, warrants and allowances made available to members of the armed forces when going on, or returning from, leave are not chargeable to tax.

Where an employer satisfies a personal obligation of an employee the amount involved will be assessable. An illustration may involve the employer who satisfies the council tax payable by an employee, unless the tax is attributable to property occupied by the employee as part of his or her employment. This may not apply to the reimbursement of expenditure relating to insurable risks, as explained on the following page.

In practice, the Inland Revenue do not seek to charge tax in respect of awards made to directors and employees as testimonials to mark long service where the period of service is not less than twenty years and no similar award has been made to the recipient within the previous ten years. This concession is broadly limited to tangible articles, for example a watch or television set, having a cost or value not exceeding £20 for each year of service but may also include the provision of shares in the employing company. Also by concession, rewards paid under a genuine suggestion scheme, the reimbursement of expenses where an employee has been required to make alternative travelling or accommodation arrangements due to industrial disputes, the cost of late night journeys where an employee is occasionally required to work late and the provision of financial assistance to severely disabled employees when travelling from home to work do not create a liability to income tax. Nor will liability arise where an employee is reimbursed the cost of car parking at or near the place of work.

Some employees receive gifts from third parties. The value of these gifts will not be taxed if they are unsolicited. It is a requirement that gifts received from the same source do not exceed £100 in any year and the exemption does not extend to cash gifts or tips. However, a payment made to an individual as an inducement to take up employment, sometimes referred to as a 'Golden Hello', is likely to be fully taxable.

Where an employee is working wholly abroad the reimbursement of travelling and hotel expenses by the employer will not create an emolument assessable to income tax. A similar exemption applies where the employer bears the cost of travel incurred by an employee's spouse and children. It is a necessary requirement that the family travel to and from the country where the employee is working and the United Kingdom. Expenses incurred by, or reimbursed to, a non-domiciled individual when travelling to the United Kingdom for employment purposes are also exempt, but this extends only to travelling within a period of five years from the initial date of arrival in this territory.

Employees who stay away from home overnight on business will often incur incidental expenses of a personal nature. These expenses may include the cost of newspapers, personal telephone calls and laundry. Where, as will frequently be the case, expenditure of this nature is borne by the employer a taxable benefit will arise. However, the creation of this benefit may be avoided from 6 April 1995 where the amount borne by the employer does not exceed £5 per night in the United Kingdom or £10 per night overseas. Should these limits be exceeded the entire amount borne by the employer will be treated as a taxable benefit accruing to the employee.

The ability of an employee to acquire shares or securities on advantageous terms will often create liability to income tax. However, exemption may be available where shares or securities are acquired under an approved profit sharing scheme, a savings-related share option scheme or an approved share option scheme.

RELOCATION PACKAGES

An employee may need to move home on being relocated by his or her employer to some other area. A move may also be necessary where an employee

takes up a new job. In circumstances such as these the employee may receive cash payments or other benefits from the employer which could become chargeable to income tax. However, liability will not arise if those items form part of a qualifying relocation package.

Several conditions must be satisfied before exemption can be obtained, namely:

a the employee must change his or her main residence as the result of commencing a new employment, a change in the duties of an existing employment or a change in the location of that employment;

b the new main residence must be within a reasonable daily travelling distance of the new normal place of work;

c the old residence must not be within a reasonable daily travelling distance of the new normal place of work; and

d the expenses must be incurred, or the benefits provided, before the end of the year of assessment following the one in which the employee commences the new job. The date on which the actual move from one residence to the other takes place is not material. The time limit may be extended at the discretion of the Inland Revenue.

Where these several requirements are satisfied, eligible expenses and benefits may fall within six broad categories, namely:

a Matters attributable to the disposal, or intended disposal, of the old residence.

b Matters attributable to the acquisition, or intended acquisition, of a new residence.

c The provision of transportation and storage of domestic belongings.

d Travelling and subsistence for the employee and members of the employee's family.

e The replacement of domestic goods for use in the new property.

f Interest on certain bridging loans which would otherwise create taxable benefits (see page 56).

These headings include not only expenses actually incurred but also the provision of some benefit, for example, the use of living accommodation. It is a requirement that exemption is confined to an aggregate of £8,000, representing both expenditure and benefits.

INSURABLE RISKS

It is sometimes necessary for a director or employee to obtain personal insurance cover against work-related risks. If the cost of obtaining this cover is borne by the employer the amount involved will create a benefit in kind on which the individual must suffer income tax. In the absence of any, or sufficient, insurance cover an employer may fund the cost of meeting an employee's uninsured liabilities. Here also the amount involved will create a taxable benefit. However, from 6 April 1995 the creation of most forms of tax liability under this heading may be avoided. In the case of insurance premiums it must be shown that the liability is work-related. Where uninsured liabilities are involved these must comprise matters capable of being insured against. Commonly this will comprise legal costs and the payment of damages but it will not extend to other liabilities, including criminal matters.

Tax liability is avoided by enabling qualifying expenditure to be included in a Schedule E expenses claim (see page 46). Therefore, although a taxable benefit may arise it is offset by subtracting the expense deemed to have been incurred.

PROVISION OF LIVING ACCOMMODATION

An additional liability to income tax may arise where an employee is provided with living accommodation by reason of his or her employment. This liability also applies where such accommodation is provided for use by the employee's wife or husband, son or daughter, son-in-law, daughter-in-law, parent, servant, dependant or guest. There are, however, exceptions and no liability will accrue where the employer is an individual and the accommodation is made available in the normal course of a domestic, family or personal relationship. Nor will it apply to most accommodation used by employees of a local authority. In addition, no liability will arise on the provision of living accommodation for an employee:

a where it is necessary for the proper performance of the employee's duties that he or she should reside in the accommodation, or

b where the accommodation is provided for the better performance of the duties of employment, and this is one of the kinds of employment in the case of which it is customary for employers to provide living accommodation for employees, or

c where, there being a threat to the employee's security, special security arrangements are in force and the employee resides in the accommodation as part of those arrangements.

The exclusions under a and b have little application to most company directors.

Where liability does arise, the employee is treated as receiving an additional emolument taxable under Schedule E. This emolument will comprise an amount equal to:

a the value of the accommodation for the period of availability in each year of assessment; less

b contributions made by the employee.

It will be clear that no additional emolument will arise where a rent is paid by the employee which equals or exceeds the value under a.

—28—
PROVISION OF ACCOMMODATION

In 1983 Company A purchased a residential property in Surrey having a gross rateable value of £2,500. Basil is an employee of the company and throughout the year ending on 5 April 1996 occupied the property as his private home. No rent was paid in return for the provision of living accommodation.

The emolument on which Basil will suffer income tax for 1995–96 must be calculated as follows:

	£
Value of accommodation – gross rateable value	2,500
Less contribution	NIL
Emolument 1995–96	£2,500

For properties in the United Kingdom, the value of the accommodation will comprise the gross rateable value used for rating purposes or, if it is greater, any rent paid by the person providing accommodation. To eliminate distortions in Scotland where properties have been uprated, the former rateable value continues to be used. Although general rates were replaced in Great Britain by the community charge, which in turn was replaced by yet another system, the council tax, rateable values continue to be used as a 'measure' for income tax purposes. In the case of new properties it will be necessary to estimate a comparable rateable value.

Expensive accommodation

A further liability to income tax may arise where an employer provides an employee with more expensive living accommodation. This is in addition to the liability mentioned above and remains subject to the exclusions and exemptions referred to earlier.

The further liability is confined to living accommodation obtained at a cost exceeding £75,000, and

29
PROVISION OF EXPENSIVE ACCOMMODATION

Using the facts of Example 28, let it be assumed that Company A paid £150,000 to acquire the residential property in 1983. Further expenditure of £40,000 was incurred before 6 April 1995 in carrying out improvements to the property. It will be assumed that the official rate of interest on 5 April 1995 was 8 per cent per annum. On this basis the emoluments arising to Basil for 1995–96 become:

		£
a Emolument as calculated in Example 28 .		2,500
b Additional emolument:		

Cost of providing accommodation:	£	
Cost of acquisition .	150,000	
Improvements . .	40,000	
Aggregate cost .	190,000	
Less to be excluded .	75,000	
Excess . .	£115,000	

		£
Emolument:		
£115,000 × 8 per cent . . .		9,200
Total emoluments from living accommodation		£11,700

can have no application where cost falls below this figure. 'Cost' includes not only expenditure laid out to acquire accommodation but includes any further outgoings on carrying out improvements, where those outgoings have been incurred before the commencement of the year of assessment concerned. In some situations, where property has been retained for more than six years before the employee enters into occupation, 'cost' may be replaced by 'market value'.

Where the cost, or market value if appropriate, of providing living accommodation does exceed £75,000, the excess over this figure must be established. The further emolument then represents 'the additional value of the accommodation', which is calculated by applying the official rate of interest at the beginning of the tax year to the excess. This rate is altered from time to time, but on 6 November 1994 was increased to 8 per cent per annum.

If the employee provides rent, or makes some other contribution for the use of living accommodation, this may be subtracted from the additional emolument, but only to the extent that it exceeds the gross rateable value of the property, or rent paid by the employer, whichever is the higher.

Therefore, for 1995–96 two different emoluments may arise where expensive living accommodation is made available. This combined liability affects all employees and is not confined to directors and the higher-paid.

EMPLOYEES EARNING £8,500 OR MORE AND DIRECTORS

The assessment of fringe benefits is broadened considerably for most company directors and many employees. The persons affected are employees earning £8,500 or more and directors, an approach which incorporates:

a all directors, except certain directors earning less than £8,500 per annum and who do not, either individually or with certain members of their family, retain a substantial shareholding interest in the company. This exception is limited to full-time working directors and directors of non-profit making companies or charitable bodies; and

b all employees earning £8,500 or more per annum.

For the purpose of establishing whether a director or employee earns £8,500 or more per annum and is therefore subject to the additional liabilities discussed below, his or her actual earnings must be increased by:

a adding the value of any benefits mentioned on the previous pages;

b adding the value of any benefits referred to below;

c ignoring any expenses which may be deducted from earnings.

This implies that many employees earning less than £8,500 per annum may become assessible on 'fringe benefits', once the adjustments have been made to the calculation of their notional income.

Assessment of benefits

The assessment of benefits is not limited to facilities and advantages made available to a director or employee personally but extends also to benefits provided for that person's spouse, his sons and daughters and their spouses, his parents, servants, dependants and guests.

Where an employer pays a sum representing 'expenses' to a director or employee this sum will comprise an additional emolument and it remains for the director or employee to submit an acceptable expenses claim if additional liability to income tax is not to arise. In many cases this formality can be avoided by obtaining a dispensation from HM Inspector of Taxes. In those cases where an employee provides his or her own motor car for business travel and receives a mileage allowance, the Fixed Profit Car Scheme outlined on page 47 may also be used to avoid the formality of a claim for expenses. This scheme will not always be available for a director.

Should an employer incur expense in providing some facility or advantage for the benefit of a director or employee the cost incurred by the employer, referred to as the 'cash equivalent', is treated as additional remuneration unless, or to the extent that, the cost is made good by the recipient. For example, should an employer purchase a television set for, say, £400 and immediately transfer the ownership of that set to a qualifying director or employee for no consideration, a benefit of £400 will be assessable to income tax. If the individual provides consideration of, say, £150, the taxable benefit becomes £250.

The calculation of the cash equivalent previously gave rise to uncertainty where an employer made facilities available to employees on advantageous terms. This could affect employees at private schools whose children were educated at a reduced fee and employees of transport undertakings able to travel at a price lower than that charged to full fare paying customers. The Inland Revenue now accept it is only the *additional* cost incurred by the employer in making these facilities available which represents the 'cash equivalent' and not the *average* cost for all children or customers.

Liability will not extend to the cost of providing meals in a canteen where those meals are available to all employees, to certain accommodation provided for an employee who is required as a condition of his employment to use the accommodation, or to the cost of providing future pensions. An employer will often incur expenses in providing a Christmas party, annual dinner dance or similar function for the benefit of employees. In practice, no taxable benefit will arise on those attending when the cost does not exceed £50 per head. Nor will liability accrue from the provision of most in-house sports facilities provided by the employer.

A taxable benefit may be provided by some person other than the recipient's employer. However, where entertainment is made available for a director or employee by a third party no benefit will arise unless the advantage arose under an arrangement with the employee's own employer or was given in return for some service or anticipated service. 'Entertainment' may also include the provision of seats at a sporting or cultural event.

Scholarship awards

The employer of a director or employee may sometimes finance the cost of scholarships awarded to a child of that individual. This is frequently achieved by a company contributing funds to the trustees of an educational trust who provide the award to selected children. Arrangements of this nature will result in the parent being assessed on the cost involved

Workplace nurseries

Benefits arising from a limited range of child care facilities are not assessable on those earning £8,500 or more. Exemption extends to nurseries run at the workplace or elsewhere by the employer. It will also extend to nurseries run by employers jointly with other employers, voluntary bodies or local authorities, and include facilities made available for older children after school or during school holidays. A condition for obtaining exemption requires that the child care facilities must comply with any local requirement for registration by the appropriate local authority. No exemption will be forthcoming if the child care facilities are made available in domestic premises.

The exemption will not extend to the provision of cash allowances for child care or the payment by an employer of an employee's bills. Nor will it be available where the employer provides vouchers which can be used by the employee to discharge child care expenses.

USE OF ASSETS

Many items of expenditure incurred, or deemed to have been incurred, by an employer will not result in the transfer of any asset to the director or employee. Detailed rules must then be applied to calculate the benefit assessable to income tax and for this purpose a distinction is drawn between the provision of motor cars, fuel for private motoring, mobile telephones, motor vans, loan facilities, and other assets or advantages. The application of these special rules is discussed below.

MOTOR CARS

Where a motor car is made available for private motoring by a director or employee the calculation of any taxable benefit will be governed in part by the amount of business mileage. Subject to the amount of this mileage, it must be emphasised that it is the availability of a motor car for private motoring which produces a benefit and not the actual use to which the vehicle is applied.

30
PROVISION OF MOTOR CAR

A company purchased a new motor car at an inclusive cost of £21,500 on 18 May 1994. The vehicle was first registered on that date and on the previous day had a 'list price', as calculated for tax purposes, of £25,200. The company had negotiated a substantial fleet discount when purchasing the vehicle from a local dealer. Immediately following purchase the car was used by a director who continued this use throughout 1995–96. There were 12,000 miles of business motoring in the year.

The list price of £25,200, and not the purchase price of £21,500, must be used to calculate the taxable benefit. This gives rise to the following basic benefit:

35 per cent × £25,200 . . . . £8,820

As there were more than 2,500 miles of business motoring the taxable benefit may be reduced as follows:

	£
Basic benefit	8,820
Less one-third	2,940
Taxable benefit 1995–96	£5,880

For 1993–94 and earlier years standard scale charges were used to calculate the taxable benefit arising from the availability of a motor car for private motoring. However, an entirely new system was introduced from 6 April 1994 which abandons the use of scale charges and determines the amount of any taxable benefit by reference to the list price of a vehicle.

Calculating the list price
The list price of a motor car will usually comprise the aggregate of:

a the manufacturer's, importer's or distributor's list price of the vehicle on the day before the date of its first registration;
b value added tax and car tax attributable to the supply;
c delivery charges, including value added tax;
d the list price of any accessory, including value added tax, which was fitted before the car was first made available to the employee (this will include delivery and fitting charges); and
e the list price of any accessory over £100, including value added tax, fitting and delivery costs, fitted after the car was first made available to the employee. This applies only to accessories fitted after 31 July 1993.

A motor car may require conversion to suit the

needs of a disabled driver. This will usually involve the installation of 'accessories' which increases the list price of the vehicle. However, from 6 April 1995 the cost of installing accessories specifically for use by a disabled driver can be ignored when calculating the list price.

For classic cars more than fifteen years old and having a market value exceeding £15,000 the list price is replaced by market value.

It is possible that an employee may provide a contribution towards the cost of acquiring a motor car or fitted accessories. Any contribution of this nature, up to a maximum of £5,000, may be deducted from the list price or market value. It is then only the net figure remaining which comprises the adjusted list price.

The maximum list price or market value is limited to £80,000. Any sum in excess of this amount is disregarded.

Calculating the benefit – 1995–96
The basic taxable benefit for 1995–96 will comprise 35 per cent of the list price (or market value). This figure will be reduced

a by one-third if the annual business mileage exceeds 2,500 miles; and
b by two-thirds if business mileage is 18,000 miles or more.

Vehicles which are four years of age or more on the last day of the income tax year will attract a further reduction of one-third when calculating the taxable benefit.

In those situations where a director or employee has more than one motor car available for his or her use only one vehicle can be identified when establishing the deductions under a and b above. This will be the vehicle which is the subject of the greater business mileage.

No benefit will usually arise from the use of a vehicle forming part of a 'pool' provided that:

a the vehicle is actually used by two or more employees;
b any private use by an employee is merely incidental; and
c the vehicle is not normally kept overnight in or near the vicinity of the employee's home.

The amount of any taxable benefit will be reduced where a vehicle is available for part only of a full year. There will also be an adjustment where the car user contributes towards the cost of private motoring.

— 31 —
MOTOR CAR –
THE ALTERNATIVES

Example 30 illustrates the taxable benefit arising from the availability of a motor car less than 4 years of age, with a list price of £25,200 and used for more than 2,500 miles of business motoring. There is a basic benefit of £8,820.

Using the same basic benefit, the possible taxable benefits are as follows:

	Age of vehicle	
	Under	Over
Business Mileage	4 years	4 years
	£	£
Not exceeding 2,500 miles	8,820	5,580
Between 2,500 and 18,000 miles	5,880	3,920
18,000 miles or more	2,940	1,960

No additional benefit will arise from the availability of a motor car unless the employer provides a chauffeur. Where a chauffeur is provided his wages and any other expenses will represent an additional benefit derived by the director or employee. The provision of a car parking space at or near the place of work will not be treated as producing a taxable benefit. The use of a car telephone will give rise to a separate benefit (see page 55).

The collection of tax on car benefits is usually achieved by using 'K' codes. The function of these codes is reviewed on page 41.

FUEL SUPPLIED FOR PRIVATE MOTORING

The scale based calculations which apply to create a taxable benefit where a motor car is provided for private motoring during 1995–96 will not necessarily exhaust all liability for the same year. There may be additional fuel benefit charges. These potential fuel benefits arise whenever a motor car is made available to a director or employee (including members of those individuals' families and households) for private motoring. Therefore, where a car benefit arises from the availability of a motor car (as discussed above), a car fuel benefit may also arise.

Car fuel benefits are measured by reference to scale charges. The scale charges for both 1994–95 and 1995–96 are shown by the tables on the following page. These tables disclose an increase of some 5 per cent for petrol driven cars and 4 per cent for diesel cars for 1995–96 when compared with the previous year.

When applying the scale charges no distinction is drawn between substantial and insubstantial use, nor is the age of the car significant. There is, however, a distinction between vehicles using petrol and those powered by diesel fuel.

Should a vehicle be available for part only of the year, or a vehicle falling within one scale charge be replaced by a vehicle falling within a different scale, the benefit must be suitably adjusted.

There will be no scale charge if the employer only provides petrol or other fuel for business travel. Contributions towards the cost of fuel supplied for private motoring will only be recognised to eliminate the scale charge if both:

a the director or employee is *required* to make good the whole of the expense incurred when providing fuel for private motoring; and

b the *whole* cost is actually satisfied.

Arrangements for collecting income tax on car fuel benefits through the PAYE system are similar to those for motor car benefits.

The restructuring of taxable benefits, which applied to the availability of a car for private motoring on 6 April 1994, has no application to the car fuel benefits. These benefits continue to be based on scale figures.

— 32 —
MOTOR CAR AND FUEL BENEFITS

A company purchased a new petrol driven 1,600 cc motor car in August 1994. The list price of the vehicle was £14,700. It was established that the car had been used by a director for both business and private travel throughout 1995–96 and 8,000 miles of business mileage was involved. All petrol used for both business travel and private motoring was supplied by the company. No contribution was made by the director.

The taxable benefits for 1995–96 will be calculated as follows:

	£
Availability of motor car	
List price – £14,700	
Basic benefit 35 per cent of £14,700	5,145
Less one-third – mileage exceeding	
2,500 miles	1,715
Taxable benefit	£3,430
Fuel for private motoring	
Scale charge – taxable benefit	£850
Total taxable benefits	£4,280

CAR FUEL SCALE BENEFITS 1994–95

Cars having a recognised cylinder capacity

PETROL FUEL				Annual benefit
Cylinder capacity:				£
1,400 or under	.	.	.	640
1,401 to 2,000	.	.	.	810
2,001 or more	.	.	.	1,200
DIESEL FUEL				**Annual benefit**
Cylinder capacity:				£
2,000 or under	.	.	.	580
2,001 or more	.	.	.	750

Cars without a cylinder capacity

Any car	.	.	.	.	1,200

CAR FUEL SCALE BENEFITS 1995–96

Cars having a recognised cylinder capacity

PETROL FUEL				Annual benefit
Cylinder capacity:				£
1,400 or under	.	.	.	670
1,401 to 2,000	.	.	.	850
2,001 or more	.	.	.	1,260
DIESEL FUEL				**Annual benefit**
Cylinder capacity:				£
2,000 or under	.	.	.	605
2,001 or more	.	.	.	780

Cars without a cylinder capacity

Any car	.	.	.	.	1,260

NATIONAL INSURANCE CONTRIBUTIONS

Before 6 April 1991, the availability of a motor car for private motoring did not create earnings for the purpose of calculating liability to Class 1 national insurance contributions. Liability arose from some arrangements involving the supply of fuel for private motoring but there were several exceptions. From 6 April 1991, however, the position changed significantly. In those cases where a director or higher-paid employee has the use of a motor car for private motoring the income tax benefit calculations are now used to establish earnings for Class 1 purposes. A similar approach is applied to the supply of fuel for private motoring, with the income tax scale charges being used. This approach does not require the satisfaction of primary Class 1 contributions by the employee. However, the employer must discharge secondary contributions. The amount of contributions arising under this heading is calculated after the end of each year of assessment and accounted for in the following June.

MOBILE TELEPHONES

Also before 6 April 1991, no taxable benefit arose from the private use of a telephone fitted in a motor car, although benefits did arise from the private use of other mobile telephones. From 6 April 1991, a standard taxable benefit is created from the private use of a mobile telephone whether fitted in a motor car or not. The standard annual charge comprises £200 for each mobile telephone. The taxable benefit will only be avoided if there is either no private use whatsoever or, where private use does arise, the employee is required to make good the whole cost, including an appropriate proportion of subscriber and other standing charges.

VANS

No special provisions were previously in place for calculating the taxable benefit arising from the availability of a van, as opposed to the availability of a motor car. Where vans were used for non-business purposes the general approach mentioned on page 57 was applied to calculate the benefit. This general approach was replaced by special provisions which apply from 6 April 1993.

These provisions impose a standard charge for the use of all vans. The word 'vans' identifies vehicles built primarily to carry goods or other loads with a gross vehicle weight not exceeding 3,500 kilograms. Where a van is made available for non-business travel, particularly involving travel from home to work, a standard benefit of £500 arises for 1995–96. This is reduced to £350 for vehicles more than four years old at the end of the tax year. In those cases where the use of a van is shared between two or more employees the standard charge of £500, or £350, must be suitably apportioned. It is possible that the allocation of the standard charge for shared vans may result in more than £500, or £350, being allocated to an individual where two or more vans are involved. However, the allocation is restricted to ensure that no individual has taxable benefits from the use of shared vans exceeding the limit of £500 or £350.

The standard charge will be reduced pro rata for

vans which become, or cease to be, available or are incapable of being used for thirty or more consecutive days during the year. In the rather unusual situation where an employee has more than two vans available simultaneously, a standard charge will arise in respect of each vehicle. No taxable benefit will arise in the case of pooled vans unless the vehicle is normally kept at or near the homes of the employees who share the van. There will be no additional charge for the provision of petrol or diesel fuel.

The standard charge for vans has no application to vehicles having a gross weight in excess of 3,500 kilograms. Nor does it extend to the private use of vehicles built primarily for the carriage of passengers, namely cars and mini-buses.

The standard charge of £500, £350 or a proportion of those amounts where vehicles are shared, will be reduced by any contribution made towards non-business use.

LOAN FACILITIES

Loans made available for the benefit of a director or employee may frequently be interest-free or carry a rate of interest falling below a commercial level. Where these facilities are obtained the director or employee may derive a taxable benefit representing the difference between the official rate of interest and the actual interest paid, if any. The official rate is changed from time to time but was increased to 8 per cent per annum on 6 November 1994.

There are alternative methods of calculating the taxable benefit using the official rate. One, 'the normal method', is to take the average rate of interest and the average amount of the loan for the entire year, or the period of the loan, if shorter. The other, 'the alternative method', which either the employee or HM Inspector of Taxes can require, calculates notional interest on the actual loan on a day-to-day basis.

For 1993–94 no liability to tax arose if the notional interest calculated on the appropriate basis did not exceed £300. If this threshold was exceeded the entire benefit became chargeable to income tax.

The £300 exemption limit has no application for later years. It still remains to calculate the difference between interest paid, if any, and the official rate. However, the next step in the calculation of income tax liability will be governed by the facts of each individual.

One possibility is that if interest had actually become payable on the loan that interest would, in whole or in part, have qualified for income tax relief.

33
LOAN USED FOR QUALIFYING PURPOSE

Albert, a married man whose only income for 1995–96 was a salary of £23,000, received an interest-free loan of £40,000 from his employers in 1991. The entire loan was applied to purchase the home occupied by Albert and his family and remained outstanding throughout 1995–96. It is assumed that an official rate of, say, 8 per cent applied throughout that year.

On the assumption that Albert is a married man entitled to the entire married couple's allowance, the tax payable for 1995–96 will be calculated as follows:

Taxable benefit:

	£
£40,000 × 8 per cent	3,200
Less interest actually paid	NIL
Taxable benefit	£3,200
Tax relief limited to £30,000 × 8 per cent	£2,400

Total income:

	£
Salary	23,000
Taxable benefit	3,200
	26,200
Less personal allowance	3,525
	£22,675

Tax payable:

	£
On first £3,200 at 20 per cent	640.00
On balance of £19,475 at 25 per cent	4,868.75
	5,508.75

	£	
Less		
Married couple's allowance – £1,720 at 15 per cent	258	
Interest – £2,400 at 15 per cent	360	618.00
		£4,890.75

Notes:
(1) Although tax is payable on 'interest forgone' on the loan of £40,000, relief is only available for interest on £30,000.
(2) It will be seen that whilst the benefit of £3,200 has been taxed at Albert's top rate of 25 per cent, relief for notional interest of £2,400 has only been given at the reduced rate of 15 per cent.

This will frequently be the case where a loan is applied to acquire an individual's home. In a situation of this nature:

a the benefit arising will be treated as income chargeable to income tax; but

34
EXEMPT LOANS

Susan received two interest-free loans aggregating £4,750 from her employers. Both loans were outstanding throughout 1995–96. The loans do not exceed in aggregate £5,000 and no taxable benefit will arise.

John received a loan of £2,000 from his employers to finance the purchase of an annual season ticket. He also received a loan of £17,500 to purchase his home. On the assumption that any interest, if actually paid, on the loan of £17,500 would qualify for tax relief, no taxable benefit will accrue by reason of the further loan amounting to £2,000. However, liability will arise for interest forgone on the larger loan of £17,500 in a manner similar to that illustrated by Example 33.

---

b relief will be available at the appropriate rate on the amount of interest which, if paid, would qualify for that relief.

This two part adjustment is necessary as whilst income of an individual may be taxable at the rate of 20 per cent, 25 per cent or 40 per cent for 1995–96, relief for some payments of interest, notably mortgage interest, is limited to 15 per cent.

No taxable benefit will arise if all loans made to an employee do not exceed £5,000. Exemption from liability is also available if all loans, excluding loans which qualify for tax relief, do not exceed £5,000. In the latter case tax will be due for 'interest forgone' on the loan qualifying for relief.

Nor will liability arise for 'interest forgone' on loans made to employees on commercial terms by employers who lend to the general public. This deals with the situation where the official rate, which is altered infrequently, actually exceeds the commercial rate of interest charged.

It may also be possible to avoid tax on benefits in kind attributable to loans where these facilities form part of a relocation package (see page 49).

Where a loan provided for a director or employee is subsequently released or written off, in whole or in part, the amount involved will be treated as part of the individual's remuneration. No liability will, however, arise where the release or writing off occurs on or after the borrower's death.

Directors or employees may sometimes be permitted to acquire shares for a consideration falling below market value. Arrangements of this nature may produce liability to income tax under several headings, including the possibility that the advantage may be treated as representing a notional loan creating a benefit in the manner discussed above.

OTHER ASSETS

Where an employer provides a director or higher-paid employee with the use of an asset which is neither living accommodation, a motor car, fuel used for private motoring, a van, a mobile telephone nor a loan of money, the annual benefit assessable to tax will comprise the aggregate of:

a the annual value, and
b the expense incurred by the employer in providing the use.

If the employer rents or hires an asset made available for use by the director or employee the rental paid will be substituted for the annual value, should this produce a higher benefit.

For land, including dwelling-houses, located in the United Kingdom the annual value will usually represent the gross annual value used for rating purposes, notwithstanding the successive replacement of rating by the community charge and the council tax. This will not apply to the provision of living accommodation, which is dealt with under a separate heading (see page 50). In other cases the annual value will be 20 per cent of the asset's value when it was first made available for use by the director or employee.

Should the ownership of such an asset subsequently be transferred to the director or employee, an additional benefit may arise. This will represent the difference, if any, between the market value of the asset when it was first made available and the aggregate of:

a the consideration given by the director or employee to acquire the asset, and
b the amount of taxable benefits arising during the employer's period of ownership.

This basis only applies if it produces a greater taxable benefit than the excess of current market value, at the time of acquisition by the director or employee, over the price paid by him or her.

9

Redundancy payments

REDUNDANCY AND LOSS of employment are matters of great concern to those affected. An outgoing director or employee may be entitled to benefit from, or to pursue, several statutory rights which are outside the scope of the present work. The individual may also receive certain payments as a result of redundancy or dismissal and the taxation liability of these sums is discussed below.

STATUTORY REDUNDANCY PAYMENTS

On leaving an employment a director or employee may well receive a statutory redundancy payment. The amount of this payment is tax-free and will not involve the recipient in any liability to taxation.

PAYMENTS DUE BY AGREEMENT

In addition to the statutory redundancy payment, if any, an outgoing director or employee may also receive other terminal payments, often described as 'golden handshakes', from his or her former employer. The treatment of these additional sums will be governed by the circumstances in which they are paid. For example, some service agreements contain a provision that, in the event of premature termination, a lump sum will be payable to the employee. Payments of this nature may well represent rewards arising from the contract of service and become assessable to income tax under Schedule E, although the Inland Revenue will not attempt to proceed if 'genuine' redundancy occurs. Whether a terminal payment is solely related to 'genuine' redundancy or represents, in whole or in part, a reward for services rendered can become a difficult

matter to decide. Employers contemplating making a terminal payment to an outgoing director or employee are encouraged to seek the views of the Inland Revenue before proceeding.

OTHER TERMINAL PAYMENTS

Many lump sum terminal payments made by an employer to an outgoing director or employee will not relate to services rendered or fail to satisfy the test of 'genuine redundancy'. The treatment of these terminal payments will then be governed by a number of complex rules.

First, an ex gratia payment made solely by reason of death or disablement by accident will not be directly assessable to income tax. Nor will severance payments made on redundancy or loss of office be assessable. These payments are subject to the £30,000 exemption rule mentioned later.

Secondly, lump sum payments made under the terms of an approved occupational pension scheme will not be treated as income.

Thirdly, other lump sum payments which are not made under the terms of an approved scheme may be exempt from tax if:

a there is only one lump sum payable to the director or employee;

b the director or employee is not a member of an approved scheme conferring benefits other than those attributable to death in service; and

c the lump sum payment does not exceed the limit placed on lump sums payable from approved schemes.

Fourthly, other ex gratia payments made on or in

connection with an individual's death or retirement, but not in relation to redundancy, may well be chargeable to income tax under Schedule E.

Finally, those lump sum payments which are made solely on the grounds of genuine redundancy and for no other reason should be subject to the £30,000 exemption rule outlined below.

In addition to making lump sum payments, an employer may fund the cost of providing counselling services for employees who have become, or are about to become, redundant. These counselling costs may be included in the redundancy package giving rise to the £30,000 exemption.

The £30,000 exemption

It remains to examine the treatment of ex gratia or other terminal payments which are neither treated as income and chargeable to income tax nor made exempt from tax under the terms of an approved occupational pension scheme. This will broadly extend to payments made to an employee on severance of an employment due to redundancy or loss of office, or because of death or disability due to accident.

The first £30,000 received is usually exempt from income tax, with any excess remaining fully chargeable. Restrictions may arise where two or more employments held with 'associated employers' terminate at the same time, or payments arising from a single termination are payable by instalments. When calculating the amount, if any, by which the terminal payment, or payments, exceed £30,000, the statutory redundancy receipt must be included, although it is not subject to tax.

Other matters

Some terminal payments arising by reason of death, injury or disability, together with those arising under superannuation scheme arrangements or for services rendered outside the United Kingdom, are immune from liability, notwithstanding the sums involved may exceed £30,000.

It will often be found that where an outgoing director or employee fails to obtain alternative

— 35 —
TERMINAL PAYMENT

Joe became redundant on 30 September 1995 and received a statutory redundancy payment of £3,250. In addition he received a golden handshake of £65,000 solely on the grounds of redundancy.

The amount taxable for 1995–96 then becomes:

					£
Statutory redundancy payment	.	.	.	.	3,250
Golden handshake	.	.	.	.	65,000
Total terminal payments	.	.	.	.	68,250
Less exempt	.	.	.	.	30,000
Taxable	.	.	.	.	.	£38,250

Assuming Joe is below the age of 65, a married man living with his wife, entitled to the entire married couple's allowance and in receipt of other income amounting to £45,000 for 1995–96, the tax payable becomes:

Total income:					£
Other income	.	.	.	.	45,000
Golden handshake	.	.	.	.	38,250
					83,250
Less Personal allowance	.	.	.	.	3,525
					£79,725

Tax payable:		£
Lower rate:		
On first £3,200 at 20 per cent	. .	640.00
Basic rate:		
On next £21,100 at 25 per cent	. .	5,275.00
Higher rate:		
On balance of £55,425 at 40 per cent	.	22,170.00
		28,085.00
Less Married couple's allowance – £1,720		
at 15 per cent	. . . .	258.00
		£27,827.00

employment, some repayment of income tax suffered under PAYE will become available for the year of assessment in which redundancy occurs. However, the ability to obtain immediate repayment during a period of unemployment may be limited (see page 41).

10

Businesses and professions

INTRODUCTION

Profits earned by an individual from carrying on a business in his or her capacity as a sole trader or practitioner are assessable to income tax. As tax is charged on profits for a year of assessment ending on 5 April the basis used to measure those profits is an important factor. This particularly affects the numerous businesses which do not prepare accounts to 5 April annually.

For many years the allocation of profits to a year of assessment has been achieved by applying the 'preceding year' basis. However, the complex rules required to administer this basis are being replaced by a new 'current year' basis of assessment. It must be emphasised that the change does not significantly affect the *calculation* of profits but only the *allocation* of those profits to different tax years.

The new current year basis applies to all businesses commenced after 5 April 1994. Businesses which were begun before that date continue to apply the preceding year basis until entering the current year basis in 1997–98, with special rules to determine taxable profits for the transitional year 1996–97.

It is therefore necessary to examine separately the assessment of profits for

a businesses commenced before 6 April 1994; and
b those commenced on and after that date.

When approaching this matter it is very important to distinguish between the two commencement dates.

BUSINESSES COMMENCED BEFORE 6 APRIL 1994

Established businesses

Profits of an established business commenced before 6 April 1994 are assessed on a preceding year basis. This requires that profits for an accounting year ending in the previous year of assessment will be taxed in the following year. For example, if accounts of a business are made up to 31 December annually the results for the year ended 31 December 1994 will form the basis of assessment for 1995–96, commencing on 6 April 1995. Special rules, which are reviewed later, then deal with the transition to the new current year basis of assessment.

New businesses

Clearly, the preceding year basis cannot apply in the first year of a new business as there was no preceding year on which to base the assessment. The rules which must be followed for a new business commenced before 6 April 1994 are then modified as follows:

a For the first tax year in which the business is commenced use profits from the date of commencement to the following 5 April.
b For the second tax year use the profits for a period of twelve months from the commencement date.
c For the third tax year it is usual to base the assessment on profits for the period of twelve months of the business accounting period preceding the commencement of the tax year.
d For later years the normal preceding year basis

36
NEW BUSINESS

Alan commenced business on 1 January 1993. His net profits, calculated as required by the Income and Corporation Taxes Act 1988, are as follows:

		£
Year to 31 December 1993	. . .	16,000
Year to 31 December 1994	. . .	12,000
Year to 31 December 1995	. . .	20,000

The normal income tax assessments for the three opening years will be:

1992–93 Actual results to 5 April 1993	
3/12ths of £16,000	£4,000
1993–94 First twelve months from commencement to 31 December 1993	£16,000
1994–95 Previous accounting year to 31 December 1993	£16,000

It is clear that the profits for the year ended 31 December 1993 form the basis of assessment for 1992–93 (part only), 1993–94 and 1994–95. To reduce any hardship which this may cause, an election may be made to adjust the assessments for the second *and* third years to the actual profits of those income tax years as follows:

	£	
1993–94 9/12ths of £16,000	12,000	
3/12ths of £12,000	3,000	
		£15,000
1994–95 9/12ths of £12,000	9,000	
3/12ths of £20,000	5,000	
		£14,000

It would be beneficial to make such an election as the assessments for both 1993–94 and 1994–95 are reduced.

37
DISCONTINUED BUSINESS

Clive closes down his business on 30 June 1995. Profits, as computed under the Taxes Acts, have been:

		£
Year to 30 September 1992	. . .	13,500
Year to 30 September 1993	. . .	15,000
Year to 30 September 1994	. . .	16,500
Nine months to 30 June 1995	. . .	12,600

In the absence of discontinuance the assessments would be:

		£
1993–94 (preceding year)	. . .	13,500
1994–95 (preceding year)	. . .	15,000
1995–96 (preceding year)	. . .	16,500

However, the assessment for 1995–96 (the year of cessation) must be adjusted to:

3/9ths of £12,600	£4,200

The actual profits for the previous years were:

	£	£
1994–95 (year to 5 April 1995)		
6/12ths × £16,500 .	8,250	
6/9ths × £12,600 .	8,400	
		16,650
1993–94 (year to 5 April 1994)		
6/12ths × £15,000 .	7,500	
6/12ths × £16,500 .	8,250	
		15,750
		£32,400

As the figure of £32,400 exceeds the original aggregate assessments of £28,500 (£13,500 + £15,000) for 1993–94 and 1994–95, the assessments for these two years will be adjusted to:

1993–94	. . . . . .	£15,750
1994–95	. . . . . .	£16,650

applies, unless or until this is replaced by the current year basis or the business comes to an end.

The application of **b** and **c** in the early years of a new business will sometimes result in an injustice to the taxpayer. To avoid this an election may be made at any time within seven years from the end of the second tax year in which the business is carried on to have the asessment for the second and third years (but not one year only) based on the actual profits of those years ending on 5 April. If the taxpayer wishes he or she may withdraw the election within a period of six years from the end of the third year.

Discontinued business

Special provisions apply for determining the assessments which must be raised in the closing years of a business which is discontinued or changes hands before 6 April 1997. These are as follows:

a For the final period of a business the assessment will be based on the actual profits of the period from the beginning of the tax year on 6 April to the date when the business closes down or changes hands.

b For each of the two previous tax years the normal basis of assessment is the profits of each preceding year. The Inland Revenue have power, however, to decide that the assessments may be based on the actual profits to 5 April for each of those years (but not one year only) if those assessments produce a higher aggregate tax liability.

It is to be assumed that this power will be exercised if the liability of the taxpayer is thereby increased.

Partnerships

The above rules governing the assessments to be raised where a new business is commenced or an existing business closes down during a period affected by the preceding year basis of assessment may require modification where changes are made in the individuals carrying on business in partnership. These changes will occur where a sole trader admits a second individual or individuals into partnership, an individual joins or leaves an existing partnership, or a business carried on in partnership reverts to a sole trader. Special adjustments and elections may apply if at least one individual continues to be involved in the business both before and after the change.

Where a change occurs after 5 April 1994 in a business commenced before that date there are two possibilities. Firstly, all individuals affected by the change may file a written notice to treat the business as continuing. The normal preceding year basis of assessment will then apply to determine the profits for each year of assessment until the subsequent introduction of the current year basis.

If no continuation election is made for a change taking place after 5 April 1994 the discontinuance rules outlined above must be applied. However, immediately following the change the current year basis of assessment discussed later must be used. In the absence of a continuation election it is not possible for members of a partnership to retain the application of the preceding year basis.

These rules apply only to changes in the persons carrying on business in partnership where those changes occurred after 5 April 1994. A finding that such a change occurred on or before that date would preserve the application of the preceding year basis, subject to a number of modifications.

Where the preceding year basis of assessment applies, profits of the partnership are shared between individal partners by reference to their profit-sharing ratios in the year of assessment. These ratios may be different from those which applied when profits were actually earned. A single assessment is raised in the partnership name and all partners have a joint liability to discharge tax becoming due.

ESTABLISHED BUSINESSES – TRANSITION TO THE CURRENT YEAR BASIS

Businesses which commenced before 6 April 1994 and continue beyond 5 April 1997 must abandon the old preceding year basis and become involved with the current year basis of assessment. This involves a transition from the old to the new with a special adjustment for the transitional year 1996–97. A number of modifications may be required if such a business ceases on or before 5 April 1999, but these are disregarded in the following comments.

Assessment for 1997–98

The current year basis requires that profits for an accounting year or period ending in a year of assessment will comprise the taxable profits for that year. No allocation is required in the case of a continuing business and it is immaterial whether the accounting year ends on 30 April, 31 December, 31 March or any other date.

For example, the profits assessable in 1997–98, the first year for which the current year basis applies for a business commenced before 6 April 1994, where accounts are prepared to, say, 31 December, will represent profits for the twelve-month period ending on 31 December 1997.

Assessment for 1996–97

There are two special transitional adjustments for businesses which commenced before 6 April 1994 and continue beyond 5 April 1997. The first adjustment is used to calculate the profit assessable for the transitional year 1996–97. The calculation of taxable profit will usually proceed as follows:

a There must be identified the period from the end of the basis period for 1995–96 (end of the preceding year basis) to the commencement of the basis period for 1997–98 (first year of the current year basis). Where accounts are prepared to the same date annually this period will extend throughout exactly twenty-four months.

b There must then be established the result of the following calculation:

$$\frac{12}{\text{number of months in period}} \times \frac{\text{profits for the}}{\text{period in } \mathbf{a}}$$

c The result will comprise the amount of profits taxable in 1996–97. If the period arising under **a** is exactly two years the calculation will produce a figure representing exactly one-half of the profits for this period, which will comprise the assess-

38
TRANSITIONAL ASSESSMENT – 1996–97

Anne commenced business in 1985 and prepares accounts for the year to 31 October annually. The business is continuing and it is to be assumed that profits were as follows:

	£
Year to 31 October 1994	20,000
Year to 31 October 1995	24,000
Year to 31 October 1996	18,000
Year to 31 October 1997	27,000

The assessment of these profits will be as follows:

	£
1995–96 – Last year of preceding year basis	
Year to 31 October 1994	20,000
1997–98 – First year of current year basis	
Year to 31 October 1997 . . .	27,000
1997–97 – Transitional year	
Period 1 November 1994 to 31 October 1996 = 24 months	
Profit for period £24,000 + £18,000 = £42,000	
Taxable	
12/24ths × £42,000	£21,000

ment for 1996–97. The remaining one-half escapes assessment entirely.

Overlap relief

The second transitional adjustment recognises that part of the profits assessed for 1997–98 will have been earned before 6 April 1997. The part identified in this manner will represent 'overlap' which can be relieved against profits at some later date. However, the ability to utilise overlap relief is restricted and in most situations it will only be available for the year of assessment in which a business comes to an end.

39
TRANSITIONAL OVERLAP RELIEF

Anne in the previous example had profits of £27,000 assessed in 1997–98. These profits arose in the twelve-month period to 31 October 1997. Overlap relief is available on that proportion of the profits falling before 6 April 1997, namely (calculated in months):

5/12ths × £27,000	£11,250

This relief may be set against future profits as explained later. It cannot affect the assessment of profits for 1997–98.

Avoidance

It will be apparent that steps could be taken to exploit the special arrangements for 1996–97 by artificially increasing profits. Similar steps might be taken to increase profits chargeable in 1997–98 to correspondingly increase the amount of transitional overlap relief. These increases could be achieved by a variety of methods, including the transfer of profits between different accounting periods. However, a range of special rules have been introduced to frustrate avoidance of this nature.

BUSINESSES COMMENCED AFTER 5 APRIL 1994

Businesses commenced after 5 April 1994 become subject to the current year basis immediately. Those businesses are not affected by the preceding year basis, nor are they in any way concerned with the special transitional rules for 1996–97 and the calculation of overlap relief for an accounting period overlapping 6 April 1997. The rules which apply to the current year basis generally are outlined below.

40
NEW BUSINESS

David commenced business on 1 August 1994, subsequently preparing accounts to 31 July annually. Profits for the opening years of the business were as follows:

	£
Year to 31 July 1995	15,000
Year to 31 July 1996	21,000
Year to 31 July 1997	18,000
Year to 31 July 1998	24,000

Assuming the business is continuing, the assessments will be:

	£
1994–95 Period to 5 April 1995	
8/12ths × £15,000	10,000
1995–96 – Year to 31 July 1995 . .	15,000
1996–97 – Year to 31 July 1996 . .	21,000
1997–98 – Year to 31 July 1997 . .	18,000
1998–99 – Year to 31 July 1998 . .	24,000

It will be seen that of the profits for the year to 31 July 1995, £10,000 has been assessed twice. Therefore overlap relief becomes £10,000 for future use.

As David commenced his business after 5 April 1994 none of the transitional provisions apply.

New businesses

Where a new business is commenced after 5 April 1994 the profits are assessable as follows:

a For the first tax year in which the business is carried on use profits from the date of commencement to the following 5 April.

b For the second tax year the basis period will usually be twelve months to the date on which accounts are made up in the second year. If this date is less than twelve months from the commencement of the business profits for the first twelve months must be used.

c For the third and subsequent years profits for the accounting year or period ending in the year of assessment will be used.

Overlap relief

The basis used in the early years of a new business will often require that some profits are assessed more than once. No relief will be immediately available but overlap relief should be forthcoming. This relief will comprise the amount of profits which have been doubly assessed.

Discontinuance

On a business being discontinued the basis period for the year in which discontinuance occurs commences immediately following the end of the basis

— 41 —
DISCONTINUED BUSINESS

Elaine had carried on business for many years, preparing accounts annually to 30 April. The business ceased on 31 March 2001. Profits were as follows:

	£
Year to 30 April 1999	24,000
Year to 30 April 2000	21,000
Period to 31 March 2001	15,000

The business ceased in 2000–2001. The previous year was 1999–2000. Profits assessable for this previous year those for the twelve months ended on 30 April 1999, namely, £24,000. The final period therefore commences on the following day, 1 May 1999, and ends on 31 March 2001 when the business ceased. As a result the assessment for 2000–2001 will be based on profits for this period, namely:

	£
12 months to 30 April 2000 . . .	21,000
11 months to 31 March 2001 . . .	15,000

Profits of twenty-three months and amounting to £36,000 must therefore be assessed in a single year.

— 42 —
USING OVERLAP RELIEF

Let it be assumed that Elaine in the previous example had unused overlap relief of £18,500 brought forward. The assessment for 2000–2001 would then be adjusted as follows:

	£
Original assessment	36,000
Less overlap relief	18,500
Revised assessment	£17,500

period for the previous year. This may establish a basis period for the final year of some considerable length. In the extreme case the profits for the final year may incorporate figures extending throughout nearly twenty-four months.

To some extent the disproportionately high level of profits assessable in the final year may be reduced by overlap relief, if of course that relief has not been used on an earlier occasion. Although the prospect of a large assessment in the final year of a business may seem unduly harsh, the theory of the current year basis of assessment is that throughout the lifetime of a business all profits are assessed exactly once only.

Partnerships

The introduction of the current year basis of assessment will profoundly affect partnerships. Once this basis applies it is still necessary to calculate partnership profits as a single entity. However, those profits must then be shared between the partners on the basis of the ratios used when profits were actually earned. There will be no assessment on the partnership as such and no joint liability. In substitution, each member of the partnership will be assessed as a 'sole trader or practitioner'. It follows that where a new partner joins a partnership he will be assessed by reference to the new business rules. When a partner leaves he will be assessed by reference to the discontinuance rules. These assessments will have no effect whatsoever on the remaining partners, who will be assessed on a continuing basis.

LOSSES

Where a loss is incurred in a continuing trade or profession and the preceding year basis applies no income tax liability arises in the following year as the assessment for that year must be based on the profits, if any, of the previous base year. A number

43
OFFSETTING LOSSES

A dealer sustains a trading loss of £23,000, in an old-established business, during the accounting year to 31 March 1995.

He has an income for the year of assessment 1994–95 of £17,000 arising from investments, on which he has suffered, or is deemed to have suffered, income tax by deduction at the basic rate.

The taxpayer may claim to set the loss against investment income of £17,000, with tax suffered on that income being repaid. If such a claim is agreed, the balance of the loss (£6,000) may be carried forward and set against future trading profits arising from the same trade, used in a similar loss claim for 1995–96 or perhaps set against chargeable gains in 1994–95. The claim must be made in writing not later than 5 April 1997 (namely, within two years following the end of the year of assessment to which the claim relates).

As the results of a business established before 6 April 1994 for the year ended 31 March 1995 form the basis of assessment for 1995–96, the assessment for that year becomes nil.

44
CARRYING LOSSES FORWARD

A trader preparing accounts to 31 October annually has the following profits and losses, as adjusted for income tax purposes:

		£
Year ended 31 October 1992	Loss	10,000
Year ended 31 October 1993	Profit	6,400
Year ended 31 October 1994	Profit	22,100

If the loss of £10,000 is carried forward the results become:

	£	Assessable profit £
Year ended 31 October 1992		NIL
Year ended 31 October 1993 –		
Profit	6,400	
Less loss brought forward (part)	6,400	NIL
Year ended 31 October 1994 –		
Profit	22,100	
Less loss brought forward (balance)	3,600	18,500

of adjustments may, however, be necessary if the calculation is affected by the new business or discontinued business rules. Once the current year basis of assessment is introduced the results of an accounting year ending in a year of assessment will usually establish the profits assessable in that year. Where the results disclose a loss there will be no profits to assess.

Subject to any adjustments which may be required, the loss arising may be utilised in several different ways.

One method, which requires the submission of a claim, is to offset the loss against the individual's income for the year of assessment in which the loss arose. Where income for the year of loss is insufficient, any unused part of the loss may usually be set against income of a different year. In the case of continuing businesses established before 6 April 1994, any unused part of the loss arising in 1995–96 and earlier years may be set against income for the year of assessment immediately following the year of loss. However, for new businesses commenced after 5 April 1994, and in the case of all businesses for 1996–97 and future years, any part of a loss which cannot be relieved in the year of loss may be offset against income for the previous year.

This method of obtaining loss relief will frequently result in a repayment of income tax suffered on investment income. It is, however, necessary to show that the loss arose from a trade or business being undertaken on a commercial basis and with a view to the realisation of profits. If there is any balance of loss in respect of which tax cannot be repaid, this may be carried forward and set against future profits of the same business. For this purpose it is immaterial whether the preceding year basis or the current year basis of assessment applies. In those cases where losses have been incurred in farming or market gardening for five consecutive years the ability to offset future losses against income will be restricted.

As the result of independent taxation it is not possible for the losses of one spouse to be offset against the income of the other.

A second method may be available where there is insufficient income to absorb the loss under the first method. This enables the unused business loss for a year of assessment to be set against chargeable gains otherwise assessable to capital gains tax in the same year.

A third method is to carry the loss forward year by year and offset it against subsequent profits arising from the same business. This process continues until the loss has been fully used or the business ends. Losses can only be carried forward to the extent that they have not been relieved under methods one and two above.

LOSSES AND NEW BUSINESSES

Where a loss arises in the first year of assessment during which a new business is carried on, or in any of the three following years, a claim may be made to set that loss against income for the three years preceding the year in which the loss occurs. The amount of any loss may usually be increased by capital allowances on business assets, but restrictions are necessary if the business is that of leasing. This claim provides a further alternative to methods one, two and three outlined above. The replacement of the preceding year basis by the current year basis has not significantly affected claims of this nature, although the method used to calculate losses for a year of assessment has changed.

45
CARRYING LOSSES BACKWARDS

An individual commenced a manufacturing business on 1 July 1993. The actual results attributable to the first four years of assessment, ending on 5 April, were as follows:

		£
1993–94 Loss	. . . . .	7,100
1994–95 Loss	. . . . .	3,400
1995–96 Profit	. . . . .	9,200
1996–97 Profit	. . . . .	15,400

If a claim is made the loss of £7,000 arising in 1993–94 may be carried back and set against income in the following order:

a Income for 1990–91
b Income for 1991–92
c Income for 1992–93

Should a separate claim be made for the loss of £3,400 arising in 1994–95 this will be set against income in the following order:

a Income for 1991–92
b Income for 1992–93
c Income for 1993–94

No relief is available for the two most recent years as both 1995–96 and 1996–97 disclosed profits.

FARMERS AND MARKET GARDENERS

The above rules for charging profits apply also to individuals who carry on the trade of farming or market gardening. However, these individuals may claim to average the results of two consecutive years of assessment if the difference between the profits of each year is at least 30 per cent, or one year

46
FARMERS AND AVERAGING

For several years Paul has carried on the business of farming. His profits for 1993–94 and 1994–95 were as follows:

		£
1993–94	. . . . .	40,000
1994–95	. . . . .	15,000

In the absence of any claim for averaging these profits are chargeable to tax in the normal manner. However, if a claim is made the results for the two years may be averaged as follows:

		£
Profit for 2 years (£40,000 + £15,000)		55,000
1993–94 – one-half	. . . .	27,500
1994–95 – one-half	. . . .	27,500

Should a similar claim be made for the two years 1994–95 and 1995–96, the averaged profit of £27,500 must be used for 1994–95 and not the actual profit of £15,000.

produces a loss. The claim must be submitted within two years following the end of the second year and cannot apply to the first year of a new business or the last year of a discontinued business. A limited claim may also be available if the difference in profits between the two years is a little less than 30 per cent.

DEDUCTIONS FROM BUSINESS PROFITS

Proper accounts are essential if business profits are to be correctly calculated and charged to tax. The absence of proper accounts may result in an overcharge, or perhaps in an undercharge which may later have serious consequences, as failure to disclose the full profits assessable to tax can involve a potential liability to interest and penalties. Many traders use the services of qualified accountants who are expert in this work. They will prepare accounts and negotiate with the Inland Revenue the most favourable assessment which the law permits.

Business and professional profits assessable under Schedule D are not usually the profits shown by the financial accounts. For income tax purposes certain items which commonly appear as expenses in the accounts are not allowed. These have to be added to the profits shown. On the other hand, there are sometimes receipts in the accounts which should not be taxed, or are chargeable to tax under some other heading. These must be deducted from the profits shown.

It should be emphasised that the replacement of the preceding year basis by the new current year basis of assessment has had little effect on the calculation of profits or losses. The real significance of the change is the manner in which profits are assessed and that on which losses are relieved. One change which has taken place involves the use of capital allowances arising on business assets. Previously, these allowances did not affect the calculation of profits but where the current year basis applies they are included as an expense.

EXPENDITURE NOT ALLOWED

The following list provides an illustration of some items of expenditure which may appear in the financial accounts of a business, but which are *not* allowed in computing income tax liability and therefore have to be added to profits, or deducted from losses, disclosed by the accounts to arrive at the profit or loss for income tax purposes.

a Expenses not wholly and exclusively laid out for the purpose of the business.

b Expenses for domestic or private purposes.

c The cost of business entertaining, including many gifts. Certain gifts made to charity may be allowed (see page 102).

d The rent of property which is not used for business purposes. The deduction allowed in respect of any dwelling-house or domestic office is not normally to exceed two-thirds of the rent, but a larger proportion may be given for hotels and boarding houses.

e Provisions for the repair of premises occupied for the business or for implements or utensils, unless sums have actually been expended.

f Any capital sums used in or withdrawn from the business.

g The cost of improvements to premises.

h Debts, other than bad debts or those estimated to be doubtful.

i Any royalty or other sum paid for the use of a patent, where tax is deducted from the payment.

j Income tax, capital gains tax, capital transfer tax or inheritance tax paid.

k Depreciation (capital allowances will usually be available, however – see page 73).

l Withdrawals by proprietors.

m Penalties for breaking the law and legal expenses in connection therewith.

n Reserves (except for discounts or for *specific* doubtful debts).

o Payments which constitute the commission of a criminal offence by the payer.

p Payments made in response to threats, menaces, blackmail and other forms of extortion.

EXPENDITURE WHICH IS ALLOWED

Any sums expended wholly and exclusively for the purpose of the business may usually be included in the computation of profits, unless the outlay is of a capital nature. Among the deductions allowable are the following:

a Advertising expenditure (but *not* the original cost of permanent signs).

b Bad and doubtful debts.

c Costs of raising business loan finance.

d Interest incurred for business purposes.

e Insurance for business purposes. Note that recoveries under the policies must usually be included in assessable profits.

f Legal expenses for recovering debts or incurred in connection with other non-capital business matters.

g National insurance contributions paid in respect of employees.

h Reasonable payments for the hire of assets. Some restriction may be necessary for the cost of hiring motor cars having a retail price exceeding £12,000 when new.

i Redundancy payments made to former employees.

j Rent of business premises. (A restriction may be necessary as shown under head **d** opposite where domestic premises are involved.)

k Repairs to premises, excluding improvements and alterations.

l Subscriptions and donations; where the society to which payment is made has agreed with the Inland Revenue to pay tax on its profits; where purely to maintain the business; or where the staff of the business benefit.

m Wages, salaries and pensions paid to employees and past employees or their dependants (but note the time limit within which payment must be made – see page 69).

The above list is not intended to be comprehensive but is indicative of the type of expenditure which may be charged against business profits to arrive at the figure on which income tax will be imposed.

Example 47 on the following page shows how the adjustments mentioned above are made.

TRADING STOCK AND WORK IN PROGRESS

Unsold trading stock or work in progress retained at the end of an accounting period is usually valued

47
ADJUSTING ACCOUNTS

The following Profit and Loss Account is prepared by a retail tradesman, using a van for the delivery of goods and living over his shop premises. It will be observed that certain items appearing in the Account are not allowable deductions for tax purposes and have to be added back to arrive at the assessable profit, while adjustment has to be made in respect of the trader's living accommodation.

Profit and Loss Account

	£		£
Wages	15,200	Gross trading profit	74,988
Rent	6,400	Dividends	1,024
Business rates	4,720		
Lighting and heating	1,274		
Repairs to premises	737		
Post and telephone	1,549		
Stationery and printing	726		
General expenses	1,002		
Income tax	5,260		
Electric name sign	1,540		
Depreciation of van	1,927		
Van running costs	4,072		
Extension of garage	7,500		
Net profit	24,105		
	£76,012		£76,012

Adjustment for Tax Purposes

		£
Net profit as Profit and Loss Account		24,105
Add Items not allowable:		
Income tax		5,260
Electric name sign		1,540
Depreciation of van		1,927
Extension of garage		7,500
Add For living accommodation (say 1/3rd):		
	£	
Rent	2,133	
Rates	1,573	
Lighting and heating	425	
Repairs to premises	246	4,377
		44,709
Less Dividends		1,024
Profit for tax purposes		£43,685

Capital allowances should be available for capital expenditure on the motor van and electric sign. If the adjusted profit is used to establish liability on the preceding year basis these allowances will be set against the assessment of adjusted business profits. Should the current year basis apply the allowances will be treated as an expense, which reduces the profits of £43,685. (See page 75 for Example.)

at the lower of original cost or market value and included as a receipt in the financial accounts. Unless the value has fallen, this will effectively eliminate the cost and transfer that cost to the next accounting period in which individual items are sold. If market value has fallen when compared with original cost, the fall will reduce the profits of the business.

Where a business comes to an end, or is sold, trading stock will frequently be transferred to another trader. The consideration received for the transfer must be included in the calculation of the transferor's profits of losses for the final period of the business. However, an adjustment may be necessary where the business is discontinued after 28 November 1994. Should trading stock be transferred between persons who are 'connected', broadly, under a common control or comprising close relatives of each other, the transfer price may be replaced by market value. It is possible that this figure of market value may exceed both the consideration received by the transferor and the original cost incurred by the transferor when acquiring trading stock. In circumstances such as these both parties to the transaction may elect to substitute the higher of these two figures for market value.

In those cases where unsold trading stock remaining on the discontinuance of a business is not transferred to another trader it is treated as sold for a consideration representing market value.

REMUNERATION

Remuneration paid to directors and employees may usually be subtracted in the calculation of business profits where the 'wholly and exclusively' requirements outlined above are satisfied. However, remuneration attributable to a period for which accounts are made up may only be deducted if it is 'paid' within nine months following the end of that period. The date on which 'payment' is treated as taking place will be identical to that which governs the time of 'receipt' (see page 44). Although any remuneration paid after the expiration of the nine-month period will usually be deductible in arriving at the profits of a later period in which 'payment' takes place, this can result in the taxable profits of the earlier period being unnecessarily inflated.

For periods of account ending not later than 5 April 1990, the nine-month period was extended to one of eighteen months. No restriction applies to remuneration for periods of account ending before 6 April 1989.

Should accounts and supporting tax computations be submitted to the Inland Revenue before remuneration is paid and in advance of the nine-month deadline, the remuneration cannot be deducted. However, if the remuneration is subsequently paid before the deadline is reached, the remuneration can be restored as a deduction, but only if a special claim is made.

POST CESSATION EXPENSES

Once a trade or profession has been discontinued and final accounts of the business properly prepared, subsequent events arising directly or indirectly out of the business will have little effect for taxation purposes. An exception concerns 'post-cessation receipts', namely, receipts which arise after the discontinuance date but which cannot be related back to the financial accounts of the business. These receipts are chargeable to income tax, usually under Case VI of Schedule D. However, no relief was previously available for 'post-cessation expenses', namely, expenditure incurred after the discontinuance date and which could not be included in the calculation of business profits. Only in very limited situations could payments of this nature be offset against post-cessation receipts.

The anomaly which this situation created has now been recognised in relation to certain payments made after 28 November 1994 and following the discontinuance of a business. It is necessary to show that the payments were made wholly and exclusively

a in remedying defective work done, goods supplied or services rendered by the previous business;

b in defraying legal and other expenses in connection with claims for that work done, goods supplied or services rendered;

c in insuring against liabilities arising out of such claims or the incurring of such expenses; or

d for the purpose of collecting a debt taken into account in computing the profits or gains of the discontinued business.

Relief is also available for a debt which was previously included in the calculation of business profits but which has become bad. If relief is obtained for this bad debt and all or any part of that debt is subsequently recovered the recovery must be charged to tax.

One further adjustment which must be noted concerns expenses which were entered into the calculation of business profits but which remain unpaid. The amount of these unpaid expenses must be subtracted from the expenditure for which relief is claimed.

Claims are limited to qualifying payments made, or bad debts arising, within a period of seven years following the discontinuance of the business. The amount of any claim is offset against income chargeable to income tax for the year of assessment during which payment takes place. Should income be insufficient for this purpose, any excess can be treated as an allowable loss for the same year and offset against chargeable gains assessable to capital gains tax.

ENTERPRISE ALLOWANCE
To provide some encouragement for unemployed individuals to set up in business, an enterprise allowance may be claimed. This is provided at the rate of £40 per week throughout the initial twelve months of the business. Although the allowance is taxable it does not enter into the calculation of business results. The recipient is separately taxed under Case VI of Schedule D by reference to the amount arising in each year of assessment.

SMALL BUSINESSES
Most proprietors of a business must usually submit proper accounts to the Inland Revenue in support of tax computations, but an exception arises in the case of some small concerns. From April 1992 it is unnecessary to submit detailed accounts where the annual turnover of a business does not exceed £15,000.

Where this limit is not exceeded it will be sufficient to disclose the following three factors:

Turnover	A
Less Purchases and expenses . .	B
Net profit	C

Tax returns contain a box where these factors can be entered.

OVERSEAS ENTERTAINERS AND SPORTSMEN
A large number of non-resident entertainers and sportsmen visit the United Kingdom each year, to undertake performances or to compete at a sporting event. These individuals include pop and film stars, actors, musicians, tennis players, golfers, boxers and motor racing drivers, among others. Whether sums arising from performances and other activities in the United Kingdom become liable to taxation will be governed by the personal circumstances of each individual and perhaps by the terms of a Double Taxation Agreement concluded between the United Kingdom and some overseas territory. However, there may well be liability to United Kingdom tax which the Inland Revenue are sometimes unable to collect.

To resolve this difficulty special collection rules apply. These require that when making certain payments to a non-resident entertainer or sportsman for services performed in the United Kingdom the promoter or other person will deduct income tax at the basic rate of 25 per cent. Deductions will also extend to associated income from sponsorship, advertising and endorsements. There will be no deductions for payments arising from record sales, nor will the deduction procedure usually apply to payments not exceeding £1,000. Any deductions made from payments must be accounted for to the Inland Revenue. The requirement to deduct income tax at the basic rate is not affected by the 20 per cent lower rate band.

Deductions made at the basic rate will not necessarily fully exhaust liability to United Kingdom income tax. Any additional liability arising at the higher rate must be recovered by direct assessment on the individual concerned.

The above rules have no application to entertainers and sportsmen who are resident in the United Kingdom for taxation purposes. Those rules are confined to non-residents, which will include both nationals of overseas territories and nationals of the United Kingdom also, if they are not resident in this territory.

SUB-CONTRACTORS
The PAYE scheme of tax deduction applies to emoluments paid to the holder of an office or employment. Certain workers employed by agencies are treated as holding an office or employment and the PAYE scheme is of application to emoluments paid to such persons. However, the PAYE scheme does not apply where payments are made to others for the supply of services. This could result in some loss of tax as the Inland Revenue may experience difficulty in tracing the persons to whom payments are made and collecting tax from those persons.

To avoid this potential loss, arrangements have been made to collect tax from payments to non-resident entertainers and sportsmen, as noted earlier. In addition, a wide ranging tax deduction scheme is in operation for persons engaged in the construction industry and this applies where a contractor makes a payment to a sub-contractor under a contract relating to construction operations.

The expression 'contractor' is widely defined and incorporates any person carrying on a business which includes construction operations, a local authority, a development corporation or New Town Commission and certain other persons. Private householders having work done on their own premises are not contractors and a business which is not normally involved in construction operations is unlikely to be treated as carried on by a contractor.

A 'sub-contractor' includes any person engaged in carrying out construction operations for a business or a public body which is a contractor, and includes companies, individuals and partnerships in addition to other persons.

'Construction operations' extend to almost anything that is done to a permanent or temporary building, structure, civil engineering work or installation. This includes site preparation, construction, alteration, many forms of repair, dismantling and demolition, but excludes some forms of installation.

Sub-contractors may apply to the Inland Revenue for a tax certificate. There are three types of certificate, namely the C certificate which is for certain companies, the P certificate which is for other companies and partnerships and the I certificate which is for use by individuals trading on their own account. Certificates are only issued to individuals, partnerships and companies who satisfy a lengthy list of requirements.

Before making any payment to a sub-contractor, the contractor must establish whether a current tax certificate is held. If a suitable certificate can be produced by the sub-contractor, the contractor will make the payment in full. In the absence of a certificate the contractor is obliged to deduct income tax at the rate of 25 per cent when making payment in 1995–96. This requirement is unaffected by the 20 per cent lower rate band.

The deduction will be made from the full amount of the payment, less the direct cost of materials used, or to be used, in carrying out the construction operations to which the contract relates. This effectively confines the deduction scheme to payments for the provision of labour.

Income tax deducted by a contractor must be paid over to the Inland Revenue. Payment usually falls due fourteen days after the end of each income tax month. Therefore deductions made for the period ending on the fifth of a month should be accounted for to the Inland Revenue by the nineteenth of that month. However, some contractors are permitted to account for deductions on a quarterly basis. If this basis is to be used it must be shown that PAYE, national insurance contributions and deductions made from payments to sub-contractors after 5 April 1995 do not exceed on average £600 per month. Where the quarterly procedure applies the contractor must account for his deductions fourteen days following 5 July, 5 October, 5 January and 5 April respectively. Failure on the part of the contractor to operate correctly the sub-contractors' deduction scheme can have serious repercussions and perhaps lead to the commencement of criminal proceedings. There may also be a liability to discharge interest where payment is made more than 14 days following the end of the year of assessment in which the deduction was made.

At the end of each year of assessment the sub-contractor will calculate the total amount of deductions suffered on payments received by him. This total amount may then be offset against the sub-contractor's liability to income tax. Should the sums deducted exceed the liability, the surplus can be reclaimed from the Inland Revenue. If the deductions fall below the full liability the sub-contractor must satisfy the excess in the normal manner.

Future developments
Some substantial changes are forthcoming in the sub-contractors' scheme, although these are unlikely to be introduced before the calendar year 1998 at the earliest. These changes are expected to involve the satisfaction of increased compliance requirements before a sub-contractor's certificate will be issued. Currently, the rate of deductions made from payments to sub-contractors who do not retain certificates is identical to the basic rate of income tax. It is anticipated that a lower tax deduction rate will be introduced. Payments to sub-contractors who retain the appropriate certificate are made gross. It is proposed that all gross payments will have to be made by electronic transfer. This will usually involve the use of bank transfer arrangements and eliminate payments in cash. The deduction scheme is being computerised and this will enable a new form of tax deduction voucher to be used. These vouchers may well be similar to those used for credit cards, with copies being forwarded to the Inland Revenue.

VOLUNTEER DRIVERS – MILEAGE ALLOWANCES
Individuals who drive for the hospital car service and other volunteer organisations usually receive mileage allowances. Any 'profit element' in these allowances will be treated as income chargeable to income tax. The profit may be calculated, at the individual's option, by

a using figures taken from the Fixed Profit Car Scheme used by employees (see page 47); or
b taking the actual mileage receipts and the actual expenses.

Profits, if any, arising before 6 October 1991 were ignored. To avoid the imposition of sudden liabilities after this date the charge was phased in over a period, with only part of the profits assessable in the transitional years. The proportion of profits assessable is as follows:

			Taxable part
a Period 6 October 1991 to			
5 April 1992	.	.	one-quarter
b Year to 5 April 1993	.	.	one-quarter
c Year to 5 April 1994	.	.	one-half
d Year to 5 April 1995	.	.	three-quarters
e From 6 April 1995	.	.	the whole

This arrangement has no application to taxi, minicab and similar operators who carry on a business.

COMPANIES

Profits, gains and income accruing to companies are chargeable to corporation tax. The assessment of companies to this tax is dealt with on page 129.

11

Capital expenditure

CAPITAL EXPENDITURE incurred by an individual carrying on a trade, profession or vocation cannot usually be subtracted when calculating business profits. However, many items of capital expenditure enable the individual to obtain capital allowances which are set against business profits, included in the calculation of business profits or perhaps absorbed against other income. Similar allowances may be available to others not carrying on business, but the ability to utilise such allowances is somewhat limited.

It should be recognised that the system of granting capital allowances has been drastically amended in recent years. In earlier times substantial initial allowances or first-year allowances were granted immediately many items of expenditure were incurred, leaving only limited, or perhaps no, annual allowances to be obtained subsequently. These accelerated allowances were largely withdrawn throughout a two-year transitional period and, with very few exceptions, ceased to apply entirely for expenditure incurred after 31 March 1986. However, following an interval in excess of six years both initial and first-year allowances were reintroduced for expenditure incurred between 1 November 1992 and 31 October 1993. After the latter date the allowances were again withdrawn.

APPLICATION OF CAPITAL ALLOWANCES

Although the calculation of capital allowances is not significantly affected by the change from the preceding year basis to the current year basis of assessment, the application of those allowances by an individual carrying on business is amended. It may be helpful to compare the approach which must be made under each heading where allowances are available for assets used in the business.

Preceding year basis

Where the preceding year basis applies capital allowances are given for a year of assessment. The factors used to calculate the allowances are those taking place in the basis year. For example, if a long-established business commenced before 6 April 1994 prepares accounts to, say, 30 September annually the profits of the year ended on 30 September 1994 will be assessed for 1995–96. Capital allowances, and indeed any balancing adjustments, for 1995–96 will be based on events taking place in the period of account ending on 30 September 1994.

Capital allowances are not subtracted when calculating profits. The allowances are given against those profits assessed to income tax.

Current year basis

In contrast, where the current year basis of assessment applies, profits for a period of account ending in a year of assessment will be taxed in that year. Capital allowances are not given for a year of assessment but form an ingredient in the calculation of business profits. It follows that the allowances to be included in the profit calculation for a period of account will reflect events taking place in that period. For example, the results for a period of account ending on 30 September 1998 will form the basis of assessment for 1998–99. The calculation of capital allowances will reflect events taking place during the period of account and not those in the full year of assessment. A further adjustment must be made if the period of account is longer or shorter than twelve months in duration. The annual allowance must then be proportionately increased or reduced to correspond with the length of the period of account.

The years of change
In the case of a business commenced after 5 April 1994 the new current year procedure will apply from the inception of that business.

Businesses established on or before 5 April 1994 and continuing after 5 April 1997 will use the old preceding year basis for 1995–96 and earlier years. Special rules affect the transitional year 1996–97 but the new current year basis will then apply for 1997–98.

Business proprietors seeking to obtain capital allowances will usually include the relevant claim when completing a tax return.

PLANT AND MACHINERY
Capital allowances are available for the capital cost of providing plant and machinery wholly and exclusively for the purposes of a business. These assets comprise many items commonly used for trading or other activities, including industrial equipment, tractors, motor cars, typewriters, desks, chairs and machinery, among others. They also include most items of computer software. Buildings and structures cannot be treated as plant for expenditure incurred after 29 November 1993, although few items of this nature would be so treated for expenditure incurred earlier.

Also from 29 November 1993, claims must be made within a period of two years from the end of the tax year in which the expenditure is incurred and to which it should be related. Late claims may still be made to obtain allowances but this will result in relief being available at a later date or year.

First-year allowances
A first-year allowance of 100 per cent was generally available for expenditure incurred before 14 March 1984. This effectively enabled the entire cost to be fully relieved in a single year. The first-year allowance of 100 per cent was rapidly reduced in amount and ceased to apply entirely for expenditure incurred after 31 March 1986.

The first-year allowance was again reintroduced for expenditure incurred in the twelve-month period commencing on 1 November 1992 and ending on 31 October 1993. No allowance of this nature was available for expenditure on ordinary motor cars, with the exception of those operated as taxis, vehicles used for short-term hire or comprising mobility allowance vehicles for the disabled. The first-year allowance was given at the rate of 40 per cent, although it remained possible to disclaim part of that allowance. There can be no first-year allowance for expenditure incurred after 31 October 1993.

Annual writing-down allowances
An annual writing-down allowance is available for expenditure incurred when acquiring plant and machinery. This allowance, given at the rate of 25 per cent, is calculated on the reduced balance of unrelieved expenditure remaining after subtracting allowances for earlier years.

In those cases where the first-year allowance was obtained for expenditure incurred in the twelve-month period ending on 31 October 1993, no

— 48 —
WRITING-DOWN ALLOWANCES THE OLD BASIS

A manufacturer who commenced business in 1970, prepares accounts to 31 March annually. The balance of expenditure remaining in the pool of plant and machinery on 31 March 1994 was £14,000. He incurred expenditure of £12,500 when acquiring new plant on 24 June 1994, and further expenditure of £10,000 was incurred on 19 February 1995. £6,500 was received from the sale of obsolete plant on 12 December 1994.

Results for the twelve months ended 31 March 1995 showed profits of £80,000.

Profits of £80,000 for the year ended 31 March 1995 will be assessed in 1995–96. Capital allowances which may be set against those profits will be calculated as follows:

	£	Pool £
Balance brought forward		14,000
Additions:		
June 1994	12,500	
February 1995	10,000	22,500
		36,500
Less sales		6,500
		30,000
Writing-down allowance 1995–96		
25 per cent of £30,000		7,500
Balance carried forward		22,500

49
WRITING-DOWN ALLOWANCES THE NEW BASIS

As the business in Example 48 commenced before 6 April 1994 it is clear that the current year basis of assessment cannot apply to the facts in that example. However, if each of the dates used was advanced by four years the calculation would be as follows:

Capital allowances	£	Pool £
Balance brought forward		14,000
Additions:		
June 1998	12,500	
February 1999	10,000	22,500
		36,500
Less sales		6,500
		30,000
Writing-down allowance – year to 31 March 1999		
25 per cent of £30,000		7,500
Balance carried forward		£22,500

Profits – Year to 31 March 1999 – Assessable 1998–99	
Original calculation	80,000
Less writing-down allowance	7,500
Adjusted profits	£72,500

writing-down allowance is available in the same year. The balance of the expenditure, usually representing 60 per cent of the outlay, remains available for the 25 per cent writing-down allowance in the second and succeeding years.

Pooling
Most items of plant and machinery, with the exception of motor cars, acquired by an individual enter into a 'pool'. Adjustments must be made to the expenditure remaining in this pool where a new asset is added or an existing asset sold. The 25 per cent annual writing-down allowance is applied to the 'pool' as a whole and it is unnecessary to identify each separate asset. Should the sale, or other proceeds, of an asset exceed the balance of unrelieved expenditure remaining in the pool, a balancing charge will be imposed to recoup allowances obtained in earlier periods. Any balancing charge will be allocated to a year of assessment or profit period on a basis identical to that used for the annual allowance.

50
ELECTION FOR NON-POOLING

Let it be assumed that the manufacturer in Example 49 also acquired a further asset at a cost of £30,000 on 5 May 1998. An election was made to exclude this asset from the common pool. The asset realised £4,000 when sold on 15 March 2001.

Capital allowances confined to this asset only are calculated as follows:

	£
Cost	30,000
Writing-down allowance – year to 31.3.99	
25 per cent of £30,000	7,500
	22,500
Writing-down allowance – year to 31.3.2000	
25 per cent of £22,500	5,625
	16,875
Sale proceeds 15 March 2001	4,000
Balancing allowance – Year to 31.3.2001	£12,875

If the asset had been included in the common pool the aggregate allowances for the year to 31 March 2001 would be considerably smaller.

Election for non-pooling
The 25 per cent reducing balance approach enables some 90 per cent of the cost of an asset to be relieved throughout a period of approximately eight years. Many items of plant and machinery have a lifespan falling below eight years and where assets acquired have a limited life expectation the taxpayer may elect to exclude these assets from the common pool. The advantage of the election is that when the excluded asset is sold a balancing adjustment will arise which is not distorted by entries in the common pool.

In those cases where plant and machinery is used only partly for business purposes a suitable restriction in the allowances granted must be made.

MOTOR CARS
Writing-down allowances are available at the rate of 25 per cent for the cost of acquiring motor cars, where the vehicles are used for business purposes. However, a restriction must be imposed for motor cars costing more than £12,000, as the annual allowance is not to exceed £3,000 on these vehicles. If the vehicle was purchased before 11 March 1992, the restriction applies to motor cars costing more than £8,000, with the annual allowance limited to £2,000. This restriction does not apply to taxis,

——— 51 ———
MOTOR CARS

A doctor, who had been in practice since 1982, purchased a motor car for use in his practice on 15 August 1994 at a cost of £23,500. Assuming the vehicle is used exclusively for business purposes and that accounts are made up to 31 October annually, the calculation of capital allowances will proceed as follows:

	£
Cost	23,500
Writing-down allowance, 1995–96:	
25 per cent of £23,500 – but restricted to	3,000
	20,500
Writing-down allowance, 1996–97:	
25 per cent of £20,500 – but restricted to	3,000
	17,500
Writing-down allowance – Year to 31 October 1997	
25 per cent of £17,500 – but restricted to	3,000
	14,500
Writing-down allowance – Year to 31 October 1998	
25 per cent of £14,500 – but restricted to	3,000
	11,500
Writing-down allowance – Year to 31 October 1999	
25 per cent of £11,500 (no restriction necessary)	2,875
Available for future writing-down allowances	£8,625

short-term hire cars and mobility allowance vehicles for the disabled.

Once the new current year basis of assessment applies and a period of account exceeds or falls below 12 months in duration, the annual allowance, as restricted, will be increased or reduced proportionally.

Should a car costing more than £12,000 (or £8,000 where appropriate) when new be leased to a business proprietor, the lessee may suffer some restriction in the hire or rental charge which can be deducted when calculating profits assessable to tax.

Only part of the available allowance may be obtained where a car is used partly for business and partly for private motoring.

INDUSTRIAL BUILDINGS

Allowances are available for expenditure incurred on the construction of buildings or structures used, or to be used, for industrial purposes. These include buildings or structures used for the purpose of the following, among others:

a a trade carried on in a mill, factory or similar premises;

b a transport, dock, inland navigation, water, electricity, or hydraulic undertaking;

c a tunnel undertaking;

d a bridge undertaking;

e a trade consisting of the manufacture of goods or materials, or the subjection of goods to a process;

f a trade which consists in the storage of certain goods;

g a trade which consists in the catching or taking of fish or shell fish;

h a trade which consists in the repairing and servicing of goods.

Relief is also available for the cost of constructing toll roads and certain other roads.

The allowances do not apply to expenditure on retail shops, offices and other non-industrial buildings.

Where part of a building is, and some other part is not, used for a qualifying purpose, allowances must usually be restricted to the cost of constructing the qualifying part. Some relaxation in this approach is, however, available where the cost of constructing the non-qualifying part does not exceed 25 per cent of the cost of constructing the entire building. In this situation, allowances may be obtained on the aggregate cost.

Initial allowances

Initial allowances were previously available for expenditure incurred on the construction of a qualifying building. For expenditure incurred after 10 March 1981, the initial allowance was 75 per cent, although an increased allowance of 100 per cent could be obtained for expenditure on small industrial workshops. The allowance was reduced throughout a transitional period and, subject to a single exception, was withdrawn completely for expenditure incurred after 31 March 1986. The exception concerned expenditure on buildings located in enterprise zones where a 100 per cent initial allowance remained available.

The initial allowance was reintroduced at the rate of 20 per cent for expenditure incurred on the construction of a building under a contract entered into between 1 November 1992 and 31 October 1993. It remained a requirement that the building was brought into use for the purposes of a qualifying trade not later than 31 December 1994. The initial allowance could also be obtained for existing unused buildings completed, or in course of construction, before 1 November 1992, if they were acquired under a contract entered into during the year ended 31 October 1993 and brought into use by the end of 1994. Subject to this, no initial allowance can be obtained for subsequent events.

Annual writing-down allowances

An annual writing-down allowance of 4 per cent is available for qualifying construction expenditure. This allowance will be given for the first year in which the building is brought into use. It is therefore possible that the 20 per cent initial allowance and the first annual allowance of 4 per cent may be available in the same year, although in many cases there will be an interval between the two allowances.

In the absence of any initial allowance, the annual writing-down allowance of 4 per cent will exhaust all construction costs once a period of 25 years has elapsed. This period will be shortened where a 20 per cent initial allowance is obtained, as the aggregate of initial and writing-down allowances cannot exceed the construction cost.

Where an industrial building, for which initial and/or annual writing-down allowances have been obtained, is sold, a balancing charge may arise. This will represent the difference between the written-down tax value of the expenditure and the disposal proceeds. However, any balancing charge cannot exceed the aggregate allowances previously granted.

—— 52 ——
INDUSTRIAL BUILDINGS

On 27 February 1994, a manufacturer entered into a contract for the construction of an industrial building. The cost was £200,000 and the completed building was first used in November of the same year. Accounts are prepared to 31 December annually and the allowances available are as follows:

	£
Cost (during accounting year to 31 December 1994)	200,000
Writing-down allowance 1995–96: 4 per cent of £200,000	8,000
	192,000
Writing-down allowance 1996–97: 4 per cent of £200,000	8,000
	£184,000

Annual writing-down allowances of £8,000 will continue until the expenditure has been exhausted, unless the building is sold or ceases to be used for a qualifying purpose.

No balancing charge will arise should the sale take place more than 25 years, or 50 years for older buildings, following the date expenditure was incurred.

A balancing allowance may arise should the sale proceeds fall below the written-down tax value.

A person who acquires an existing building from the previous owner cannot base annual writing-down allowances on the price paid, unless the building is bought unused. However, some future annual writing-down allowances will usually be available, based on the previous owner's 'residue of expenditure'.

SMALL INDUSTRIAL WORKSHOPS

Where expenditure was incurred on the construction of a small industrial workshop, comprising an industrial building as defined above, an initial allowance of 100 per cent could be obtained. A building was regarded as 'small' if the gross internal floor space did not exceed 2,500 square feet. Where a larger building was divided into parts, each part qualified as a separate building only if it was permanently separated from the remainder of the building and intended for separate occupation. The increased initial allowance applied only to expenditure incurred in the three-year period ending on 26 March 1983. However, for a further period of two years, ending on 26 March 1985, the 100 per cent allowance remained available if the internal floor space did not exceed 1,250 square feet. In the case of converted large buildings, it was sufficient if the average size of each unit within the building did not exceed 1,250 square feet.

The special 100 per cent initial allowance for small industrial workshops cannot apply to construction expenditure incurred after 26 March 1985. However, the significance of the allowance for the future is that it will explain a written-down tax value of nil should the building be sold and the need to calculate a balancing charge arise.

HOTELS

Expenditure incurred on the construction, extension or improvement of hotels may qualify for capital allowances. It is a necessary requirement that the hotel has at least ten letting bedrooms, is not normally in the same occupation for more than one month, regularly provides guests with breakfast and evening meals and is open for at least four months between April and October. Additionally, all sleeping accommodation offered at the hotel must consist wholly or mainly of letting bedrooms. Any expenditure on that part of the premises occupied by the proprietor or his family must be disregarded but accommodation used by employees may usually be included.

Qualifying expenditure incurred before 1 April 1986 produced an initial allowance of 20 per cent and an annual writing-down allowance of 4 per cent until the expenditure had been exhausted. No initial allowance was available for expenditure incurred after 31 March 1986, but an annual writing-down allowance could be obtained at the rate of 4 per cent until the expenditure had been entirely written off.

An initial allowance at the rate of 20 per cent was reintroduced for expenditure incurred between 1 November 1992 and 31 October 1993. The annual writing-down allowance may also be obtained until the expenditure is exhausted. No initial allowance will be forthcoming for expenditure incurred subsequently.

Should an hotel for which allowances have been obtained be sold, the vendor may be taxed on a balancing charge, or receive relief for a balancing allowance, and the purchaser may obtain future writing-down allowances, in a manner similar to that which applies for industrial buildings.

Where an hotel is located in an enterprise zone, it is advisable to claim the alternative allowances discussed below.

ENTERPRISE ZONES

Substantially increased capital allowances are available for expenditure incurred on assets located in enterprise zones. The cost of constructing an industrial building, a qualifying hotel or a commercial building or structure qualifies for an initial allowance, which unlike other allowances, was not withdrawn for expenditure incurred after 31 March 1986. It is a requirement that the expenditure must be incurred, or a contract entered into, within a period of ten years following the date on which the area first became designated as an enterprise zone.

An initial allowance of 100 per cent can be obtained to absorb the entire expenditure. Alternatively, the initial allowance may be reduced to some smaller amount with annual writing-down allowances, not exceeding 25 per cent of original cost, until the expenditure has been fully used. Where a building located in an enterprise zone is sold, balancing adjustments must be calculated on a basis similar to that applied on the sale of an industrial building.

53
ENTERPRISE ZONES

During the year ended on 5 April 1996, Mr X incurred £100,000 on the construction of a commercial building in an enterprise zone. He decided to claim an initial allowance of £50,000 in 1995–96 which resulted in annual writing-down allowances of £25,000 for both 1996–97 and 1997–98.

In 1995–96 Mr X received rent of £10,000 from letting the building to a tenant. This rent must be set against the initial allowance of £50,000, leaving a balance of £40,000.

The other income of Mr X for 1995–96 was £85,000. Assuming he was a married man aged 47 entitled to the full married couple's allowance, and made a claim to set the unused initial allowance against other income, the tax payable for 1995–96 becomes:

	£	£
Total income		85,000
Less		
Personal allowance . .	3,525	
Surplus initial allowance .	40,000	43,525
		£41,475

Tax payable:	£
Lower rate:	
On first £3,200 at 20 per cent . .	640.00
Basic rate:	
On next £21,100 at 25 per cent . .	5,275.00
Higher rate:	
On balance of £17,175 at 40 per cent	6,870.00
	12,785.00
Less Married couple's allowance – £1,720	
at 15 per cent	258.00
	£12,527.00

AGRICULTURAL BUILDINGS

Expenditure incurred by the owner or tenant of agricultural land on the construction of farm buildings, fences, cottages and other works, such as ditches and drains, will usually qualify for capital allowances. The cost of constructing a farmhouse will also be included but must be restricted to one-third of the capital cost, or a smaller fraction where the amenities of the farmhouse are considered excessive in relation to the agricultural holding.

The calculation of allowances and the effect on those allowances where property is subsequently demolished or sold differs substantially for expenditure incurred before 1 April 1986 and that incurred subsequently.

Expenditure incurred on or before 31 March 1986

For expenditure incurred before 1 April 1986, an initial allowance of 20 per cent could be claimed and usually granted in the year of assessment following that in which the outlay took place. At the taxpayer's option, the initial allowance could be reduced to some smaller amount. An annual writing-down allowance of one-tenth of the expenditure was also granted for the year of assessment following that in which expenditure was incurred and each of the succeeding years until the cost had been fully relieved. Where the maximum initial allowance of 20 per cent was claimed, aggregate allowances of 30 per cent were available in one year and allowances of 10 per cent in each of the seven following years.

Once qualifying expenditure has been incurred allowances remain available and cannot subsequently be withdrawn. Nor will any balancing charge or balancing allowance arise on the sale of an interest in agricultural property. Where an interest in such property changes hands before all allowances have been obtained the benefit of remaining future allowances accrues to the purchaser.

Expenditure incurred after 31 March 1986

For several years no initial allowance was forthcoming to absorb expenditure incurred after 31 March 1986. However, an initial allowance of 20 per cent was available for expenditure incurred between 1 November 1992 and 31 October 1993. No such allowance can be obtained for expenditure incurred subsequently.

Writing-down allowances are given at the rate of 4 per cent annually for the year of assessment in which expenditure is incurred and succeeding years. These allowances are given in addition to the initial allowance, although the aggregate allowances obtained cannot exceed the cost incurred.

Subject to the election mentioned below, no balancing charge or allowance will arise if the property is sold or assets cease to exist. Any purchaser of property will become entitled to the annual writing-down allowance at the rate of 4 per cent annually throughout the remaining part of the 25-year period or, where an initial allowance has been obtained, throughout a shorter period. This writing-down allowance is based on the vendor's original cost and not on the purchase price paid by the purchaser.

However, an election may be submitted where a building, fence or other work on which expenditure has been incurred is demolished, destroyed or other-

———————— 54 ————————
AGRICULTURAL BUILDINGS

On 12 April 1990, A incurred capital expenditure of £50,000 on the construction of a farm building. He sold the farm to B on 6 October 1994 with £47,000 being allocated to the building.

If *no election is made* annual allowances will be granted at the rate of £2,000 (4 per cent × £50,000) for 1990–91 and each of the next twenty-four years. These will be allocated as follows:

A

1990–91 to 1993–94 inclusive	£2,000 annually
1994–95 (to 5 October) . .	Half × £2,000

B

1994–95 (from 6 October)	Half × £2,000
1995–96 and the following nineteen years . . .	£2,000 annually

If *an election is made* the effect on A will be:

	£
Cost	50,000
Less writing-down allowances: 1990–91 to 1993–94 inclusive (4 × £2,000)	8,000
	42,000
Sale price	47,000
1994–95 balancing charge . . .	£5,000

B may obtain annual writing-down allowances calculated on the 'residue of expenditure' of £47,000 (£42,000 + £5,000), which represents that part of A's original cost not covered by allowances, with the addition of the balancing charge. These allowances will be available to B throughout the remaining part of the twenty-five year period, namely twenty and a half years, at the annual rate of £2,293. No initial allowance is available to B as he incurred no cost of construction.

wise ceases to exist. This election will establish a balancing allowance arising at the time of the event and representing the balance of unused expenditure. No future annual writing-down allowances will then be available.

An election may also be made, jointly by the vendor and purchaser, where property on which qualifying expenditure has been incurred is sold. Where such an election is made the disposal proceeds must be compared with the written-down tax value. Should the proceeds exceed this value a balancing charge will be made on the vendor to recoup previous writing-down and initial allowances. If the proceeds fall below the written-down tax value the vendor will receive a balancing allowance. The effect on the purchaser is that he will then receive future annual writing-down allowances throughout the remaining twenty-five year, or shorter, period based on the 'residue of expenditure'.

Broadly stated, the effect of submitting an election is similar to that which applies to industrial buildings and structures. It does, however, remain a matter for decision by the parties whether or not to take advantage of the election procedure.

FORESTRY LAND AND BUILDINGS
Capital expenditure incurred by the owner or tenant of commercial forestry land on the construction of forestry buildings, fences and other structures previously produced an entitlement to capital allowances. These allowances were calculated on a basis similar to those for expenditure on agricultural buildings. It was necessary to demonstrate that an election had been made for the occupation of woodlands to be assessed under Case I of Schedule D. Liability to assessment in this manner generally terminated in 1988, although it continued until 5 April 1993 where an election had been made. No capital allowances are available after the date on which commercial woodlands cease to be within the charge under Case I of Schedule D. It inevitably follows that all entitlement to capital allowances ceased once the special transitional period ended on 5 April 1993.

OTHER CAPITAL EXPENDITURE
Other expenditure for which allowances are available includes the cost of acquiring patents, 'know-how', expenditure on scientific research, ships, and the capital outlay incurred in working mines and sources of mineral deposits.

PARTNERSHIPS
The allowances mentioned earlier are also available to individuals carrying on business in partnership.

COMPANIES
Capital expenditure incurred by companies will enable the various capital allowances to be claimed, but different rules apply for determining the basis periods into which those allowances fall.

NON-TRADERS
Many of the capital allowances discussed on the previous pages are also available to individuals who incur expenditure on investment assets leased or used by others. This includes expenditure on industrial buildings, hotels, agricultural property and property located in enterprise zones. Allowances must be primarily offset against income arising from the investment, but it is usually possible to absorb surplus allowances against other income. A non-trader who incurs capital expenditure on plant and machinery leased to others may obtain the appropriate capital allowances, but these are generally only available to be offset against income arising from leasing and cannot be used against other forms of income.

12

Treatment of income

Property income

One of the many changes in the tax structure which have been made to remove complexity and smooth the path to self-assessment affects the taxation of income arising from land and buildings located in the United Kingdom. The change to a new system mainly applies from 6 April 1995 and concerns both the calculation of income and the nature of expenditure which can be subtracted when determining the amount of taxable income. The former practice of providing relief for interest paid on a loan applied to acquire property is altered by allowing that interest to be included in the calculation of income. Some features of the earlier system have largely emerged unscathed, including the taxation of premiums, the rent-a-room scheme and the treatment of furnished holiday accommodation.

It is therefore advisable to briefly outline the system in operation before 6 April 1995 and then to examine the new system which applies on and after that date. In those cases where premiums and other matters apply on a similar basis before, on and after 6 April 1995 they will be dealt with separately.

LIABILITY BEFORE 6 APRIL 1995

Before 6 April 1995 rent and other income from land, buildings and real property located in the United Kingdom was chargeable to income tax under Schedule A. Liability extended to:

a rents under leases of land;

b rent-charges, ground annuals and feu-duties and any other annual payments reserved in respect of, charged on, or issuing out of, land; and

c any other receipts arising to a person from his or her ownership of an estate or interest in, or right over, land.

Liability did not extend to yearly interest, mortgage interest, building society interest, or rents and royalties payable in respect of the exploitation of mines, quarries and similar undertakings. These matters were dealt with under different headings.

Calculation of liability

The income chargeable to tax was that to which the landlord became entitled, but did not necessarily receive, in the year of assessment. There could be some departure from this 'entitlement' rule where rent was paid in arrears by a tenant closely associated with the landlord.

A deduction could be made from the rent or other income for expenditure incurred in respect of the following, among others:

a maintenance, repairs, insurance and management;

b services which the landlord was obliged to provide but for which he received no separate payment;

c rates or other charges on the occupier which the landlord was obliged to pay;

d any rent-charge, ground annual, feu-duty or other periodical payment in respect of the land, or charged on or issuing out of the land.

Relief could not be obtained for expenditure relating to a period before the landlord acquired the property, or for expenditure incurred by reason of dilapidations which accrued in such a period. Thus, a person who purchased property in a dilapidated condition and incurred substantial expenditure on repairs to the premises could obtain no relief for the cost of those repairs, if the necessity to repair arose on some earlier date.

Excess expenditure

It sometimes happened that expenditure incurred by the landlord in respect of a single property exceeded in any year the rental income for that year. This excess could usually be set against rental income accruing to the landlord from other properties in the same year. However, the right of set-off was precluded where properties were let under abnormal conditions. Where expenditure was not offset against other rental income the excess could be carried forward to succeeding years and set against income subsequently arising from property. Owners of agricultural property could elect to set excessive expenditure against income generally, but other landlords were unable to relieve expenditure in this manner.

Lost rents

The charge to income tax under Schedule A was based on the rent or other receipts to which the landlord was entitled during the year of assessment. Failure to obtain payment did not necessarily provide sufficient grounds for avoiding liability to satisfy tax becoming due. However, if the person entitled to receive rents or other sums could show that

a the non-receipt was attributable to the default of the person liable to pay and all reasonable steps have been taken to enforce payment; or

b the payment had been waived without consideration and to avoid hardship,

the landlord could claim that the sum outstanding should be disregarded. If this claim was accepted no liability to tax arose on the 'lost' rents.

Furnished lettings

Profits from furnished lettings, calculated after deducting expenses including rent, rates, lighting and wages paid for household assistance, do not arise from a trade. The actual profits of a year of assessment could be assessed, at the taxpayer's option, under Schedule A or Case VI of Schedule D. The selection of a proper charging provision could be important where some deficiency was capable of being relieved against amounts chargeable under one heading only. Assessment remained subject to the special treatment of income arising under the 'rent-a-room' scheme and from the provision of furnished holiday accommodation.

Assessment

Income tax due by an individual in respect of rental and other income arising from land or buildings was payable on 1 January during the year of assessment. Thus the tax due in respect of income for the year ended 5 April 1995 was payable on 1 January 1995.

It will be apparent that in many cases accurate details of the annual incomings and outgoings could not be ascertained until after the end of the year of assessment. At the same time, if tax otherwise due on 1 January was held over, considerable delay in collection would inevitably result. This problem was overcome by using the agreed figures of net income for the immediately preceding year. For example, income tax payable on 1 January 1995 would be provisionally based on net income for the year ended 5 April 1994. When the final results for the year ended 5 April 1995 were known the original assessment would be adjusted, thereby producing either a repayment of tax or additional liablility. The necessity to estimate income on this basis could only be avoided if, since the beginning of the previous year, property had been sold or ceased to produce income.

LIABILITY AFTER 5 APRIL 1995

The 'old' basis for calculating liability under Schedule A often produced difficulty, particularly where an individual retained two or more properties, some of which were unlet and others let on different terms. Many of these difficulties have been removed by new provisions coming into operation on 6 April 1995. These provisions may not necessarily apply to a source of income which existed in 1995–96 but which was discontinued in the following year. Nor do the new provisions have any application to companies, which continue to adopt the old approach.

The new provisions treat income from land and buildings as arising from a Schedule A business. Such income will include profits or gains arising from the exploitation of any estate, interest or right in or over land in the United Kingdom. This will incorporate receipts in the form of rent but may also extend to other items from the exploitation of land. However, there must be excluded from liability under Schedule A

a the receipt of yearly interest;

b profits or gains arising from the occupation of woodlands managed on a commercial basis and with a view to the realisation of profits;

c profits from farming and market gardening;

d profits from the operation of mines, quarries and other concerns;

e rents arising from mines, quarries and similar undertakings.

Calculation of liability

All receipts accruing to an individual from the exploitation of property and forming part of a Schedule A business are gathered together in a single 'pool'. It is no longer necessary to isolate the different transactions which may produce profits, gains or income.

Unlike the previous approach, the type of expenditure which can be entered in the pool is not closely defined. The pool is attributable to a Schedule A business and both the expenditure which can be included and the receipts which must be gathered together will be determined on a basis similar to that used to calculate profits from a trade or profession assessable under Case I and Case II of Schedule D. Therefore many of the comments made on pages 66 and 67 are now of application when calculating the profits of a Schedule A business. The former calculation was based on rents to which a person became 'entitled' in a year of assessment, with relief for 'lost' rents. Although the right to receive rent will be an important matter when completing the Schedule A calculation, neither entitlement nor the special relief for 'lost' rents is a necessary ingredient.

Where income arises from furnished lettings this will be incorporated in the profits of the Schedule A business. That part of the receipts attributable to the use of furniture will be included also unless the provision of furniture comprises an activity of a trade. It is no longer possible to invoke an option to assess income from furnished lettings under Case VI of Schedule D or under Schedule A.

Excess expenditure

The entries made in a Schedule A business 'pool' may disclose a deficiency at the end of the year of assessment. This deficiency, treated as a Schedule A loss, may be carried forward and offset against Schedule A business profits for the following year or years until the deficiency or loss has been absorbed. It will not generally be possible to offset a Schedule A loss against the taxpayer's other income. However, where the loss is attributable to certain capital allowances or relates to agricultural land the position may be otherwise.

Any unused Schedule A expenditure being brought forward on 6 April 1995 and arising under

---

55
SCHEDULE A BUSINESS

During the year ended 5 April 1996 Keith received the following income:

	£
Rent from letting commercial property on a tenant's repairing lease . . .	19,500
Rent from letting unfurnished flats . .	6,200
Rent from letting furnished accommodation to students	4,800
Rent from letting agricultural property on a full repairing lease . . .	10,000
	£40,500

Expenses incurred 'wholly and exclusively' for the purposes of the business amounted to £11,600. In addition, Keith paid interest of £9,000 on a loan applied to acquire the agricultural property.

Based on these short facts, the Schedule A assessment for 1995–96 will be calculated as follows:

	£	£
Rent received . . .		40,500
Expenses . . .	11,600	
Interest	9,000	20,600
Schedule A profit . .		£19,000

---

the 'old' provisions may be carried forward and utilised against Schedule A business profits arising subsequently, unless the source of income for which that expediture was incurred ceased before 6 April 1996.

Assessment

The assessment of profits from a Schedule A business will represent the full amount of the profits or gains arising in each year of assessment and calculated after subtracting any Schedule A loss relief. The previous requirement that provisional liability should be discharged on 1 January and a balancing adjustment made later will cease to apply with the introduction of self-assessment for 1996–97. Special rules will, however, operate for the transitional Schedule A year 1995–96.

Relief for interest paid

Relief for interest paid before 6 April 1995 on a loan applied to acquire property was only available against income from that property where a number of requirements were satisfied. Relief for interest ceases to be given in this manner after 5 April 1995 as the interest merely forms an ingredient in the calculation of Schedule A business profits or losses.

In those cases where interest is paid under the MIRAS scheme in relation to let property, the payer may exercise an option to exclude MIRAS and bring the interest payment into the calculation of profits or losses from the Schedule A business.

PREMIUMS

Premiums received on the grant of a lease for a term not exceeding fifty years in duration are liable to taxation. The amount of the premium received must be reduced by 2 per cent for every complete twelve months of the lease, excluding the first twelve months, and only the balance remaining will produce liability. Only the reduced sum will be included in the Schedule A computation of profit.

Any part of a premium excluded from assessment under Schedule A may enter into other calculations of income or gains requiring assessment to income tax or capital gains tax.

The calculation is not affected by the changes which took place on 6 April 1995.

——— 56 ———
PREMIUMS ON LEASES

On 25 June 1995 Tom granted a 21-year lease of property in return for a premium of £40,000. That part of the premium which must be treated as income for 1995–96 and included in the calculation of profit from a Schedule A business will be calculated as follows:

	£
Number of complete years of the lease	21
Less first year	1
	20

	£
Premium received	40,000
Less	
20 years at 2 per cent = 40 per cent	16,000
Schedule A receipt 1995–96	£24,000

FURNISHED LETTINGS – RENT A ROOM SCHEME

Introduced on 6 April 1992, an exemption from tax applies to individuals who receive rent from letting rooms in their own homes. This exemption, known as the 'rent a room' scheme, extends to owners and tenants who let rooms furnished in their only or main residence. It is a necessary requirement that all income from this activity is either attributable to the letting of furnished accommodation assessable to income tax under Case VI of Schedule D before 6 April 1995 or Schedule A on and after this date or

——— 57 ———
RENT A ROOM SCHEME – EXEMPTION

David owns 'Fairways' and resides in the property with his wife and family as their only residence. He lets part of the property furnished to a lodger, and information for 1995–96 was as follows:

	£
Gross rents	2,700
Expenses	600

Apart from David, no other person receives any income for letting 'Fairways'. As the gross rents do not exceed £3,250 there will be no taxable profit, nor can relief be obtained for the expenses of £600.

represents profits from a trade chargeable under Case I of Schedule D. The scheme is confined to the letting of rooms and accommodation in an individual's only or main residence and has no application to similar activities undertaken in some other property.

Gross rents up to a maximum of £3,250 received in a tax year may qualify for complete exemption, but this figure is halved to £1,625 if two or more individuals each receive income from lettings in the same property. The limitation could arise, for example, where an owner lets part of his or her home to a tenant who sub-lets to a sub-tenant. Both the owner and the tenant may each obtain a maximum exemption of £1,625, if of course each individual can treat the property as his or her only or main residence.

Complete exemption

Where gross rents do not exceed £3,250 (or £1,625 where appropriate) in a tax year both receipts and expenses will be disregarded and the rent received incurs no liability to taxation. It remains possible to file an election to avoid taking advantage of this exemption. An election may be beneficial where the expenses incurred exceed rental income, as it will then be possible to carry forward surplus outgoings to a subsequent year or years.

Partial exemption

Gross rents arising in a tax year may exceed the ceiling of £3,250 (or £1,625). The taxpayer is then provided with a choice, namely:

a The individual may elect to suffer tax on that proportion of the gross rents which exceeds the

58
RENT A ROOM SCHEME –
PARTIAL EXEMPTION

Using the basic facts in Example 57, let it be assumed that the figures for 1995–96 were:

						£
Gross rents	.	.	.	.		8,000
Expenses	.	.	.	.	.	4,100

David is now provided with a choice, namely:

a He may file an election and pay tax on the following profit without obtaining any relief for expenses:

					£
Gross rents	.	.	.	.	8,000
Less basic exemption	.	.	.	3,250
Taxable profit	.	.	.	.	£4,750

b He may decline to file an election and pay tax on the following:

					£
Gross rents	.	.	.	.	8,000
Actual expenses	.	.	.	4,100
Taxable profit	.	.	.	.	£3,900

It would be advisable not to file any election.

ceiling of £3,250 (or £1,625). No relief will then be available for outgoings

b In the absence of an election the individual will incur liability to tax on the difference between gross rents received and expenses paid with no relief under the 'rent a room' scheme.

The election must be made within a period of twelve months following the end of the year to which it relates.

FURNISHED HOLIDAY ACCOMMODATION

A relaxed approach is available for individuals deriving income from the commercial letting of furnished holiday accommodation. Several requirements must be satisfied before these relaxations can apply, including the following:

a the property must be located in the United Kingdom;

b there must be a letting on a commercial basis and with a view to the realisation of profit;

c the tenant or occupier must be entitled to the use of furniture;

d accommodation must be available for commercial letting as holiday accommodation to the public

generally for periods which aggregate at least 140 days;

e the property must actually be so let for at least 70 days; and

f in a period of seven months the property must not normally be in the same occupation for a continuous period exceeding 31 days.

Special rules must be applied to determine whether these requirements are satisfied in a year of assessment. It also remains possible to submit a claim for averaging where some properties in the same ownership would, and others would not, satisfy the requirements.

Once the existence of qualifying lettings has been established, there are several taxation advantages. Income remains chargeable under Case VI of Schedule D, or under Schedule A after 5 April 1995, but for all practical purposes that income is deemed to be derived from a trade. Income is treated as 'earned', losses may be relieved against other income, profits will be calculated by applying trading principles and income can be used to provide cover for personal pension or retirement annuity premiums.

An additional benefit from establishing qualifying furnished holiday lettings is that the disposal of property used for this purpose may enable roll-over relief and retirement relief to be obtained when calculating capital gains tax liability.

The relaxed treatment of furnished lettings is confined to property in the United Kingdom and has no application to property situated overseas, perhaps in Spain, Portugal or France.

SAND AND GRAVEL QUARRIES

Rents and royalties for the use and exploitation of quarries of sand and gravel, sand-pits and brickfields are payable after deduction of income tax at the basic rate of 25 per cent. Deduction at this rate is not affected by the 20 per cent lower rate band. Income from such sources is not assessable under Schedule A.

It is often possible for the recipient of mineral royalties to divide the sums received into two equal parts. One part will be regarded as a chargeable gain assessable to capital gains tax and the other remains assessable to income tax. This does not affect the deduction of income tax at the rate of 25 per cent from the aggregate gross sum received.

FARMERS

Farmers who carry out farming on a commercial basis and with a reasonable expectation of profit, and persons who occupy land managed on a commercial basis and with a view to profit, are chargeable in the same manner as other persons who carry on a trade (see page 60). A claim may be made to average profits from farming between two consecutive years. Relief for farming losses may be obtained by setting those losses against other sources of income derived by the farmer, but there may be some limitations in the relief available where losses have been sustained for five consecutive years.

The allowances in respect of plant and machinery referred to on page 73 are available to farmers, and other allowances will frequently be obtained for capital expenditure on agricultural buildings and works (see page 78).

AGRICULTURAL LAND

Owners of agricultural land let to tenants are entitled to special relief for expenses. In the ordinary case where property outgoings exceed income in a year of assessment, the excess must be carried forward and set against income accruing in future years. However, if the expenditure was incurred on land, houses or other buildings comprised in an agricultural estate, the excess may be set against any income of the landlord for the same year.

This relief applies to excess expenditure arising both before 6 April 1995 and on or after that date.

FORESTRY AND WOODLANDS

In earlier times the occupation of woodlands did not give rise to a tax liability unless the woodlands were managed on a commercial basis and with a view to the realisation of profit. If woodlands were managed in this manner the occupier was provided with a choice. He could either choose to be assessed under Schedule B on an assumed annual value or elect to be assessed under Case I of Schedule D as a person carrying on a trade. Persons having the use of woodlands for the purpose of felling and removing timber in connection with an actual trade could not be assessed under Schedule B.

This basis for dealing with commercial woodlands was substantially amended and has now been withdrawn entirely as shown by the following timetable:

a Schedule B cannot apply after 5 April 1988.

b Subject to **d** below, no new election for assessment under Case I of Schedule D could be made after 14 March 1988.

c Elections for assessment under Schedule D and made before 15 March 1988 continued until 5 April 1993.

d Persons who had entered into commitments or made applications for grants received from the Forestry Commission before 15 March 1988 could also elect to be assessed under Case I of Schedule D until 5 April 1993.

The effect of these measures is that from 6 April 1993, the occupation of commercial woodlands has been entirely removed from income tax liabilities, reliefs and commitments, unless those woodlands are occupied for the purpose of felling and removing timber in connection with a bona fida trade.

Short rotation coppice

Some farmers produce fuel from the use of short rotation coppice. This involves planting willow or poplar cuttings on farm land. After a year or so the plantings are cut back to ground level which causes the production of shoots. These shoots are harvested every three years or so and made into chips which are then used as fuel. Arguably, the activity could involve commercial woodlands and support exemption from tax on profits arising. However, from 29 November 1994 the activity cannot comprise a use of commercial woodlands but income and expenditure will be included in the calculation of farming profits.

Investment Income

INDIVIDUALS retaining surplus funds, or maintaining an investment portfolio, will be concerned to obtain the maximum income or capital yield from the investment of capital. There are many investment opportunities and the eventual choice will also be influenced by tax considerations. Income from certain investments, notably National Savings Certificates and Children's Bonus Bonds, is exempt from liability to income tax. Exemption also extends to dividends and other revenue arising from Personal Equity Plans and Venture Capital Trusts, together with interest from TESSA arrangements. However, most other forms of income are liable to tax where the investor's income is sufficiently substantial.

In the case of husband and wife 'living together', it is necessary to allocate income between the couple, particularly where income-producing assets are jointly owned. Caution must be taken to ensure that any attempt to transfer future income from one spouse to the other cannot be set aside by the Inland Revenue on the grounds the transaction represents a 'settlement'.

These and other matters affecting investment income are discussed below.

TAXATION OF INVESTMENT INCOME

Income arising on many investments may be received 'net' after deduction of income tax at the basic rate of 25 per cent. Examples include interest received from debentures, loan interest payable by a company and interest on many Government stocks. Depositors with building societies and banks also receive interest after deduction of income tax, although those not liable to tax can arrange to receive income gross. Where the recipient is liable to income tax at the basic rate only, the income has been fully taxed by deduction and no further tax is due. Recipients who are not liable, or not wholly liable, to tax at the basic rate may obtain a partial or complete repayment of the tax deducted as shown on page 109. The gross income, calculated before deduction of income tax, must be included in the figure of total income where the recipient is liable to income tax at the higher rate of 40 per cent, but tax will only be charged at the rate in excess of the basic rate suffered, namely at 15 per cent.

Certain income, such as interest on holdings of $3\frac{1}{2}$ per cent War Loan, Income Bonds and Deposit Bonds issued by the National Savings movement, together with interest on National Savings Investment Accounts and Government stocks purchased through the National Savings Stock Register, is received gross, without deduction of income tax, and the recipient is taxed directly on the basis of the previous year's income. In the early years of ownership of every new source of income, and also in the closing years, a special basis of assessment applies. This basis will no longer be relevant when all income is taxed on a current year basis for 1997–98 and future years. Special adjustments will be needed for the transitional year 1996–97.

There are complex rules for dealing with certain forms of indirect income. For example where an investment in an offshore 'roll-up' fund is realised, surplus proceeds may be treated as income. Accrued income may also arise on the realisation of deep-discounted stock, namely stock issued at a large discount. The special rules which affect interest on National Savings Capital Bonds are reviewed later.

DIVIDENDS

Dividends paid by United Kingdom companies are not subject to deduction of income tax. However, each dividend is treated as having attached to it a 'tax credit'. The amount of this tax credit and the effect on the liability of individual shareholders changed significantly on 6 April 1993. It is therefore advisable to briefly examine the system in operation before that date and then to review the new system introduced on 6 April 1993 and which applies for 1995–96.

Dividends paid on or before 5 April 1993

For 1992–93 the tax credit was equal to one-third of the dividend paid. When calculating the total income of an individual who received such a dividend, the tax credit was added to the dividend received. For example, a cash dividend of £75 would have a tax credit of £25 thereby creating gross income of £100.

The tax credit was regarded as income tax suffered on the aggregate dividend at the rate of 25 per cent, with the following results:

a An individual who was not liable to income tax, due to an insufficiency of income, could obtain a repayment of the tax credit in full.

b An individual who only became liable following the receipt of dividends could recover part of the tax credit.

c An individual liable to tax at the lower rate of 20 per cent could also recover part of the tax credit.

d An individual liable at the basic rate only would neither pay nor recover tax on the dividend unless the dividend increased taxable income beyond the basic rate band of £23,700.

e An individual liable to tax at the higher rate of 40 per cent would be assessed on the aggregate of the dividend and the tax credit, but received a reduction in the tax otherwise payable equal to the amount of the tax credit. This involved an effective higher rate liability of 15 per cent on the gross sum.

Dividends paid on or after 6 April 1993

Dividends paid on or after 6 April 1993 also have a tax credit but for 1995–96 this is equal to one-quarter (and not one-third) of the dividend paid. Here also an individual receiving such a dividend will calculate total income by adding the tax credit to the dividend received. Thus a dividend of £75 will have attached to it a tax credit of £18.75 (one quarter of £75) which gives rise to a gross sum of £93.75.

The tax credit will be regarded as income tax suffered on the aggregate dividend at the rate of 20 per cent. However, the dividend is not liable at the basic rate of 25 per cent and will only involve an individual in liability to income tax at the higher rate of 40 per cent to the extent that the dividend

59
DIVIDENDS RECEIVED

Andrew is a single man aged 54. During 1995–96 he received dividends of £1,600 (tax credit £400).

Using these basic facts, it will be assumed that other income of Andrew chargeable to income tax was £4,500, £10,000, £27,000 and £40,000 respectively.

Other income £4,500

	£
Other income	4,500
Less Personal allowance . . .	3,525
	975
Add Dividends – gross . . .	2,000
	£2,975

Tax payable:	£
On £2,975 at 20 per cent . . .	595.00
Less tax credits	400.00
	£195.00

Other income £10,000

	£
Other income	10,000
Less Personal allowance . .	3,525
	6,475
Add Dividends – gross . . .	2,000
	£8,475

Tax payable:	£
On first £3,200 at 20 per cent . .	640.00
On next £3,275 at 25 per cent . .	818.75
On dividends of £2,000 at 20 per cent .	400.00
	1,858.75
Less tax credits	400.00
	£1,458.75

The dividends have been taxed in full and no further tax is due on those dividends.

Other income £27,000

	£
Other income	27,000
Less Personal allowance . . .	3,525
	23,475
Add Dividends – gross . . .	2,000
	£25,475

Tax payable:	£
On first £3,200 at 20 per cent	640.00
On next £20,275 at 25 per cent . .	5,068.75
On dividends:	
On first £825 at 20 per cent . .	165.00
On balance of £1,175 at 40 per cent .	470.00
	6,343.75
Less tax credits	400.00
	£5,943.75

This calculation ensures that only to the extent that total income exceeds the basic rate band of £24,300 by £1,175 will the excess gross dividend of £1,175 give rise to liability at 40 per cent.

Other income £40,000

	£
Other income	40,000
Less Personal allowance . . .	3,525
	36,475
Add Dividends – gross . . .	2,000
	£38,475

Tax payable:	£
On first £3,200 at 20 per cent . .	640.00
On next £21,100 at 25 per cent . .	5,275.00
On balance of £14,175 at 40 per cent	5,670.00
	11,585.00
Less tax credits	400.00
	£11,185.00

It is clear that the entire gross dividend of £2,000 is fully taxable at the higher rate of 40 per cent.

---

increases taxable income above the basic rate band of £24,300. To achieve this result the dividend is treated as comprising the highest slice of the taxpayer's income.

This will support the following conclusions:

a An individual who is not liable to income tax, due to an insufficiency of income, may obtain a repayment of the tax credit in full.

b An individual who only becomes liable following the receipt of dividends may recover part of the tax credit.

c An individual liable to tax at the lower rate of 20 per cent will neither pay additional tax nor recover any part of the tax credit.

d An individual liable at the basic rate only will neither pay nor recover tax on the dividend unless the dividend increases taxable income beyond the basic rate band of £24,300.

e An individual liable to tax at the higher rate of 40 per cent will be assessed on the aggregate of the dividend and the tax credit but will receive a reduction in the tax otherwise payable equal to the amount of the credit. As the tax credit is given at the reduced rate of 20 per cent, this will involve a higher rate liability of 20 per cent on the gross sum.

BUILDING SOCIETY INTEREST

When making payments of interest, or crediting interest to a depositor's account, in 1995–96, a building society will deduct income tax at the basic rate of 25 per cent, leaving only the net sum payable or to be credited. Depositors not liable, or not fully liable, to income tax at the basic rate may recover part, or all, of the tax deducted. Those incurring liability at the higher rate will be assessed to further tax on the gross sum. The 20 per cent lower rate band has no effect on the requirement to deduct income tax at the basic rate of 25 per cent. Nor does the tax credit system, which applies

─── 60 ───
BUILDING SOCIETY INTEREST – BASIC RATE

Jean, a married woman aged 42, earns a salary of £9,000 for 1995–96. She receives interest of £342 on an ordinary building society deposit account and has not registered to receive interest gross. An election has been made to transfer one half of the married couple's allowance to the wife.

Total income:	£	£
Salary		9,000
Building society interest received	342	
Add Tax deducted at 25 per cent	114	
		456
		9,456
Less Personal allowance . . .		3,525
		£5,931

Tax payable:		£
On first £3,200 at 20 per cent . .		640.00
On balance of £2,731 at 25 per cent		682.75
		1,322.75
Less Married couple's allowance (one-half) – £860 at 15 per cent . .		129.00
		1,193.75
Less Tax deducted on building society interest		114.00
		£1,079.75

The total tax due is £1,193.75 of which £114 has been suffered by deduction from interest received, leaving the balance to be collected from the salary under the PAYE deduction scheme.

─── 61 ───
BUILDING SOCIETY INTEREST – HIGHER RATE

Marcus is a single man and receives building society interest of £1,245 on a non-TESSA account in 1995–96. His other income for the year amounts to £30,000.

Total income:	£	£
Other income . . .		30,000
Building society interest received . . .	1,245	
Add Tax deducted at 25 per cent . . .	415	
		1,660
		31,660
Less Personal allowance . . .		3,525
		£28,135

Tax payable:		£
Lower rate:		
On first £3,200 at 20 per cent . .		640.00
Basic rate:		
On next £21,100 at 25 per cent . .		5,275.00
Higher rate:		
On balance of £3,835 at 40 per cent		1,534.00
		7,449.00
Less Tax deducted on building society interest		415.00
Tax payable		£7,034.00

to dividends, have any application to interest payments.

It is apparent that substantial administrative problems would arise if small savers received interest after deduction of income tax at the basic rate and in the absence of tax liability had to reclaim the tax suffered from the Inland Revenue. This problem has been recognised and investors who do not expect to pay income tax may complete a simple registration form. Once this form has been completed and forwarded to the building society concerned, interest will subsequently be paid or credited gross without any deduction of income tax. Should the circumstances of the investor change, the building society must be notified immediately to ensure that in future income tax is deducted from interest. It is possible that some investors may fraudulently complete the registration form or fail to notify the building society of changed circumstances. This is a serious matter as following detection a penalty of up to £3,000 may be incurred.

Many minor children have building society accounts into which pocket money, gifts or earnings are deposited. If sums deposited in a minor child's account by that child's parents, but not by grandparents or others, produce interest in excess of £100 the interest may well be treated as that of the parents. In this situation no registration should be made in an attempt to receive interest gross.

A considerable number of individuals entitled to receive interest gross have failed to register. There will be others having anticipated income close to, or a little in excess of, the threshold at which income tax liability commences who subsequently find there is no liability. These individuals may apply for repayment of excess income tax deducted from payments made.

No tax is deducted from building society TESSAs (see page 94).

BANK DEPOSIT AND OTHER INTEREST

With limited exceptions, which include National Savings Ordinary Accounts, Investment Accounts and Income Bonds, items of interest paid or credited on bank deposits in 1995–96, are discharged net after deduction of income tax at the basic rate of 25 per cent. Those investors unlikely to incur income tax liability may complete a simple registration form which will enable the bank or other person to discharge interest gross. The formalities of registration, the penalties for false declarations and procedures for the recovery of excessive basic rate income tax deductions are identical to those which affect building society deposits (see above). Banks also may take deposits within the TESSA arrangements and interest credited under these arrangements is not subject to income tax (see page 94).

Individuals over the age of 64 may obtain an increased personal allowance and married couple's allowance. The amount of any increase will require restriction, or perhaps elimination, where total income exceeds £14,600 in 1995–96. When calculating income for this purpose it should not be overlooked that the gross amount of bank, building society or other interest must be included and not only the net sum received or credited.

NATIONAL SAVINGS BANK INTEREST

Interest received on deposits with the National Savings Bank is chargeable to income tax. The assessment for any tax year is based on income received in the preceding year, but special adjustments must be made where a new source arises or an existing source is discontinued. The preceding year basis will cease to apply once the new current year basis is introduced for 1997–98, with special adjustments made for 1996–97.

62
BANK INTEREST RECEIVED AND INCREASED PERSONAL ALLOWANCE

Cyril, a married man aged 78, receives pensions amounting to £15,300 in 1995–96. He also receives net building society interest of £1,650 in the same year. No TESSA account was involved and Cyril is entitled to the full married couple's allowance.

Total income is calculated as follows:	£	£
Pensions . . .		15,300
Building society interest received	1,650	
Add Tax deducted at 25 per cent	550	2,200
Total income . . .		£17,500

As total income exceeds £14,600, the increased personal allowance of £4,800 must be reduced as follows:

	£
Increased allowance	4,800
Less one-half of excess over £14,600 (£17,500–£14,600)	1,450
	£3,350

The allowance cannot be reduced below the basic allowance of £3,525. Therefore of £1,450, only £1,275 is needed to produce this result. The increased married couple's allowance will be:

	£	£
Increased allowance .		3,035
Less one-half of excess as above . . .	1,450	
Deduct subtracted from personal allowance . .	1,275	175
Reduced allowance . . .		2,860

The calculations may now be completed:

Total income	17,500
Less Personal allowance . . .	3,525
	£13,975

Tax payable:	£
On first £3,200 at 20 per cent . .	640.00
On balance of £10,775 at 25 per cent	2,693.75
	3,333.75
Less Married couple's allowance – £2,860 at 15 per cent	429.00
	2,904.75
Less Tax deducted on building society interest	550.00
	£2,354.75

The gross building society interest of £2,200 has been included to calculate total income. This has had the effect of reducing allowances by £1,450 (£1275 + £175).

63
SAVINGS BANK INTEREST

Charles is a married man and receives a salary of £16,750 for 1995–96 and his wife, Sandra, has business profits of £5,120 assessable in the same year. Both have ordinary deposits with the National Savings Bank and the amounts of interest from these deposits otherwise assessable for 1995–96 are as follows:

	£
Husband	90
Wife.	37

Assuming neither spouse has reached the age of 65 and the husband is entitled to the full married couple's allowance, the tax payable by Charles will be:

Total income:	£	£
Salary		16,750
Interest	90	
Less exemption . .	70	
		20
		16,770
Less Personal allowance . . .		3,525
		£13,245

Tax payable:	
On first £3,200 at 20 per cent . .	640.00
On balance of £10,045 at 25 per cent	2,511.25
	3,151.25
Less Married couple's allowance – £1,720 at 15 per cent	258.00
	£2,893.25

The liability of Sandra will become:

Total income:	£	£
Profits		5,120
Interest	37	
Less exemption . .	37	
		—
		5,120
Less Personal allowance . . .		3,525
Tax chargeable on		£1,595

Tax payable:	
On £1,595 at 20 per cent . . .	£319.00

However, when calculating the total income of an individual for 1995–96, the first £70 of interest received from deposits, other than investment deposits, with the National Savings Bank, is disregarded. If husband and wife each receive interest, both may obtain the £70 exemption. This applies also where husband and wife have a joint holding. Should interest received by one spouse fall below £70 the unabsorbed balance cannot be used to increase the other's exemption limit above £70.

NATIONAL SAVINGS CAPITAL BONDS

National Savings capital bonds offer a guaranteed return of interest throughout a five-year period. Interest is not paid out but added, without deducting income tax, to the value of the bond. However, the amount of interest added is liable to income tax as if it was actually received by the bond holder. Liability arises by reference to the interest added in the previous year of assessment, with special adjustments for the opening years of a new source and the closing years of a discontinued source. This basis of assessment alters when the new current year basis is introduced.

GOVERNMENT AND OTHER SECURITIES

A special scheme applies for dealing with interest arising on large holdings of securities. The scheme has no application to shares but extends to Government securities, together with most securities issued by companies and local authorities, among others.

Normally, the price paid to acquire securities, together with proceeds arising from the disposal of those assets, will be calculated by inserting an adjustment for accrued interest. This adjustment has no effect for income tax purposes as the holder actually receiving interest is liable to bear tax on the entire amount of that interest at his or her appropriate rate.

64
GOVERNMENT SECURITIES

On 1 May 1995 Jack acquired a holding of securities. Interest at the rate of £6,000 was payable half-yearly on 1 July and 1 January. Interest of £6,000 (less tax) was received by Jack on 1 July 1995. He sold his holding, with settlement on 15 December 1995. If Jack is not within the special scheme his income for 1995–96 will comprise £6,000, representing the gross equivalent of interest actually received.

However, if, as seems probable, the special scheme applies, Jack's income will be calculated as follows:

	£
Interest period to 1 July 1995 – 181 days	
Period of ownership – 61 days	
Taxable 61/181 × £6,000 . . .	2,022
Interest period to 1 January 1996 – 184 days	
Period of ownership – 167 days	
Taxable 167/184 × £6,000 . .	5,446
Taxable income	£7,468

65
PURCHASED LIFE ANNUITY

Mabel is a widow aged 67. She receives a social security retirement pension and a pension from her late husband's former employers aggregating £9,800 for 1995–96. She also receives £1,500 (gross) annually from a purchased life annuity. The annuity contains a capital element of £850 and an income element of £650.

The actual sum received from the annuity in 1995–96 will be:

	£	£
Capital element		850.00
Income element	650.00	
Less Tax at 25 per cent . .	162.50	487.50
Cash received		£1,337.50

The tax payable will be:

Total income:	£
Pensions	9,800
Annuity (income element only) . .	650
	10,450
Less Personal allowance . .	4,630
	£5,820

Tax payable:	£
On first £3,200 at 20 per cent . .	640.00
On balance of £2,620 at 25 per cent	655.00
	1,295.00
Less Deducted on annuity . .	162.50
	£1,132.50

However, the position is otherwise for securities brought within the scheme as interest is treated as accruing on a day to day basis and this will determine the individual's liability to tax where securities are purchased and sold. For example, where securities are purchased between interest payment dates the purchaser will only bear tax on that part of the interest for the period from the purchase date to the end of the interest period. Similarly, where securities are sold the vendor will bear tax on interest from the commencement of the interest period to the date of settlement.

The scheme will only apply if the nominal value of all securities held by an individual in the year of assessment during which the interest period ends, or in the previous year, exceeds £5,000. The threshold of £5,000 applies separately to a husband and to his wife. Personal representatives are brought within the scheme if the nominal value of securities held in the deceased person's estate exceeds £5,000.

Individuals and personal representatives who do not retain holdings of this magnitude remain unaffected by the special scheme and continue to suffer income tax on the actual amount of interest received.

PURCHASED LIFE ANNUITIES
Life annuities can be purchased from insurance companies and other financial institutions. Each annuity, which may be paid on an annual or some other periodic basis, contains two elements, namely a capital element and an income element. The amount of each element will be determined by the insurance company or institution responsible for the arrangement.

The capital element is effectively a return of the purchase price and will not be liable to income tax. However, the income element is taxable and payments will be received after deduction of income tax at the basic rate. Only the income element will enter into the calculation of the annuitant's total income. The use of the basic rate is not affected by the 20 per cent lower rate band.

These purchased life annuities must be distinguished from those acquired as part of a pension scheme arrangement. The latter annuities are wholly taxable.

STOCK DIVIDEND OPTIONS
Companies residing in the United Kingdom sometimes offer shareholders the option of receiving a cash dividend or an issue of shares. Where the shareholder decides to accept shares the market value of the holding will usually exceed the corresponding cash dividend. However, these arrangements, called stock dividend options, may involve the shareholder in liability to income tax. The value of the shares issued is deemed to represent a sum remaining after deducting income tax at the lower rate of 20 per cent for 1995–96. There can be no assessment to tax at either the lower rate or the basic rate. However, where income is sufficiently substantial the gross sum will incur liability to higher rate income tax, less a notional credit of 20 per cent. Shareholders not liable, or not fully liable, to income tax cannot obtain any repayment of the notional tax deducted. This arrangement effectively ensures that a shareholder opting to obtain shares will suffer income tax in a manner similar to that which is applied to dividends, but without the ability to recover any tax credit.

LIFE POLICIES
There are a range of products, including life policies, life annuities and capital redemption policies, which

66
STOCK DIVIDEND OPTIONS

Henry has substantial income which attracts considerable liability to higher rate income tax for 1995–96. He retains shares in a United Kingdom company and during the year was provided with an option to take either

a a cash dividend of £4,000; or
b shares issued by the company.

Henry opted to take shares, which had a market value of £5,000 at the time of issue.

For assessment purposes the shares are treated as representing a gross sum of £6,250 from which income tax at the lower rate of 20 per cent has been deducted to produce £5,000. As Henry is already liable to tax at the higher rate of 40 per cent he will incur the following additional liability:

	£
Tax on £6,250 at 40 per cent . . .	2,500
Less deemed tax suffered – £6,250 at	
20 per cent	1,250
Additional liability	£1,250

may produce liability to income tax on maturity, surrender or assignment. These will not usually comprise normal policies of life assurance but broadly reflect other arrangements, often involving single premium policies. Liability may arise on the occurrence of a chargeable event which affects the underlying policy. The amount of any gain arising by reason of this event will be both calculated and notified by the insurance company or other financial institution marketing the product. The gain does not incur liability to income tax at the lower rate or the basic rate. Liability is confined to higher rate income tax. A policyholder not liable to tax at the higher rate is unable to recover any of the notional income tax deemed to have been suffered.

SAVE AS YOU EARN

Save As You Earn contracts enable monthly investments to be made throughout a period of five years. At the end of this period, or at the investor's option two years later, the investment may be withdrawn together with a terminal bonus. The bonus is not liable to income tax. Most Save As You Earn contracts are share option related and enable employees to purchase shares in their employing company with the proceeds arising on maturity.

No new 'non' share option related schemes are now available.

PERSONAL EQUITY PLANS

As an incentive to encourage wider share ownership, personal equity plans have been available for several years. Individual plans are managed by plan managers, usually financial institutions, which must be approved by the Inland Revenue. Investment is confined to individuals aged 18 years and above who must be either resident and ordinarily resident in the United Kingdom, or performing duties on behalf of the Crown in some territory overseas.

There are basically two kinds of available plan, namely a general plan and a single company plan. For 1995–96 the maximum permitted cash investment capable of being made by an individual in a general plan is £6,000. The entire sum may be invested in investment or unit trusts. It remains a condition that at least one-half of the investments made by the investment or unit trusts are in United Kingdom ordinary shares or comparable shares in companies incorporated within a Member State of the European Community, in certain United Kingdom corporate bonds, or preference shares in United Kingdom and European Community companies. Where this 50 per cent level is not achieved the maximum amount of investment capable of being made in unit or investment trusts is limited to £1,500. It is a further condition that this limited investment will only be recognised if the underlying unit or investment trust holds at least one-half of its investments in shares, which need not necessarily be issued by a United Kingdom company or one in the EC.

It is also possible for an individual to invest up to £3,000 in a single company plan during 1995–96. This is in addition to an investment in a general plan. However, an individual cannot invest in more than one general plan during the year of assessment.

The attraction of a personal equity plan is the exemption from taxation offered to investors. Any dividends paid on investments made by plan managers will have the usual tax credit attached. Managers may obtain repayment of the tax credit from the Inland Revenue on behalf of investors. This ensures that dividend income received by the plan will effectively be realised 'gross' without suffering the inroads of income tax. Some relief may also be available for interest on investments made within the plan. Should gains arise from the disposal of assets held by the plan no liability to capital gains tax will arise.

Plan managers charge a fee for their services and the investor cannot obtain any tax relief for this outlay.

Since their introduction in 1986 personal equity plans have grown in popularity and now provide many investors with a convenient method of achieving tax-free investment.

TAX EXEMPT SPECIAL SAVINGS ACCOUNT

A further facility conferring taxation benefits is the Tax Exempt Special Savings Account (TESSA), which is operated by authorised banks and building societies. Among the conditions which must be discharged before the account will be recognised for taxation purposes are the following:

a the account holder must be an individual aged at least 18 years;

b the account must be identified as a TESSA;

c the holder of the account must not have any other TESSA;

d the account must not be held on a joint basis;

e the account must not be held for the benefit of any person except the holder;

f the account must not be connected with any other account.

A maximum is placed on the amount which can be deposited in a TESSA throughout a five-year period. Deposits must not exceed £3,000 in the first year or £1,800 in each of years two, three, four and five. In addition, the total deposited must be limited to £9,000.

Where these conditions are satisfied, any interest or bonus added to the account will not become liable to income tax if the account is maintained throughout a full five-year period, or until the death of the account holder, whichever event occurs first. Once the five-year period has come to an end any future interest will become chargeable to income tax but the account holder may close the account and open another TESSA attracting similar tax advantages.

It is possible to contemplate the withdrawal of some interest during the five-year period. The amount withdrawn is not to exceed the interest credited less income tax at the basic rate. However, should interest in excess of the amount calculated on this basis be withdrawn, or any extraction of capital take place, the tax advantages will be lost. All interest will then be treated as the depositor's income, with that interest deemed to arise at the date exemption is abandoned.

Reinvestment

TESSA's were first made available in January 1991. It follows that many account holders will reach the five-year anniversary in January 1996. As an inducement for those with maturing TESSA accounts to reinvest the proceeds, a relaxation is being made in the maximum investment into a new TESSA during the first year. Up to a maximum of £9,000 can be invested in the new TESSA using proceeds arising from the maturity of the old deposit. Only the capital part of the earlier deposit can be used for this purpose and not any accrued interest. The restrictions on the amount which can be deposited in the new account for years two, three, four and five remain. Those who receive the maximum repayment of £9,000 on the maturity of the old TESSA and reinvest the entire sum in a new deposit account cannot invest any further amounts in that account. It is a requirement that the proceeds must be reinvested within a period of six months following the maturity of the original TESSA.

VENTURE CAPITAL TRUSTS

Yet a further facility conferring substantial tax benefits, the venture capital trust, became available for investment on and after 6 April 1995. The general nature of these new trusts has been outlined on page 36. Subject to a maximum investment of £100,000 in any year of assessment the investor may obtain income tax relief at the rate of 20 per cent. In addition, any dividends or other distributions received from the investment will be immune from income tax, where of course the underlying requirements are satisfied. It is possible that the investments made by an individual in a year of assessment may exceed £100,000. In such a situation it is only dividends and other distributions attributable to the initial £100,000 qualifying for relief which are exempt from liability to income tax. Dividends and distributions on any excess will be chargeable to tax in the normal manner.

An additional attraction of venture capital trusts is freedom from capital gains tax liability where a qualifying holding is retained throughout a five-year period.

INCOME FROM ABROAD

A taxpayer may receive income from abroad which must suffer United Kingdom taxation. As this income has probably been taxed in a foreign country also, it is effectively taxed twice. To avoid the problems of double taxation, agreements have been entered into between the United Kingdom and many foreign countries. These agreements contain a variety of features. Some exempt income from tax in either the foreign country or the United Kingdom and others provide that the foreign tax suffered shall be deducted from the United Kingdom tax due on the same income.

Even where no double tax agreement has been concluded a taxpayer who would otherwise pay tax on the same slice of income both here and abroad is entitled to similar relief.

No relief from double taxation will be granted unless it is claimed by the taxpayer, who must be resident in the United Kingdom. A person not liable to United Kingdom taxation, where, for example, personal allowances exceed income, cannot claim any repayment of foreign tax from the United Kingdom authorities.

Dividends received from overseas companies are not within the United Kingdom 'tax credit' system discussed on page 87. However, the income tax charged on those overseas dividends was reduced from 25 per cent to 20 per cent from 6 April 1993. Increased liability will arise for individuals liable at the higher rate of 40 per cent.

HUSBAND AND WIFE – JOINT PROPERTY

A husband and wife 'living together' may jointly retain the ownership of income-producing assets. It is then necessary to allocate any income arising between each party. The general rule is that the income from jointly held assets must be apportioned equally between each spouse. This does not apply to earned income, income from a partnership or to some special types of income where the legislation requires a specific allocation.

Where equal apportionment is appropriate it remains possible for this to be varied by making a joint declaration. The declaration does not enable the parties to impose their own allocation but requires income to be apportioned on the basis of each individual's beneficial interest in the asset.

A declaration may be made at any time, but unless it was made before 6 June 1990 the declaration will only apply to income arising subsequently. The declaration cannot be related back to some earlier period.

A separate declaration is required for each jointly owned asset. For example, a husband and his wife may jointly own perhaps five assets. The declaration may apply to any number between one and four, extend to all assets, or the parties may choose not

67
JOINT ASSETS

Bob and Betty are married and the joint owners of commercial property with the husband retaining a beneficial interest of two-thirds and his wife the remaining one-third. Net rental income taxable under Schedule A amounted to £3,000 for 1995–96.

In the absence of a declaration the income will be allocated as follows:

	£
Bob – one-half	1,500
Betty – one-half	1,500
	£3,000

If a declaration is made before the commencement of the year of assessment on 6 April 1995, the allocation becomes:

	£
Bob – Beneficial ownership two-thirds .	2,000
Betty – Beneficial ownership one-third .	1,000
	£3,000

A finding that the declaration was only made on, say, 6 October 1995 and income accrued evenly throughout the year would support the following allocation:

	Bob £	Betty £
Income to 5 October 1995 – £1,500		
Bob – one-half . . .	750	
Betty X – one-half . . .		750
Income from 5 October 1995 – £1,500		
Bob – two-thirds . . .	1,000	
Betty – one-third . . .		500
	£1,750	£1,250

to make any declaration whatsoever. A declaration is only valid if it reaches HM Inspector of Taxes within a period of 60 days from when it was made.

A declaration once made cannot subsequently be withdrawn and will only cease to apply where the couple separate, one spouse dies or there is a change in the beneficial interests.

HUSBAND AND WIFE – TRANSFER OF ASSETS

A deceptively simple method of transferring future income from one spouse to the other is to transfer the ownership of the asset producing that income. Where the transfer is made by way of outright gift, and without any strings attached, the transfer should achieve the required objective. The position will, however, be otherwise if the transferee does not obtain an interest in all income arising, is bound to apply that income for the benefit or advantage of the transferor, or the transferor can benefit from either income or capital in any circumstances whatsoever. Some caution must therefore be exercised when contemplating the transfer of income-producing assets between a husband and his wife.

13

Deeds of covenant

THROUGHOUT A PERIOD of many years payments made under a properly drawn deed of covenant have formed a popular method of transferring income from one person to another. In some cases payments have been made for valuable and sufficient consideration but the great majority have been devoid of any consideration whatsoever. The continuing use of deeds of covenant as a tax efficient arrangement was severely restricted by the withdrawal of relief for many covenants made after 14 March 1988. This withdrawal has no effect on covenants in favour of recognised charities, nor did it apply to the rapidly diminishing list of non-charitable covenants entered into before that date.

To achieve a proper understanding of the effect which payments made under deed of covenant may have on taxation liabilities a distinction must be drawn between:

a charitable covenants; and
b other covenants.

CHARITABLE COVENANTS

Charitable covenants must require payments to be made to a named charity throughout a period capable of exceeding three years. Many deeds drawn in simple form will be suitable but professional advice should be obtained before entering into deeds containing unusual provisions.

If a covenant is capable of being terminated within the initial three-year period it will not be recognised for tax purposes. To avoid this some covenants are drawn in a form which enables termination to occur after the end of three years.

Previously such covenants ceased to be recognised immediately the power arose, but in 1992 a change was made enabling this type of covenant to continue, should the parties so require, without the need for a fresh deed.

When making payments under a deed of covenant drawn in favour of a charity the payer should deduct income tax at the basic rate. This will involve a deduction at the rate of 25 per cent for payments made in 1995–96. The rate at which tax must be deducted is not influenced by the 20 per cent lower rate band. If the payer has taxable income equal to, or in excess of, the gross sum payable, and chargeable at the basic rate, he or she may retain the income tax deducted. This effectively provides relief from income tax at the basic rate if, but only if, the payer exercises the right to deduct tax.

Where the payer's taxable income is not sufficiently substantial to incur liability at the basic rate on an amount equal to payments made under deed of covenant, income tax similar to the amount of tax deducted must be accounted for to the Inland Revenue. This situation may arise where income is exceeded by allowances and reliefs, or occasionally where liability arises at only the lower rate of 20 per cent. The possibility of such a development should not be overlooked by those of modest means.

Some married couples enter into joint covenants. The Inland Revenue will treat payments made under such covenants as discharged in equal proportions by each spouse, unless there is evidence supporting a different conclusion.

In those cases where the payer's income is

68
CHARITABLE COVENANTS

Richard is a married man aged 54 earning an annual salary of £22,000 and entitled to the full married couple's allowance. During 1995–96 he made a payment of £500, less tax, to a charity as required by a properly drawn deed of covenant.

The actual payment made will be:

	£
Gross sum	500
Less Income tax at 25 per cent	125
Actual payment	£375

The income tax payable by Richard in 1995–96 will be:

	£
Total income	22,000
Less Personal allowance	3,525
	£18,475

Tax payable:

On first £3,200 at 20 per cent	640.00
On balance of £15,275 at 25 per cent	3,818.75
	4,458.75
Less Married couple's allowance – £1,720 at 15 per cent	258.00
	£4,200.75

As Richard suffers tax at the basic rate on an amount of income in excess of the gross covenanted payment, he may retain the tax deducted of £125.

69
RESTRICTION OF RELIEF

Margaret, a married woman aged 40 living with her husband, has earnings of £3,400 for 1995–96. During the year she makes an annual payment of £300, less tax, under a charitable covenant. The actual payment made will be:

	£
Gross sum	300
Less Income tax at 25 per cent	75
Actual payment	£225

The income tax payable will be:

	£
Total income	3,400
Less Personal allowance	3,525
	NIL

Tax payable:

On £300 at 25 per cent	£75.00

Although income is fully covered by the personal allowance, income tax must be charged at the basic rate of 25 per cent on £300. This ensures that tax of £75 deducted from the annual payment is fully accounted for.

70
COVENANTS – HIGHER RATE RELIEF

Peter is a married man and has business profits of £75,000 assessable for 1995–96. During the year he made payments under deed of covenant aggregating £20,000 (gross) to several charities.

The actual aggregate payments made to charity in 1995–96 will be:

	£
Gross sums	20,000
Less Income tax at 25 per cent	5,000
Actual payments	£15,000

The income tax payable, assuming Peter is entitled to the full married couple's allowance, will be calculated as follows:

	£
Total income	75,000
Less Personal allowance	3,525
	£71,475

Tax payable:

	£
Lower rate:	
On first £3,200 at 20 per cent	640.00
Basic rate:	
On next £21,100 at 25 per cent	5,275.00
On next £20,000 at 25 per cent (re covenanted payments)	5,000.00
Higher rate:	
On balance of £27,175 at 40 per cent	10,870.00
	21,785.00
Less Married couple's allowance – £1,720 at 15 per cent	258.00
	£21,527.00

Note: Relief at the basic rate on £20,000 has been obtained by deducting, and retaining, tax at 25 per cent on payment. It is therefore necessary to ensure that the above calculation confines relief to rates in excess of 25 per cent on this outlay. This has been achieved by imposing tax of 25 per cent on £20,000 of taxable income.

sufficiently substantial to incur income tax liability at the higher rate of 40 per cent, covenanted payments may be offset against income otherwise chargeable at that rate.

Thus an individual having suffered sufficient tax on income at the top rate of 40 per cent and making payments of, say, £10,000 (less tax) to a charity obtains the following tax reliefs for 1995–96:

a £2,500 (£10,000 at 25 per cent) by deduction; and

b £1,500 (£10,000 at 40 per cent less 25 per cent) against higher rate liability.

The net cost of the payments becomes £6,000 (£10,000 less £2,500 plus £1,500).

The charity receiving payments under a properly drawn deed of covenant may expect to recover income tax suffered at the basic rate.

Further matters relating to payments made under charitable deeds of covenant are discussed on page 100. In addition, single donations made under the Gift Aid scheme are effectively treated as discharged in a manner similar to payments under deed of covenant (see page 101).

OTHER COVENANTS

Payments made under a non-charitable deed of covenant entered into before 15 March 1988 continued to be recognised for taxation purposes. It remained a condition that the deed of covenant was examined by HM Inspector of Taxes not later than 30 June 1988. In the absence of such an examination the deed could not be accepted and payments made after 5 April 1988 were entirely disregarded for taxation purposes.

Where a non-charitable covenant had been accepted by the Inspector the payer would deduct and retain or account for income tax at the basic rate of 25 per cent for 1994–95 in a manner identical to that which applied to a charitable deed of covenant. However, relief was restricted to the deduction of income tax at the basic rate on payment. It was not possible to obtain relief at the higher rate of 40 per cent.

Recognition of these pre 15 March 1988 non-charitable covenants ceased to apply for all payments made after 5 April 1995. The payer cannot deduct income tax at the basic rate and must satisfy payments 'gross'. The recipient will not treat the amount received as taxable income, nor can any attempt be made to recover income tax allegedly deducted. Shortly stated, payments under a non-charitable deed of covenant, whether entered into before 15 March 1988 or on or after that date now have no effect whatsoever for income tax purposes.

71
OTHER COVENANTED PAYMENTS

A father receives a salary of £26,000 in 1994–95 and makes an annual payment of £2,500, less tax, to his 24-year-old son who is attending university. The covenant was made before 15 March 1988 and has been accepted as qualifying by the Inland Revenue.

The actual payment made in 1994–95 will be:

	£
Gross sum	2,500
Less Income tax at 25 per cent . .	625
Actual payment	£1,875

On the assumption the father is entitled to the married couple's allowance, his tax liability becomes:

	£
Total income	26,000
Less Personal allowance . . .	3,445
	£22,555

Tax payable:	
On first £3,000 at 20 per cent . .	600.00
On balance of £19,555 at 25 per cent	4,888.75
	5,488.75
Less Married couple's allowance – £1,720	
at 20 per cent	344.00
	£5,144.75

As tax is chargeable at the basic rate on a sum in excess of £2,500, the father may retain the tax of £625 deducted when making the annual payment. If the income of the father had been sufficient to incur liability at the higher rate of 40 per cent, the covenanted payment would not support any further relief.

It may be possible for the son to obtain a complete or partial repayment of the tax deducted on application to the Inland Revenue.

The above example applies only for 1994–95 as recognition of the covenant is withdrawn for 1995–96 and future years.

14

Charitable bodies

GENERAL EXEMPTION

Recognised charities are provided with a general exemption from tax where income is applied for charitable purposes. This exemption extends to rents and other receipts from land, together with dividends and interest, among others. Therefore a charity may invest surplus funds and obtain a return which is not eroded by taxation liabilities. Where income is received after deduction, or deemed deduction, of tax, for example interest and dividends, the charity may obtain a repayment of tax suffered from the Inland Revenue.

Trading profits earned by a charity are, however, exempt only where either:

a the trade is exercised in the course of the actual carrying out of a primary purpose of the charity; or

b the work in connection with the trade is mainly carried out by beneficiaries of the charity.

Failure to satisfy one of these conditions will result in the trading profits remaining liable to tax, notwithstanding that the proprietor of the business is a charity.

INDUCEMENTS FOR CHARITABLE FUNDING

In addition to exemptions from tax for income arising on investments made, or profits earned, by a charity, several reliefs are available to encourage charitable funding.

Deeds of covenant

On making payments under deed of covenant to a charity an individual may deduct and usually retain income tax at the basic rate of 25 per cent for 1995–96. Additionally, the charity may obtain repayment of the tax deducted from the Inland Revenue. Where the payer is liable to tax at the higher rate of 40 per cent he or she may obtain further relief as shown on page 98. Thus the cost to the covenantor is reduced and the charity obtains the full benefit of the gross payment. If the donor merely made a cash gift equal to the gross sum, no deduction of income tax could be made and the cost to the donor would be correspondingly increased. The position may be otherwise if sufficiently large gifts are made to qualify for relief under the Gift Aid arrangements outlined on the following page.

The advantages of making payments under deed of covenant are not confined to individuals, as similar payments may be made by companies. These payments enable the corporate payer to obtain relief for corporation tax and also confer an entitlement on the recipient charity to recover tax suffered by deduction.

Deeds of covenant often provide for the payment of a fixed annual sum which must be grossed up at the basic rate prevailing at the time of payment. The advantage of this arrangement is that the covenantor may continue to make the same cash payment annually, notwithstanding any change in the basic rate of income tax.

As a general rule, payments made under deed of covenant will only be recognised for tax purposes if they produce no benefit for the payer and place no obligation on the payee to provide some advantage. Small benefits or advantages may be disregarded but those of any substance may not. This prevents subscriptions being paid in the form of covenanted payments and qualifying for tax relief. However, a relaxation affects payments made to a limited range of charities whose sole or main purpose is the preservation of property or the conservation of wildlife for the public benefit. This also includes museums and supporters' organisations having charitable status. For payments made to these charities, any right of entry to view property or perhaps a collection will not be treated as a benefit which may otherwise disqualify a deed, if the right is limited to the covenantor, or members of the covenantor's family.

Company donations

Although payments made under covenant provide the payer with tax relief, there is no general relief for isolated donations. An exception concerns donations made by a limited range of companies. The maximum amount of qualifying donations is not to exceed 3 per cent of the ordinary dividends paid by the company concerned. Closely controlled companies are excluded from this arrangement, which is therefore confined to larger public companies. On making a qualifying donation the paying company will deduct income tax at the basic rate of 25 per cent and account for the deduction to the Inland Revenue. This will usually enable the company to subtract the gross sum when calculating liability to corporation tax. The recipient charity may then claim repayment of the tax deducted in a manner similar to that available for tax suffered on payments under deeds of covenant. An alternative and substantially more widely used method of obtaining relief is available under the Gift Aid arrangements (see below).

Payroll deduction scheme

Limited income tax relief will be available where charitable donations are made under an approved payroll deduction scheme. These schemes must be operated by an employer through an approved charity agency. Membership is voluntary but those employees who join may contribute up to £900 in 1995–96. Contributions are subtracted from each employee's earnings and the aggregate sums collected paid to an approved agency which is responsible for distributing those funds to the selected charities.

The qualifying contributions are also deducted from earnings when calculating the net sum chargeable to income tax. This effectively provides contributing employees with tax relief for payments made under the payroll deduction scheme.

Costs incurred by an employer when operating the scheme may be subtracted when calculating the employer's liability to taxation. In addition, relief can be obtained where the employer contributes towards the costs of a charitable agency administering the employer's scheme.

Gift Aid scheme

As a further inducement to charitable giving, a Gift Aid scheme is available. This scheme encourages individuals to make lump sum donations to charity and obtain income tax relief. If the donations are to qualify the following conditions, among others, must be discharged:

a There must be a payment in money.
b The payment must not be subject to any condition leading to repayment.
c The payment must not comprise a covenanted payment to charity.
d The payment must not fall within the payroll deduction scheme.
e No benefit of any substance must be receivable by the donor in return for the donation.
f The sum paid must not be less than £250. An increased threshold of £400 applied for payments made before 16 March 1993.

Where the above conditions are satisfied the donor is provided with a choice. He or she may decline to make any attempt to obtain tax relief, in which eventuality the transaction is entirely disregarded for taxation purposes. However, the individual may provide a certificate confirming that the above conditions have been satisfied and that any tax liability will be discharged. This certificate will identify the donation made as a net sum after deduction of income tax at the basic rate of 25 per cent for 1995–96. The donor must treat the payment on a basis identical to payments made under deed of covenant. The tax deemed to have been deducted can usually be retained and relief will be available at the higher rate of income tax on the gross equivalent. Should the donor have insufficient income to absorb the gross payment he or she will be required to account to the Inland Revenue for the income tax deemed to have been deducted.

Companies also may make single donations under the Gift Aid scheme. Income tax will be deducted

72
GIFT AID SCHEME

Simon, a married man aged 42, has business profits of £75,000 assessable for 1995–96. During the year he made a single donation of £15,000 to a recognised charity. The payment satisfied the requirements of the Gift Aid scheme and a certificate was provided.

The actual payment of £15,000 must be treated as a net sum calculated as follows:

	£
Gross sum	20,000
Less Income tax at 25 per cent	5,000
Actual payment	£15,000

The income tax payable by Simon, assuming the full married couple's allowance can be obtained, will be calculated as follows:

	£
Total income	75,000
Less Personal allowance	3,525
	£71,475

Tax payable:

	£
Lower rate:	
On first £3,200 at 20 per cent	640.00
Basic rate:	
On next £21,100 at 25 per cent	5,275.00
On next £20,000 at 25 per cent	5,000.00
Higher rate:	
On balance of £27,175 at 40 per cent	10,870.00
	21,785.00
Less Married couple's allowance – £1,720 at 15 per cent	258.00
	£21,527.00

Note: Relief at the basic rate on £20,000 is deemed to have been obtained by deducting, and retaining, tax at 25 per cent on payment. It is therefore necessary to ensure that the above calculation confines relief to rates in excess of 25 per cent on the outlay. This is achieved by imposing tax at the basic rate of 25 per cent on £20,000.

It will be noted that the tax liability in this case is identical to that shown by Example 70 on page 98 which involved actual payments of £20,000 made under deed of covenant.

at the basic rate on payment and accounted for to the Inland Revenue, if of course the required certificate is forthcoming. The gross amount of donations can then be set against profits chargeable to corporation tax.

No upper limit is placed on the maximum lump sum which individuals or companies may contribute

under Gift Aid, providing the minimum of £250 (or £400 where appropriate) is exceeded.

Gifts of business equipment
A novel form of relief is made available for business gifts to educational establishments. The relief can be obtained by individuals, partnerships and companies carrying on a trade. Only the transfer of 'equipment' is brought within this relief, with 'equipment' comprising plant and machinery.

Where the equipment is either manufactured or sold by the business the gift of that equipment will not require any adjustment in the calculation of trading profits. However, as the cost of the equipment, or the raw materials and other costs involved in manufacture, will be included in the computation of profits, relief is effectively obtained. In those cases where the equipment has qualified for capital allowances, its transfer will be treated as taking place for no consideration.

The transfer must be made to a recognised educational establishment, which can include a university, polytechnic, college and school.

Company dividends
The tax credit of one-third attaching to dividends paid by United Kingdom companies in 1992–93 was reduced to one-quarter for 1993–94 and for future years. Charities able to reclaim the amount of the tax credit from the Inland Revenue therefore suffered a reduction in income. For example, the tax credit on a dividend of £75 paid in 1992–93 was £25. The credit on the same dividend for the next three years has been reduced to £18.75. Charities receiving a great deal of dividend income would therefore suffer a substantial reduction in aggregate receipts.

To offset this reduction, special claims may be made by charities in 1993–94 and each of the three following years. In addition to claims for repayment of the tax credit, charities may recover from the Inland Revenue an amount representing:

a one-fifteenth of dividends received in 1993–94;
b one-twentieth of dividends received in 1994–95;
c one-thirtieth of dividends received in 1995–96; and
d one-sixtieth of dividends received in 1996–97.

These special payments will have no effect whatsoever on companies paying the dividends involved.

Other reliefs
Wide-ranging reliefs from capital gains tax and inheritance tax are also available where assets are transferred to charitable bodies.

15

Husband and wife

Marriage

FOR THE YEAR of assessment in which a couple marry, each will receive the normal personal allowance, suitably increased for those over the age of 64.

A married couple's allowance of £1,720 will be available for 1995–96 if the ceremony takes place before 6 May 1995. The married couple's allowance may be increased to some higher figure for those over the age of 64 or 74 years.

However, the amount of the married couple's allowance will be reduced by one-twelfth for each complete month after 5 April until marriage occurs.

73
RESTRICTED MARRIED COUPLE'S ALLOWANCE

Janet and Mark, both aged 24, were married on 14 November 1995. The married couple's allowance for 1995–96 is £717, calculated as follows:

	£
Full married couple's allowance . .	1,720
Deduct period before marriage	
7/12ths of £1,720	1,003
Married couple's allowance available. .	£717

In addition, each individual will obtain a full year's personal allowance of £3,525.

74
YEAR OF MARRIAGE

Michael and Sarah were married on 19 October 1995. Michael earns a salary of £17,000 per annum and Sarah £9,000 per annum. Michael is to obtain the full married couple's allowance. The tax payable for 1995–96 is calculated as follows:

Michael		£
Total income	.	17,000
Less Personal allowance . .	.	3,525
		13,475
Tax payable:		
On first £3,200 at 20 per cent .	.	640.00
On balance of £10,275 at 25 per cent		2,568.75
		3,208.75
Less Married couple's allowance:		
Maximum . . .	1,720	
Deduct period before		
marriage (one-half of		
£1720) . . .	860	
£860 at 15 per cent .	.	129.00
		£3,079.75

Sarah		£
Total income . . .	.	9,000
Less Personal allowance . .	.	3,525
		£5,475
Tax payable:		
On first £3,200 at 20 per cent .	.	640.00
On balance of £2,275 at 25 per cent		568.75
		£1,208.75

In those cases where the amount of the increased married couple's allowance for older persons must be restricted by reason of the husband's income exceeding £14,600 the restriction must firstly be applied and the one-twelfth limitation then made applicable to the reduced married couple's allowance only.

It is possible that the husband will be entitled to the additional personal allowance for a child or children in the year of marriage. He may then choose whether to retain that allowance or abandon the allowance and obtain the married couple's allowance. This choice applies for the year of marriage only. Whilst the additional personal allowance will be greater, when making the choice it should not be overlooked that any part of this allowance which cannot be used by the husband is incapable of being transferred to the wife. In contrast, any unused part of the married couple's allowance can be transferred.

The wife may retain the additional personal allowance for the year of marriage if the qualifying child was resident with her before the ceremony took place. Any unused blind person's allowance can be transferred between the couple in that year.

It is possible that a married man already entitled to the married couple's allowance for a year of assessment re-marries in the same year, perhaps following the death of his first wife. In such a situation there will be no restriction to the married couple's allowance, which may be obtained in full. However, only one married couple's allowance can be obtained and not a separate allowance for each wife.

Although a husband may have more than one wife as permitted by his religious or other beliefs, only a single married couple's allowance will be available for each year.

The wife may elect to obtain one-half of the basic married couple's allowance. Husband and wife may jointly elect that the entire basic allowance should be transferred to the wife (see page 8). This election must be made during the year of marriage, if it is to apply for that year.

Death of spouse

WHERE A HUSBAND and wife are 'living together' and the husband dies, no apportionment of allowances is made. A full year's personal allowance will be granted when calculating the liability of the deceased husband. In addition, a full year's married couple's allowance will be available. It is possible for the personal representatives administering the estate of the deceased husband to transfer any unused married couple's allowance for 1995–96 to the widow.

In the year of her husband's death the widow will obtain the normal personal allowance. In addition, she will qualify for a widow's bereavement allowance. This allowance will be available for the following year also, unless she re-marries in the year of her husband's death. If the widow has a qualifying child she should be entitled to receive the additional personal allowance.

On the death of his wife the surviving widower is entitled to a full year's married couple's allowance for the year in which death occurs, unless an election has been made to transfer any part of that allowance to the wife. The allowance will not be available for later years unless the widower re-marries. Although a widow may obtain a widow's bereavement allowance, usually for two consecutive years, no similar allowance is available to a widower.

PENSIONERS AND ELDERLY PERSONS
Pensioners and elderly persons are liable to tax in exactly the same manner as other individuals but the increased personal allowance and increased married couple's allowance mentioned on pages 7 and 8 may be available to those who are in receipt of income falling below, or not substantially exceeding, £14,600 for 1995–96.

Retirement pensions payable under the state scheme and those received from a former employer are subject to tax. A state retirement pension received by a married woman is treated as her income, whether or not it arises from contributions made by the wife or by her husband. Where only small sums of tax are involved on retirement pensions and other income the Inland Revenue may refrain from raising assessments (see page 43).

CHILDREN'S INCOME
Income accruing to a child will not usually be treated as that of the child's parents. Special rules apply, however, where a parent creates a settlement for, or makes gifts to, such a child. Income arising from the settlement or gift may then be treated as that of the parent until the child reaches the age of 18 or marries, whichever event first occurs. This only arises if the income exceeds £100 in 1995–96.

A minor child can obtain the benefit of a personal allowance of £3,525 for 1995–96 if income received is chargeable to income tax as the child's income.

75
DEATH OF HUSBAND

Mr and Mrs G had been married for many years but the husband died on 3 September 1995. Income assessable in 1995–96 was as follows:

Before death

Mr G

	£
Earnings	10,500
Investment income (gross) . .	520

Mrs G

Earnings	4,000
Investment income (gross) . .	240

After death

Mrs G

	£
Pension and taxable social security benefits	5,100
Earnings	5,000
Investment income (gross) . .	340

Neither individual was over the age of 64 and no election had been made to transfer the married couple's allowance.

Tax payable will be calculated as follows:

Deceased husband (to date of death)

Total income:	£
Own earnings . . .	10,500
Own investment income . .	520
	11,020
Less Personal allowance . . .	3,525
	£7,495

Tax payable:

	£
On first £3,200 at 20 per cent . .	640.00
On balance of £4,295 at 25 per cent	1,073.75
	1,713.75
Less Married couple's allowance – £1,720 at 15 per cent . . .	258.00
	£1,455.75

Mrs G

Total income:	£
Pension and social security benefits	5,100
Own earnings (£4,000 + £5,000) .	9,000
Own investment income (£240 + £340)	580
	14,680
Less Personal allowance . . .	3,525
	£11,155

Tax payable:

	£
On first £3,200 at 20 per cent . .	640.00
On balance of £7,955 at 25 per cent	1,988.75
	2,628.75
Less Widow's bereavement allowance – £1,720 at 15 per cent . . .	258.00
	£2,370.75

Divorce and separation

MARRIAGE BREAKDOWN

Where a husband and wife are separated under an order of a court of competent jurisdiction, by deed of separation, or are in fact separated in such circumstances that the separation is likely to be permanent, the couple will be treated as not 'living together' for income tax purposes. The loss of this status may affect the future availability of allowances. It may also have some application for capital gains tax purposes on the treatment of assets transferred between the parties.

Year of separation

For the year of assessment in which separation occurs a full year's married couple's allowance is available. There will be no reduction in the amount of the allowance, providing the couple were 'living together' at some time during the year of assessment. It will remain possible for the husband to transfer any unused part of the married couple's allowance to his separated wife for the year of separation.

The wife will receive the normal personal allowance for 1995–96, perhaps increased to some higher amount if she is over the age of 64. In addition, where a wife has a qualifying child living with her after the date of separation she may obtain the additional personal allowance of £1,720.

Exceptionally, a husband who was separated from his wife on 5 April 1990 may obtain the married couple's allowance if he is wholly maintaining her but obtains no tax relief for his outlay (see page 15).

MAINTENANCE PAYMENTS

Payments will frequently be made by a husband to his separated wife, or by a former husband to his divorced wife, under a binding legal agreement recorded in a separation deed or similar document or under the terms of a United Kingdom court order. The nature and treatment of these and other

76
YEAR OF SEPARATION

Mr and Mrs H, both in their thirties, were living together until July 1995 when they permanently separated. There were two children, aged 10 and 7 years, who continued to reside with their mother after the separation. Both parents were employed, with Mr H receiving earnings of £22,000 and his wife earnings of £10,000 in 1995–96. No maintenance payments were made and the husband was entitled to the full married couple's allowance.

The tax payable by Mr H will be:

	£
Total income	22,000
Less Personal allowance . . .	3,525
	£18,475

Tax payable:

On first £3,200 at 20 per cent . .	640.00
On balance of £15,275 at 25 per cent .	3,818.75
	4,458.75
Less Married couple's allowance – £1,720 at 15 per cent . . .	258.00
	£4,200.75

The tax payable by Mrs H becomes:

	£
Total income	10,000
Less Personal allowance . .	3,525
	£6,475

Tax payable:

On first £3,200 at 20 per cent . .	640.00
On balance of £3,275 at 25 per cent .	818.75
	1,458.75
Less Additional personal allowance – £1,720 at 15 per cent . . .	258.00
	£1,200.75

As the husband was living with his wife during part of the year, a full year's married couple's allowance is available. The wife can obtain the additional personal allowance as she has at least one qualifying child.

---

payments for taxation purposes will be governed by the date on which the order or agreement was concluded. It is therefore necessary to examine separately:

a payments made under 'old' orders and agreements, and

b payments made under 'new' orders and agreements.

OLD ORDERS AND AGREEMENTS

The first group incorporates payments under:

a court orders made before 15 March 1988;

b court orders applied for before 16 March 1988 and made not later than 30 June in the same year;

c maintenance agreements made before 15 March 1988; and

d court orders or maintenance agreements made on or after 15 March 1988 which vary or replace earlier orders or agreements.

The maintenance agreements referred to in c and d must be binding documents concluded between the parties. Not only is it necessary for these agreements to have existed before 15 March 1988 but they must also have been examined by HM Inspector of Taxes not later than 30 June in the same year if they are to be recognised for taxation purposes. Failure to achieve recognition destroys relief for subsequent payments.

To obtain relief for payments in 1995–96 under 'old' orders or agreements it must be shown that the payments were made:

a to one of the parties of a marriage, including a marriage which has been dissolved or annulled, to or for the benefit of the other party to the marriage and for the maintenance of the other party; or

b to any person under 21 years of age for his own benefit, maintenance or education; or

c to any person for the benefit, maintenance or education of a person under 21 years of age.

All payments falling in the 'old' group will be made gross without deducting income tax.

The payer will obtain income tax relief for payments made in each year of assessment up to an amount not exceeding the payments qualifying for relief in 1988–89 (12 months ending on 5 April 1989). These limits will take account of any amending court order or agreement made before 6 April 1989, but subject to this any future increase will not obtain relief.

For 1993–94 and earlier years, the amount of any qualifying maintenance payment could be fully relieved when calculating the payer's liability to income tax. However, a restriction has been imposed for later years. This requires that relief for the first £1,720 of any maintenance payments made in 1995–96 will be restricted to the reduced rate of 15 per cent. The excess of any payments over £1,720 will continue to attract relief in full at the taxpayer's highest rate suffered.

The reason for this restriction is to align relief

—— 77 ——
PAYMENTS UNDER 'OLD' ORDERS

A husband and wife were divorced in 1983. Under the terms of a pre-1988 court order the former husband was required to pay maintenance at the rate of £6,000 per annum, payable monthly. His income for 1995–96 was £28,000. The former wife had no other income.

The aggregate maintenance payments of £6,000 must be broken down into two parts, namely

a the first £1,720, and

b the excess of £4,280.

The tax liability of the former husband may now be calculated as follows:

	£	£
Total income		28.000
Less Personal allowance . .	3,525	
Excess maintenance		
payments . .	4,280	7,805
		£20,195
Tax payable:		
On first £3,200 at 20 per cent . .		640.00
On balance of £16,995 at 25 per cent		4,248.75
		4,888.75
Less Maintenance payments – first £1,720		
at 15 per cent . . .		258.00
		£4,630.75

The tax liability of the former wife becomes:

	£
Total income	6,000
Less Exempt	1,720
	4,280
Less Personal allowance . .	3,525
Tax chargeable on . . .	£755
Tax payable:	
On £755 at 20 per cent . .	£151.00

for maintenance payments with that obtained for the married couple's allowance.

The change in relief for payments made does not affect the recipient. Throughout the application of the old arrangements the recipient has been taxable on the amount received or, if lower, the amount taxable in 1988–89, after subtracting an amount equal to the married couple's allowance for the year of receipt. This approach continues unaltered.

An election may be made to adopt the 'new' rules outlined on page 108. This could be beneficial where the level of payments made in 1988–89 fell below the married couple's allowance for a future year.

—— 78 ——
VARIATION OF ORDER

Using the basic facts in Example 77, let it be assumed that in September 1988 the former wife obtained an order increasing the monthly payments from £500 to £700, with the first revised payment falling due in October of that year.

The payments made by the former husband in 1988–89 became:

	£
6 × £500	3,000
6 × £700	4,200
	£7,200

The aggregate amount payable in 1988–89, namely £7,200, will establish the amount which can be recognised for future years. For 1995–96 relief for the first £1,720 will be restricted to 15 per cent, with the balance of £5,480 obtaining relief at the top rate suffered. The revised calculation of tax payable then becomes:

Former husband

	£	£
Total income		28,000
Less Personal allowance . .	3,525	
Excess maintenance		
payments . .	5,480	9,005
		£18,995
Tax payable:		
On first £3,200 at 20 per cent . .		640.00
On balance of £15,795 at 25 per cent .		3,948.75
		4,588.75
Less Maintenance payments – first £1,720		
at 15 per cent . . .		258.00
		£4,330.75

Former wife

	£
Total income:	
Maintenance payments – restricted .	7,200
Less Exempt	1,720
	5,480
Less Personal allowance . .	3,525
	£1,955
Tax payable:	
On first £1,955 at 20 per cent .	£391.00

Although the actual maintenance payments made in 1995–96 were £8,400 (£700 × 12) the amount in excess of payments due in 1988–89 must be disregarded.

NEW ORDERS AND AGREEMENTS

The second group incorporates payments made under 'new' court orders and maintenance agreements concluded after 14 March 1988 other than:

a Court orders applied for before 16 March 1988 and made not later than 30 June in the same year; and

b Court orders or maintenance agreements varying orders or agreements made before 15 March 1988 or falling within **a**.

All payments made under orders and agreements of this nature will be discharged gross in 1995–96 without deducting income tax.

Where a divorced former spouse or separated spouse is required to make payments to the other spouse income tax relief can be obtained on the smaller of:

a the payments made in 1995–96, and

b £1,720, which is equal to the basic married couple's allowance for the year.

This relief continues to apply, subject to an adjustment for any changes in the basic married couple's allowance, until the recipient re-marries, if at all. In the somewhat unusual case where an individual is making payments to more than one divorced former spouse or separated spouse all payments must be aggregated when establishing the £1,720 limitation.

Apart from limited relief where payments are made to a divorced former spouse or a separated spouse, no other tax relief whatsoever will be available to the payer. It follows that relief cannot be obtained for payments made to a child or those falling due under an affiliation order.

The relief based on the smaller of **a** or **b** was available at the payer's top rate suffered in 1993–94. However, for payments made in later years relief is restricted and for 1995–96 is limited to 15 per cent.

In the case of all payments falling within the second group and made under a court order or maintenance agreement, the recipient is immune from any taxation liability.

79
PAYMENTS UNDER 'NEW' ORDERS

Norman separated from his wife in 1990. Under a court order made on 12 August 1990, Norman was required to make monthly payments of £500 to his separated wife; the first payment falling due on 15 August 1990. Norman received a salary of £26,000 for 1995–96 but his separated wife received no other income.

Payments made under the court order in 1995–96 will aggregate £6,000 (12 × £500). Norman will obtain relief on £1,720, which is less than the payments made. His liability for 1995–96 then becomes

					£
Total income	.	.	.	.	26,000
Less Personal allowance		.	.	.	3,525
					£22,475

Tax payable:
On first £3,200 at 20 per cent		.	.	640.00
On balance of £19,275 at 25 per cent		.	4,818.75
			5,458.75
Less Maintenance payments –			
£1,720 at 15 per cent	.	.	.	258.00
			£5,200.75

The separated wife has no taxable income as the payments received from her husband are ignored. There is no liability to tax, nor can the wife obtain any tax repayment as no tax has been suffered.

CHILD SUPPORT AGENCY

In April 1993 the Child Support Agency became responsible for a great deal of work associated with child maintenance. Included in this work is the collection of certain maintenance payments which are then forwarded to the person entitled. This function will not affect the treatment of maintenance payments for tax purposes, notwithstanding the involvement of an 'intermediary'.

RECONCILIATION

It is possible that a separated couple achieve a reconciliation. For the year of assessment in which this occurs a full year's married couple's allowance will be available.

16

Administration

Repayment of tax

SOME ITEMS OF investment income are received after deduction of income tax at the basic rate of 25 per cent for 1995–96. These may include interest on building society and bank deposits, although many depositors not liable to income tax may arrange to receive interest gross. Other examples of income received after deduction of income tax include interest on many Government securities and annuities. Income tax is not strictly deducted from dividends paid by United Kingdom companies but each dividend has a tax credit equal to one-quarter of the

sum received which effectively represents income tax at the rate of 20 per cent on the aggregate amount.

80
REPAYMENT CLAIM

The total income of Robin, a widower aged 72, for 1995–96, was as follows:

	£	£
State retirement pension . .		3,060
Dividends received . . .	960	
Add Tax credits at 1/4th . .	240	
		1,200
Total income		4,260

The taxpayer is entitled to a personal allowance of £4,630 and as total income does not exceed this amount no tax is due. The tax credits of £240 on dividends received may be reclaimed from the Inland Revenue.

81
REPAYMENT CLAIM

Gwen is a single woman aged 58. She receives an annuity of £8,000 (tax deducted £2,000), building society interest of £600 (tax deducted £150) and cash dividends of £1,200 for 1995–96.

	£	£
Annuity (gross)		8,000
Building society interest (gross) . .		600
		8,600
Less Personal allowance . . .		3,525
		5,075
Plus Dividends received . .	1,200	
Add Tax credits at 1/4th . .	300	1,500
		£6,575

		£
Tax payable:		
On first £3,200 at 20 per cent . .		640.00
On next £1,875 at 25 per cent . .		468.75
On dividends of £1,500 at 20 per cent		300.00
		1,408.75
Less		
Tax on annuity . . .	2,000.00	
Tax credits	300.00	
Tax on interest . . .	150.00	
		2,450.00
Repayment due		£1,041.25

82
REPAYMENT CLAIM

Ralph, a married man entitled to the full married couple's allowance, receives interest on investments of £2,400 gross (tax deducted £600) in 1995–96. He has National Savings Bank interest of £90 on an ordinary deposit account, National Savings Income Bonds interest (paid gross) of £275 and business profits of £4,000 chargeable in the same year.

	£	£
Total income:		
Business profits		4,000
Investment income (gross) . . .		2,400
National Savings Bank interest	90	
Less Exempted . . .	70	
		20
Income Bond interest . . .		275
		6,695
Less Personal allowance . . .		3,525
		£3,170
Tax payable:		
On £3,170 at 20 per cent . . .		634.00
Less Married couple's allowance – £1,720 at 15 per cent		258.00
		376.00
Less Tax suffered by deduction . .		600.00
Repayment due		£224.00

Where tax has been suffered by deduction it may be possible to obtain a complete or partial repayment. This may arise where the recipient is exempt from income tax and does not receive the full benefit of personal and other allowances from direct assessment on other income, or is not fully liable to tax on the amount deducted or that treated as deducted. Repayment situations are not confined to income tax suffered on investment income but may arise where excessive deductions have been made under the PAYE scheme, where there are claims for loss relief or claims are submitted for some other relief.

For 1992–93 and earlier years the tax credit attaching to a dividend effectively represented tax suffered at the basic rate of 25 per cent. The credit was then reduced to 20 per cent for subsequent years. It follows that shareholders entitled to any repayment for these years will only receive the appropriate sum at the rate of 20 per cent.

Stringent time limits apply for submitting claims and elections and there is a wide range of different limits which must be observed. However, claims for the repayment of income tax suffered may be forwarded within a period of six years following the end of the year of assessment to which the claim relates. Before submitting any repayment claim the claimant should consider whether it is possible to arrange for interest to be received 'gross', or indeed that a claim for repayment is justified.

For 1996–97 and later years the introduction of self assessment will often require that claims for repayment of income tax are made when completing a tax return, for delivery not later than 31 January following the end of the year of assessment to which the claim relates.

The effect of claims for the repayment of tax suffered by deduction in 1995–96 is shown by examples on this and the previous page.

Where a repayment of tax claimed for a year of assessment has not been made within twelve months after the end of that year, the taxpayer may become entitled to receive a repayment supplement. The amount of this supplement is amended from time to time but rates used in the last six years are as shown below:

From	To	Per cent
6 January 1989	5 July 1989	11.5
6 July 1989	5 November 1989	12.25
6 November 1989	5 November 1990	13
6 November 1990	5 March 1991	12.25
6 March 1991	5 May 1991	11.50
6 May 1991	5 July 1991	10.75
6 July 1991	5 October 1991	10
6 October 1991	5 November 1992	9.25
6 November 1992	5 December 1992	7.75
6 December 1992	5 March 1993	7
6 March 1993	5 January 1994	6.25
6 January 1994	5 October 1994	5.5
6 October 1994		6.25

Schedules and Cases

TO FACILITATE the collection of income tax each source of income is allocated to a Schedule. The scope of each Schedule is given below but it must be borne in mind that there is only one income tax and the use of the various Schedules in no way affects this principle.

Schedule	Source of income includes
A	Income from land and property in the United Kingdom.
B	Previously woodlands managed on a commercial basis and with a view to the realisation of profit but this Schedule has now been abolished.
C	Interest and dividends on Government or public authority funds and certain payments made out of the Public Revenues of overseas countries.
D	This Schedule is divided into the following Cases: Case I – trades; Case II – professions and vocations; Case III – interest, annuities, annual payments and discounts; Case IV – securities located outside the United Kingdom; Case V – possessions located outside the United Kingdom; Case VI – annual profits or gains not chargeable under any other Case or Schedule.
E	This Schedule includes three Cases and extends to emoluments from offices and employments of profit and also to pensions arising in the United Kingdom.
F	Company distributions.

INCOME LIABLE TO ASSESSMENT

In general, liability to United Kingdom income tax extends to all income arising in England, Scotland, Wales and Northern Ireland. Additionally, individuals who are regarded as resident in the United Kingdom are usually liable to income tax on income arising overseas. However, in the case of individuals resident in the United Kingdom but either domiciled abroad, or, being British subjects, ordinarily resident abroad, only overseas income actually remitted to, or received in, the United Kingdom will suffer income tax.

RESIDENCE

Liability to United Kingdom income tax may arise on overseas income if an individual becomes resident here and this is of particular importance to visitors and other persons whose stay is only intended to be temporary. In the absence of residence no part of the visitor's income arising overseas will be subject to United Kingdom taxation, whether remitted here or retained abroad.

A visitor is regarded as resident for any income tax year (commencing on 6 April) if he or she is present in the United Kingdom for periods amounting to six months or more during that year. There are no exceptions to this rule.

Difficult cases arise where an individual is in the United Kingdom for a period falling short of six months, but if visits are made year after year, and are for substantial periods, residence will be acquired. For this purpose visits are usually regarded as substantial if they average three months or more per annum over a four-year period. When establishing the duration of visits for this purpose, days spent in the United Kingdom which were beyond the individual's control may be ignored. This may arise in the case of illness and also in the case of individuals affected by the outbreak of hostilities overseas. Where an individual comes to the United Kingdom to commence permanent residence or with the intention of remaining for at least three years, he or she will be treated as becoming resident from the date of arrival.

At earlier times the retention of a place of abode in the United Kingdom could sometimes be sufficient to indicate residence for any year during which visits, however short, were made. The existence of such a place was disregarded if the individual worked full-time in a trade, profession or vocation, no part of which was carried on in the United Kingdom, or if that individual worked full-time in an office or employment, all the duties of which were performed overseas. From 6 April 1993, the existence of a place of abode has little influence on the determination of an individual's residential status.

An individual's status of residence strictly applies throughout a full year of assessment. In practice, however, where an individual comes to the United Kingdom and acquires the status of 'resident' this will apply only from the date of arrival. A similar approach is adopted where an individual leaves the United Kingdom and ceases to be both resident and ordinarily resident in this territory.

Following the introduction of independent taxation the residence status of a wife must be determined separately from that of her husband. However, where the husband leaves the United Kingdom to take up employment overseas and is accompanied by his wife at or about the time of departure, the residential status of the husband may be adopted by the wife also.

The significance of 'splitting' a year of assessment is that certain items of income arising in the 'non-resident period' may be exempt from United Kingdom taxation.

Date tax payable

WAGES, SALARIES and other remuneration arising from an office or employment will usually be paid after deduction of income tax under the PAYE scheme. The deductions will extend to tax at the lower rate, the basic rate and the higher rate also where earnings are sufficiently substantial. Pensions paid by a former employer will frequently be subject to PAYE deductions. The PAYE deduction scheme is also extended to include the taxation of statutory maternity and short-term sickness benefits payable by an employer.

Many payments of interest, together with various annual payments, will be received net after deduction of income tax at the basic rate of 25 per cent for 1995–96. No deduction of income tax will be made from dividends paid by United Kingdom resident companies, but each dividend carries a tax credit and the recipient will not be assessed to income tax at the lower or basic rates.

In those cases where the recipient of income is assessable direct the tax will generally fall due for payment on whichever is the later of:

a 1 January in the year of assessment; or
b thirty days after the date on which an assessment is made.

The income tax assessable in this manner will include tax at the lower rate, the basic rate and the higher rate.

Income arising from a trade, profession or vocation is payable by two equal instalments, namely on:

a 1 January in the year of assessment; and
b 1 July following.

Here also the tax will extend to the lower rate, the basic rate and the higher rate.

Any higher rate tax attributable to the following income will be separately charged and become payable on 1 December after the end of the year of assessment to which the charge relates, or on the expiration of thirty days from the date of making the assessment, whichever is the later:

a Dividends from United Kingdom companies.
b Investment income taxed at source at the basic rate of 25 per cent.

Where an assessment is under appeal an application may be made to defer payment of some, or all, of the tax, pending determination of the disputed liability. This application must usually be made within a period of thirty days from the issue of the notice of assessment and it is necessary to specify the grounds for believing there has been an overcharge of tax.

The dates of payment will be different for 1996–97 and future years following the introduction of new arrangements for collecting tax. These dates and other matters affecting self assessment are discussed on page 140 et seq.

REMISSION OF TAX
By concession, the collection of arrears of income tax or capital gains tax may be wholly or partly waived where those arrears have arisen through the failure of the Inland Revenue to make proper and timely use of information supplied by

a the taxpayer about his or her own income, gains or personal circumstances;
b an employer, where the information affects the taxpayer's coding; or
c the Department of Social Security, where the information affects a taxpayer's entitlement to the retirement or widow's pension.

However, the concession will only be given where

a the taxpayer could reasonably have believed that his or her tax affairs were in order; and
b he or she was notified of the arrears after the end of the tax year following that in which the arrears arose. Exceptionally, where the Inland Revenue have made repeated errors within that period, or the arrears have built up over two whole years in succession as a direct result of the Department's failure to make proper and timely use of information, arrears arising at an earlier date may be waived.

The amount of tax waived has been changed from time to time but will be calculated as follows in the case of arrears notified after 16 February 1993:

a Where gross income is not greater than £15,500, no attempt will be made to recover the arrears.
b Where the income exceeds £15,000 but is not greater than £18,000, only one-quarter of the arrears will be recovered.
c If the income exceeds £18,000 but is not more than £22,000, one-half of the arrears will be recovered.

d If the income exceeds £22,000 but is not greater than £26,000, three-quarters of the arrears will fall due for payment.

e If the income exceeds £26,000 but is not greater than £40,000, nine-tenths of the arrears will be collected.

f Where the gross income exceeds £40,000 no remission of tax will be granted.

A measure of relief may be given where income marginally exceeds these limits, or the taxpayer has exceptional family responsibilities.

When applying this concession (based on previous figures) to a husband and wife 'living together' where notification of the arrears took place before 6 April 1990, the joint income of the couple had to be taken. With the introduction of independent taxation consideration is now confined to the taxpayer's own income, without reference to that of his or her spouse.

INTEREST AND PENALTIES
Failure to discharge, or to disclose, tax liabilities promptly may have serious repercussions resulting in an obligation to satisfy interest and penalties. The law on this subject is extremely complex and the comments made below provide little more than broad guidelines. Individuals should never disregard the possibility of additional obligations arising where there is a failure to comply with statutory requirements.

INTEREST ON OVERDUE TAX
When tax falls due for payment, it must be satisfied not later than the due and payable date. Overdue tax incurs a liability to interest, calculated from the 'reckonable date' to the date of payment. The

From	To	Per cent
6 January 1989	5 July 1989	11.5
6 July 1989	5 November 1989	12.25
6 November 1989	5 November 1990	13
6 November 1990	5 March 1991	12.25
6 March 1991	5 May 1991	11.50
6 May 1991	5 July 1991	10.75
6 July 1991	5 October 1991	10
6 October 1991	5 November 1992	9.25
6 November 1992	5 December 1992	7.75
6 December 1992	5 March 1993	7
6 March 1993	5 January 1994	6.25
6 January 1994	5 October 1994	5.5
6 October 1994		6.25

reckonable date is broadly that on which tax falls due, but may be affected by such matters as an appeal against an assessment and the increase of an estimated assessment which is adjusted to the proper amount later.

The rate of interest has changed on numerous occasions in recent years. Rates for the last six years have been calculated at the percentage rates shown by the table at the foot of the left hand column.

Any interest paid cannot be subtracted when calculating the payer's income chargeable to tax.

INTEREST ATTRIBUTABLE TO OFFENCES
If an assessment is raised to make good a 'loss of tax' due to failure on the part of a taxpayer to provide notice, complete a tax return or to supply proper accounts or other information, a liability to satisfy interest may also arise. This situation often develops where a taxpayer has failed to disclose details of taxable income in sufficient time for assessments to be raised before the normal due and payable date. Interest runs from the date on which tax ought to have been satisfied, and not from the date when an assessment is issued, to the date of payment. It is by no means uncommon for interest calculated on this basis to extend over several years, and it may actually exceed the tax payable which must be satisfied in addition.

In recent years the rate of interest has changed on several occasions. Rates for the last six years are shown by the table opposite.

The Revenue have powers to mitigate the interest charged. Interest arising under this alternative heading displaces interest otherwise chargeable where overdue tax is satisfied late. Here also, any interest paid cannot be subtracted when calculating income chargeable to tax.

PENALTIES
The Taxes Acts provide a wide range of penalties for failure to notify the Inland Revenue of tax liabilities and other matters. This broadly involves the commission of fraud, wilful default or neglect.

Among the offences is failure to complete properly a tax return within a reasonable time, or to provide notification of liability where no return form has been received. There may also be a failure to provide many other returns required by the legislation. A much more serious offence giving rise to penalties is the deliberate understatement or omission of profits, gains or income.

The maximum amount of penalties chargeable

may vary considerably between relatively nominal sums and 100 per cent of the under-assessed tax. In very serious situations a criminal prosecution may result.

Where penalties fall due, these must be satisfied in addition to tax and interest, but the Inland Revenue retain wide powers to mitigate amounts otherwise payable. Like interest, penalties incurred cannot be deducted when calculating the payer's income chargeable to income tax.

How to appeal

APPEALS AGAINST income tax assessments must be made in writing to HM Inspector of Taxes within thirty days of the date appearing on the notice of assessment. The required notice of appeal must state the grounds on which the appeal is made, for example, 'on the grounds that the assessment is excessive'.

Most appeals can be settled by agreement with the local Inspector, but it is as well to be represented professionally if the appeal is to be heard personally by the General (Local) or Special Commissioners.

If no appeal is made against an assessment, or if an assessment is confirmed on appeal, it cannot afterwards be reopened unless, exceptionally, it was made on the basis of an error or mistake in the taxpayer's return.

No award of costs is made at the conclusion of appeal hearings before the General Commissioners, nor are details of the hearings made available for examination by the public. However, the Special Commissioners do retain powers to award costs where either party has acted 'unreasonably' in pursuing the appeal. In addition, the Special Commissioners retain powers to publish details of important decisions.

17

Capital gains tax

WHERE A SURPLUS arises from the disposal of land, securities or other assets it is necessary to establish whether that surplus forms part of the profits from a business. A finding that the surplus is derived from a business of dealing will require that the profit must be assessed to income tax in a manner identical to that applicable for other business profits as illustrated on page 60. In those cases where surplus proceeds do not represent business profits and are not otherwise chargeable to income tax, those proceeds may be chargeable to capital gains tax.

The application of capital gains tax has been changed on many occasions, with the most significant recent change affecting transactions taking place after 5 April 1988. Not only was the method used to calculate gains and losses altered but the calculation of tax payable was radically reformed. There have been further subsequent changes of considerable importance, which illustrates the speed with which many areas of the tax code alter in the United Kingdom.

The following comments are of application to more recents events and have little application to those occurring on earlier occasions.

DISPOSAL OF ASSETS
Liability to capital gains tax may be incurred where chargeable gains arise on the disposal of assets. The expression 'disposal' usually involves a change of ownership but certain 'deemed' disposals are treated as having taken place and these also may produce liability to capital gains tax. 'Assets' include nearly all forms of 'property'; an expression which extends to stocks, shares, unit trust holdings, land, buildings, jewellery and antiques, among others.

EXEMPTIONS AND RELIEFS
The potential scope of liability to capital gains tax is extremely wide but numerous exemptions are available. For example, gains arising on the disposal of private motor vehicles, National Savings Certificates and Premium Savings Bonds, together with sums received on the maturity or surrender of normal policies of life assurance and sums received from the sale of most chattels which have a predictable life of less than fifty years, are exempt. Gains arising on the disposal of goods and chattels not otherwise exempted, usually those with a life expectation of more than fifty years, will be exempt if the disposal proceeds, but not the gains, do not exceed £6,000. Should the proceeds exceed £6,000 by a small amount, the gains otherwise arising on disposal may be reduced. The disposal of gilt edged securities, marketable securities issued by public corporations and guaranteed by the government, together with most fixed interest stocks, are also exempt.

No liability to capital gains tax arises on assets retained at the time of an individual's death. However, personal representatives, legatees and others taking assets on death are deemed to acquire those assets for a consideration representing market value at the time of death. This use of market value will establish the notional cost of acquisition should the personal representatives, or other persons, subsequently undertake the disposal of assets in circumstances requiring the calculation of chargeable gains.

The disposal of assets to a recognised charity, or to certain national institutions, will incur no liability to capital gains tax. Further, a claim may be made to exclude from liability gains arising on the disposal of works of art, historic houses, and other assets of national interest, if a number of conditions are satisfied.

These exemptions are given in addition to the annual exemption of £6,000 which applies for 1995–96.

TRANSFERS BETWEEN HUSBAND AND WIFE

Transfers of assets between a husband and wife 'living together' will incur no liability to tax. This is achieved by applying the assumption that assets are transferred for a consideration which produces neither gain nor loss to the transferor. It is immaterial whether the transfer has taken place before or after the introduction of independent taxation.

In those cases where the parties are not 'living together', for example by reason of separation, liability to tax will arise in the normal manner.

PRIVATE RESIDENCES

An exemption which is of considerable interest to many individuals arises on the disposal of a private residence. Where the property has been used as an individual's only or main residence throughout the period of ownership, or from 31 March 1982 if later, no chargeable gain will arise on disposal by that individual. In other situations, involving such use throughout part only of the ownership period, some portion of the gain may be chargeable. However, where a property has been occupied for a qualifying purpose at some time in the ownership period, it will be treated as so occupied in the closing years whether occupied or not. This previously extended to the final twenty-four months of ownership but in recognition of the difficulty experienced by many when attempting to find a buyer of property, was increased to thirty-six months for disposals taking place after 18 March 1991.

An individual can have only one qualifying residence at any time. If two or more main residences are held simultaneously, perhaps a town house and a seaside cottage, the individual may select which property should qualify for exemption. In the case of husband and wife 'living together', the couple cannot each have a qualifying residence sim-ultaneously. Any selection must be made by written notice within a period of two years from the date an additional property is acquired.

In addition, where an individual derives gains from the disposal of a private residence previously occupied by a dependent relative, rent-free and without other consideration, exemption from capital gains tax may be forthcoming. This exemption cannot be obtained where the dependent relative first commenced to occupy the property after 5 April 1988.

Employees occupying job-related accommodation and self-employed individuals required to occupy accommodation in connection with their business may also establish a qualifying residence which is either used or intended to be used on some future occasion.

RETIREMENT RELIEF

Where an individual undertakes the disposal of business assets the gain arising may be reduced or eliminated by retirement relief. This relief is available for gains realised on the disposal of:

a the whole or part of a business carried on by a sole trader or by individuals in partnership;
b assets used for the purposes of a business in **a** which has ceased; and
c shares or securities issued by a company where the following requirements are satisfied:
  i the company was a trading company;
  ii the individual retained a sufficient percentage holding of voting rights; and
  iii the individual was a full-time working director, officer or employee of that company or an associated company.

For disposals undertaken before 16 March 1993, the requirement under **ii** was only satisfied if the individual personally retained at least 25 per cent of the voting rights, or held at least 5 per cent of those rights personally with that individual and members of his or her family having more than 50 per cent. For subsequent disposals it is only necessary for the individual to personally retain at least 5 per cent of the voting rights. A further relaxation taking effect from the same day was the widening of **iii** to include officers and employees in addition to directors.

For disposals made after 18 March 1991, and before 30 November 1993, the maximum amount of retirement relief comprised:

a 100 per cent of gains up to £150,000, plus
b 50 per cent of the gains between £150,000 and £600,000.

These figures were increased to the following levels for disposals made on and after 30 November 1993:

a 100 per cent of gains up to £250,000, plus
b 50 per cent of the gains between £250,000 and £1,000,000

This latter formula could produce maximum retirement relief of £625,000 calculated as follows:

	£
On first £250,000 at 100 per cent	250,000
On balance of £750,000 at 50 per cent	375,000
	£625,000

In most situations the total gains arising on disposal will fall substantially below £1,000,000. However, the above approach may be used to establish the amount of available retirement relief.

Maximum relief will only be forthcoming where the business has been carried on, or the shares retained, throughout a minimum ten-year period. If those conditions are satisfied for less than ten years, but more than twelve months, the amount of retirement relief will be reduced. Relief is then governed by the 'appropriate percentage', which represents that part of the ten-year period throughout which the conditions are satisfied and comprises the aggregate of:

i the appropriate percentage of £250,000 plus
ii one-half of the gains exceeding the product of **i** but which do not exceed the appropriate percentage of £1,000,000.

Retirement relief cannot exceed the gains less losses arising on disposal, as it merely serves to reduce or eliminate the net gains. However, apart from premature retirement on the grounds of ill-health, physical retirement is usually unnecessary and 'retirement relief' may be available for two or more separate disposals until maximum relief has been obtained. In most cases involving disposals after 18 March 1991, it is only necessary to show that the individual was at least 55 years of age on the disposal date. Retirement relief may also be available for disposals made by an individual before reaching this age if the individual was compelled to retire from business early on the grounds of ill-health.

ROLL-OVER RELIEF – BUSINESS ASSETS

Gains arising from the disposal of many assets used for the purpose of a business may be 'rolled over' and offset against the cost of acquiring a replacement asset. This avoids any liability on the gain, but as

83
RETIREMENT RELIEF

On 17 September 1995, John realised gains of £530,000 from the disposal of business assets. At the time of disposal John was 58 years of age and had carried on business for more than 10 years.

As the maximum 10 year period is satisfied the appropriate percentage becomes 10/10ths. The chargeable gain assessable to capital gains tax will be calculated as follows:

	£
Aggregate gains	£530,000

Maximum relief 10/10ths × £1,000,000 = £1,000,000

	£
Available relief:	
On first £250,000 at 100 per cent . .	250,000
On balance of £280,000 at 50 per cent	140,000
Total relief	£390,000

	£
Aggregate gains	530,000
Less retirement relief – maximum . .	390,000
Assessable chargeable gains, 1995–96	£140,000

A finding that John had only carried on the business for exactly 4 years would limit retirement relief to the following:

Appropriate percentage = 4/10ths

	£
Maximum relief 4/10ths × £1,000,000 = £400,000	
Available relief:	
On 4/10ths of £250,000 = £100,000 at	
100 per cent	100,000
On £400,000 less £100,000 = £300,000	
at 50 per cent	150,000
Total relief	250,000

	£
Aggregate gains	530,000
Less retirement relief	250,000
Assessable chargeable gains, 1995–96	£280,000

the cost of the replacement asset is reduced a correspondingly increased gain may arise from the eventual disposal of that asset. A written claim must be made if roll-over relief is to be forthcoming.

It remains a requirement that both the old and the replacement assets fall within a restricted list. This list includes land and buildings occupied and used for the purposes of the business, goodwill, fixed (but not moveable) plant and machinery, aircraft, hovercraft and ships. It also includes milk quotas, potato quotas and other agricultural quotas, together with qualifying property used to provide furnished holiday accommodation and commercial woodlands.

——— 84 ———
ROLL-OVER RELIEF
BUSINESS ASSETS

On 30 August 1995, Bob sold freehold premises used for the purposes of his business. The chargeable gain arising on disposal was calculated as follows:

	£
Disposal proceeds	150,000
Less cost	60,000
	90,000
Less indexation allowance – say . .	38,000
Chargeable gain	£52,000

Bob purchased replacement premises at a cost of £200,000 on 17 July 1995, and submitted a claim for roll-over relief. The claim was duly accepted with the following results:

	£
Gain arising on disposal . . .	52,000
Less roll-over relief . . .	52,000
Chargeable gain 1995–96 . . .	NIL

	£
Cost of replacement premises . .	200,000
Less roll-over relief . . .	52,000
Deemed cost of acquisition . . .	£148,000

If a disposal is to be matched with an acquisition, the replacement asset must usually be acquired within a period commencing twelve months before and ending thirty-six months following the disposal of the old asset.

Only limited roll-over relief will be available where the consideration used to acquire the replacement asset falls below the amount of consideration received from the disposal of the old asset.

A similar form of roll-over relief may be available where an interest in land is disposed of to an authority possessing compulsory purchase powers. In circumstances such as these it is frequently possible to roll-over the chargeable gain arising against the cost of acquiring some other interest in land. The only limitation is that the interest acquired must not be the acquirer's qualifying only or main residence.

ROLL-OVER RELIEF – SHARES
Gains arising on the disposal of shares issued by unquoted trading companies could be rolled over against the cost of acquiring shares in similar companies where the disposal occurred after 15 March 1993. Stringent conditions were imposed and it was necessary for the individual involved to have retained a minimum 5 per cent shareholding interest in the 'old' company and to have worked full-time for that company.

The application and availability of general roll-over relief for a reinvestment in shares was substantially extended for disposals taking place on and after 30 November 1993. In addition, a further form of roll-over relief was introduced for disposals taking place on or after 29 November 1994 where the proceeds were invested in shares qualifying for enterprise investment scheme relief. Finally, yet a further form of roll-over relief is available where a disposal is made after 5 April 1995 and the proceeds are used to subscribe for qualifying shares issued by a venture capital trust.

Although different rules apply to each form of investment, the availability of roll-over relief retains a common factor. In all situations it is now possible for an individual realising a chargeable gain from the disposal of any type of asset to contemplate the availability of roll-over relief where disposal proceeds are applied to acquire shares. It follows that the gains arising may be attributable to the disposal of any asset, including land and buildings, shares and jewellery, among others.

The general requirements and effect of each of the three different forms of roll-over relief are briefly outlined below.

General roll-over relief
General roll-over relief is available where the disposal of an asset takes place on or after 30 November 1993 and the proceeds are applied to acquire shares in an unquoted trading company or the holding company of a trading group. It is a requirement that the reinvestment must take place within a period commencing twelve months before and ending thirty-six months following the disposal date.

Not all acquisitions of shares in trading companies are available for roll-over relief. Previously farming companies and property dealing companies were excluded. In addition, companies retaining substantial interests in land were also excluded from the list of qualifying companies. However, none of these exclusions now applies where the disposal of assets occurred on or after 29 November 1994.

Where a reinvestment in shares takes place and a claim for roll-over relief is submitted, the amount of that relief will represent the smaller of

a the gain arising on disposal;

b the actual consideration given to acquire new

85
ROLL-OVER RELIEF
SHARES GENERALLY

On 22 March 1995, Betty realised a gain of £75,000 from the sale of a painting. She invested £51,000 when acquiring shares in A Ltd, a qualifying company, on 9 June 1995, and made a claim for roll-over relief. No entitlement to enterprise investment scheme relief arose.

Roll-over relief will be available on the smaller of

a the gain of £75,000
b the consideration given to acquire shares, namely £51,000
c any amount which may be specified, falling between £1 and £50,999

Assuming Betty claims maximum relief under **b**, the effect on capital gains tax liability will be as follows:

	£
Gain on disposal of painting . . .	75,000
Less Roll-over relief . . .	51,000
Chargeable gain 1994–95 . . .	£24,000

	£
Cost of acquiring shares . . .	51,000
Less roll-over relief . . .	51,000
Deemed cost of acquisition . . .	NIL

shares, or market value where those shares are acquired otherwise than by way of a transaction at arm's length; and
c the amount which the claimant may specify.

Heading **c** is a most important factor as this may enable the claimant to restrict the amount of roll-over relief for the purpose of absorbing the annual exemption, or perhaps losses, on the balance remaining.

The amount for which a roll-over relief claim is submitted will be deducted from the gain arising on disposal of the 'old asset' and subtracted from the cost of acquiring qualifying shares.

Any gain which has been rolled over will become chargeable to capital gains tax if the claimant emigrates from the United Kingdom within a period of three years following the acquisition of shares. Liability will also arise should the share issuing company cease to qualify within the three-year period, perhaps because the company's activities change.

Roll-over relief is primarily available to individuals. However, it may also be obtained by many trustees administering settled property for the benefit of individuals.

86
ROLL-OVER RELIEF
ENTERPRISE INVESTMENT SCHEME

Barry realised a gain of £80,000 on 17 May 1995 from the disposal of some land. Four months later, on 16 September, he subscribed £60,000 when acquiring shares in X Ltd. The subscription qualified for enterprise investment scheme relief. This relief reduced Barry's income tax liability by

£60,000 at 20 per cent	£12,000

In addition, Barry claimed roll-over relief on the maximum sum available, namely, the subscription cost of £60,000.

On 31 October 2000 Barry sold his holding. The substantial gain arising on disposal was not chargeable to capital gains tax as all requirements had been satisfied throughout a five-year period.

The effect of the claim for roll-over relief will be as follows:

	£
Gain on disposal of land	80,000
Less Roll-over relief	60,000
Chargeable gain 1995–96 . . .	£20,000

Postponed gain becoming chargeable in 2000–2001 on the disposal of shares (£80,000 less £20,000) . . .	£60,000

A similar set of calculations would apply if Barry had subscribed £60,000 for shares in a capital venture trust.

Enterprise investment scheme shares

Investments up to a maximum of £100,000 during any year of assessment in shares issued by a company to which the enterprise investment scheme applies qualify for income tax relief at the reduced rate of 20 per cent (see page 34). In addition, where a chargeable gain arises from a disposal taking place on or after 29 November 1994 a claim for roll-over relief may be made to match that gain with the cost of acquiring qualifying shares. The sum matched in this manner will comprise the smaller of

a the gain arising on disposal;
b the cost of acquiring shares qualifying for enterprise investment scheme relief; and
c the amount which the claimant may specify.

Unlike many other forms of roll-over relief, the amount established by this calculation is not subtracted from the cost of acquiring enterprise investment scheme shares. The amount involved, representing all or part of the chargeable gain arising from the disposal of an asset, will be deferred until the eventual disposal, or some other event, of enterprise investment scheme shares takes place. Therefore this form of roll-over relief is in the nature of a deferment of liability and not a liability which is rolled over into the cost of acquiring shares. Although this may seem harsh it will not be overlooked that gains arising on the eventual disposal of enterprise investment scheme shares may well be exempt from capital gains tax liability. It is therefore necessary to ensure that this exemption does not include the amount of rolled-over gains.

It is a requirement that enterprise investment scheme shares must be acquired within a period commencing twelve months before and ending thirty-six months following the disposal of other assets.

Venture capital trust shares

Yet a further form of roll-over relief is available where the disposal of an asset takes place after 5 April 1995 and the chargeable gain arising is matched with an investment in shares issued by a venture capital trust. The nature of these trusts is outlined on page 36 but an individual may invest up to a maximum of £100,000 in a year of assessment. It then becomes possible to match the disposal of an asset with the cost of acquiring shares qualifying for venture capital trust relief. Should a claim for roll-over relief be submitted, this will be based on the smaller of

a the amount of the gain arising on disposal;

b the consideration applied to acquire qualifying shares in a venture captial trust; and

c the amount which the claimant may specify.

Here also, the amount on which roll-over relief is claimed will not be subtracted from the cost of acquiring shares in a venture capital trust. The amount involved, representing all or part of the chargeable gain arising on disposal, will be deferred until a disposal of qualifying venture capital trust shares takes place or some other event occurs. Only at that time will the amount of the rolled-over gain become chargeable to capital gains tax.

It is a necessary requirement that the subscription for shares in a venture capital trust takes place within a period commencing twelve months before and ending twelve months following the disposal of the other asset.

GIFTS AND HOLD-OVER RELIEF

Where assets are transferred by way of gift, or for an inadequate consideration, the disposal proceeds actually passing, if any, and the corresponding cost

87
GIFTS AND HOLD-OVER RELIEF

On 14 October 1995, a father gifted shares in a family trading company to his son. The shares, which retained a market value of £50,000 at the time of the transfer, had been acquired by the father for £6,000 in 1984 and the transaction satisfied the requirements for hold-over relief.

If no claim is made the chargeable gain accruing to the father will be:

	£
Disposal proceeds (market value) . .	50,000
Less cost	6,000
	44,000
Less indexation allowance – say . .	3,900
Chargeable gain 1995–96 . . .	£40,100

However, should a claim for hold-over relief be made there will be no chargeable gain accruing to the father. The son's cost of acquisition must then be adjusted as follows:

	£
Cost of acquisition (market value) . .	50,000
Less father's chargeable gain . .	40,100
Deemed cost of acquisition . .	£9,900

of acquisition to the transferee, will be deleted and replaced by market value. A similar adjustment must be made for all transactions between 'connected persons' an expression which applies to near relatives and many other closely associated individuals and companies.

The insertion of market value may well produce chargeable gains accruing to the transferor which are not actually realised gains. However, where the transferor is an individual and the transferee resides in the United Kingdom a claim for hold-over relief may be available. The effect of this claim is that the chargeable gain will be reduced to nil and the amount of the reduction subtracted from the cost of acquisition (namely market value) to the transferee. As the transferee's cost is reduced, he or she may well incur an increased chargeable gain from the eventual disposal of the asset. A similar claim is available for assets transferred by trustees residing in the United Kingdom.

Only limited hold-over relief may be available if the transferee provides some consideration for the asset. Any hold-over relief previously granted may be withdrawn should the transferee emigrate from the United Kingdom within the succeeding six-year period before undertaking a disposal of the asset transferred.

Only a limited range of assets qualify for hold-over relief. These comprise:

a Assets used for the purposes of a business carried on by the transferor, or by a company in which the transferor retains a significant interest.

b Agricultural property.

c Shares or securities in unquoted trading companies.

d Shares or securities in quoted trading companies and companies dealt in on the Unlisted Securities Market, where the transferor retains a significant interest.

No restriction is placed on the nature of an asset where the transfer is a lifetime transfer, other than a potentially exempt transfer, which is recognised for inheritance tax purposes.

INDEXATION ALLOWANCE

Many capital gains are created or swollen by inflation. This phenomenon will often increase the apparent value of assets and produce substantial paper gains on disposal without creating gains in real terms. For disposals made before 6 April 1982, there was no relief for the inroads caused by inflation but for disposals taking place on or after this date the gain arising may be reduced by an indexation allowance. The availability, calculation and application of the indexation allowance has changed from time to time and the following comments are confined to disposals taking place after 5 April 1988.

The indexation allowance is calculated using monthly figures taken from the retail prices index. There are two components, namely:

RI – which represents the figure extracted from the index for the month of March 1982, or the month in which expenditure is incurred, whichever is the later; and

RD – which is the index figure for the month in which the disposal takes place.

The allowance will then comprise:

$$\frac{RD - RI}{RI} \times \text{Expenditure}$$

Where two or more items of expenditure have been incurred in relation to an asset in different months, separate calculations must be prepared for each item. Retail prices index figures used to establish factors RI and RD are shown by the Tables on the following page.

88
INDEXATION ALLOWANCE

Cyril purchased shares at a cost of £10,000 on 12 June 1982. He realised £42,000 from selling the shares on 24 October 1994. Figures extracted from the retail prices index were as follows:

June 1982 (RI)	322.9
January 1987	394.5
October 1994 (RD)	145.2

The indexation allowance becomes:

$\dfrac{145.2 \times 394.5}{322.9} =$		177.4
Less		100.0
		77.4

£10,000 × 77.4 per cent . . .		£7,740

The chargeable gain for 1994–95 will be:

		£
Disposal proceeds		42,000
Less Cost		10,000
		32,000
Less indexation allowance . .		7,740
Chargeable gain 1994–95 . . .		£24,260

89
INDEXATION ALLOWANCE – LOSSES

Jane purchased property at a cost of £80,000 on 14 September 1987. The property realised £95,000 when sold on 27 August 1995. Retail prices index figures were:

September 1987	102.4
August 1995 (say)	148.7

The indexation allowance will be:

$\dfrac{148.7 - 102.4}{102.4} =$		45.2
£80,000 × 45.2 per cent . . .		£36,160

The calculation continues:

		£
Disposal proceeds		95,000
Less cost		80,000
		15,000
Less Indexation allowance (restricted)		15,000
Gain or loss 1995–96 . . .		NIL

Although an indexation of £36,160 is available, this cannot be used to create a loss and can only apply to reduce the gain to nil. As the disposal occurred after 5 April 1995, no relief can be obtained under the transitional provisions shown by example 90 on page 123.

RETAIL PRICES INDEX 1982–1987

Month	1982	1983	1984	1985	1986	1987
Jan		325.9	342.6	359.8	379.7	394.5
Feb		327.3	344.0	362.7	381.1	100.4
Mar	313.4	327.9	345.1	366.1	381.6	100.6
Apr	319.7	332.5	349.7	373.9	385.3	101.8
May	322.0	333.9	351.0	375.6	386.0	101.9
Jun	322.9	334.7	351.9	376.4	385.8	101.9
Jul	323.0	336.5	351.5	375.7	384.7	101.8
Aug	323.1	338.0	354.8	376.7	385.9	102.1
Sep	322.9	339.5	355.5	376.5	387.8	102.4
Oct	324.5	340.7	357.7	377.1	388.4	102.9
Nov	326.1	341.9	358.8	378.4	391.7	103.4
Dec	325.5	342.8	358.8	378.9	393.0	103.3

RETAIL PRICES INDEX 1988–1994

Month	1988	1989	1990	1991	1992	1993	1994
Jan	103.3	111.0	119.5	130.2	135.6	137.9	141.3
Feb	103.7	111.8	120.2	130.9	136.3	138.8	142.1
Mar	104.1	112.3	121.4	131.4	136.7	139.3	142.5
Apr	105.8	114.3	125.1	133.1	138.8	140.6	144.2
May	106.2	115.0	126.2	133.5	139.3	141.1	144.7
Jun	106.6	115.4	126.7	134.1	139.3	141.0	144.7
Jul	106.7	115.5	126.8	133.8	138.8	140.7	144.0
Aug	107.9	115.8	128.1	134.1	138.9	141.3	144.7
Sep	108.4	116.6	129.3	134.6	139.4	141.9	145.0
Oct	109.5	117.5	130.3	135.1	139.9	141.8	145.2
Nov	110.0	118.5	130.0	135.6	139.7	141.6	145.3
Dec	110.3	118.8	129.9	135.7	139.2	141.9	146.0

The compilation of the retail price index was amended by introducing a revised unit of 100 for January 1987. Changes in subsequent months are measured against the new unit of 100. To calculate the indexation allowance for acquisitions taking place before the month of February 1987 and corresponding disposals made in or after that month the procedure is as follows:

a Take factor RD for the month of disposal
b Mutltiply factor RD by the January 1987 indexed figure of 394.5
c Divide the product of b by factor RI, the figure taken from the index for the month of acquisition
d Subtract 100 from the result to produce the required percentage change.

Example 88 on the previous page shows how the calculation is made.

The use and application of the indexation allowance changed significantly for disposals taking place on and after 30 November 1993. In the case of disposals made before that date the full indexation allowance entered into the calculation of gain or loss. The effect was to reduce a gain, to convert a gain into a loss or to increase the amount of a loss. This frequently gave rise to considerable capital losses where the value of an asset had fallen due to the recession, or modest increases in value had not kept pace with changes in the retail prices index.

However, for disposals taking place after 29 November 1993, the application of the indexation allowance is restricted. The allowance can no longer be used to create a loss or to increase the amount of a capital loss. It follows that

a an indexation allowance remains available to reduce a gain to some smaller amount;
b the indexation allowance may be used to eliminate a gain but not to convert that gain into a loss; and

c where a loss arises without incorporating the indexation allowance, no such allowance can be used to increase the loss.

For most disposals taking place after 5 April 1988, and involving assets acquired before 31 March 1982, the computation of the indexation allowance will proceed by applying the assumption that assets were actually acquired for a consideration reflecting market value on the latter date. In the case of assets acquired, or expenditure incurred, subsequently the actual amounts involved will be used as representing cost.

Before an indexation allowance can be calculated the disposal must be matched with the corresponding acquisition of an asset. This should not give rise to difficulty where there is a single acquisition followed by a single disposal. However, problems do arise when dealing with a holding of shares or securities. The holding may have been created by acquisitions made on two or more occasions, only part of the aggregate holding may be realised and many quoted holdings will be affected by bonus issues, rights issues, exchanges and reorganisations. Complex rules must then be followed to identify a disposal with the matching acquisition before the calculation of gain or loss can proceed and the indexation allowance be established.

INDEXATION LOSSES

In recognition that the unexpected withdrawal or restriction of an indexation allowance on 29 November 1994 would reduce relief for losses, a limited

---
90
INDEXATION LOSSES

Molly had no capital gains transactions taking place in 1993–94. However, in 1994–95 she made two disposals producing aggregate gains of £21,000 after subtracting the indexation allowances attributable to those disposals.

In addition, during the same year Molly made a third disposal which produced a gain of £1,500 before subtracting an indexation allowance of £18,000. The gain of £1,500 must be reduced to nil by using part of the available indexation allowance. This leaves £16,500 of the allowance unrelieved. Relief for indexation losses must be limited to a maximum of £10,000 and the gains assessable for 1994–95 become:

Aggregate gains	21,000
Less indexation losses	10,000
Taxable gains	£11,000

91
INDEXATION ALLOWANCE – ASSETS ACQUIRED BEFORE APRIL 1982

Using the facts in Example 88 let it be assumed that the shares were acquired in 1973. On 31 March 1982, the holding retained a market value of £20,000.

As the shares were acquired before 31 March 1982, they will be treated as having been acquired on that date for a consideration representing market value, both for the purpose of calculating the gain and also when determining the indexation allowance. Factor RI will represent the index figure of 313.4 for March 1982.

The indexation allowance becomes:

$\dfrac{145.2 \times 394.5}{313.4} =$	182.8
Less	100
	82.8
£20,000 × 82.8 per cent	£16,560

	£
Disposal proceeds	42,000
Less cost (*i.e. market value at 31.3.82*)	20,000
	22,000
Less indexation allowance . . .	16,560
Chargeable gain 1994–95 . . .	£5,440

---

form of special relief was made available to individuals and trustees for disposals taking place between 29 November 1993 and 5 April 1995. For disposals within this period but before 6 April 1994 it was necessary to calculate the amount of any indexation allowance which would have been available but for the existence of, or creation of, losses. This amount, referred to as an indexation loss, was then subtracted from gains assessable to capital gains tax for 1993–94 to the extent those gains exceeded the exemption limit of £5,800. A similar calculation was made of indexation losses arising from disposals in the following year ended 5 April 1995. The indexation losses, including any similar losses not utilised in the previous year, were then available to be offset against gains arising in 1994–95, to the extent that those gains exceeded the exemption limit of £5,800. The maximum amount of indexation losses capable of being utilised in this manner was limited to £10,000. It followed that if the full £10,000 was utilised in 1993–94 no balance would be available for 1994–95. If indexation losses were not utilised by 5 April 1995 they cannot be carried forward to any future year.

92
CALCULATION OF GAIN

Norman purchased an asset at a cost of £8,000 on 27 March 1972. The asset realised £100,000 when sold on 9 October 1995. Market value at 31 March 1982 was agreed to be £52,000.

The chargeable gain arising on disposal becomes:

	£
Disposal proceeds	100,000
Less deemed cost – market value at 31 March 1982	52,000
	48,000
Less indexation allowance – say . .	42,800
Chargeable gain 1995–96 . . .	£5,200

CALCULATION OF GAINS AND LOSSES

Before the application of the indexation allowance to a gain or loss can receive consideration, the amount of that gain or loss must be determined. In some cases the calculation used for disposals taking place before 6 April 1988 will differ from that used for disposals undertaken on or after that date. The following comments apply only to disposals occurring after 5 April 1988.

The gain or loss will broadly reflect the difference between acquisition cost and the disposal proceeds, with an adjustment for incidental costs of both acquisition and disposal and costs incurred when carrying out improvements to the asset. There is, however a significant alteration in the computation procedure for assets acquired before 31 March 1982. These assets are deemed to have been acquired for a 'cost' representing market value on that date. The position will only be otherwise where this approach produces an excessive gain or loss exceeding the actual gain or loss incurred, converts a gain into a loss or a loss into a gain. It is, however, possible to file an election to adopt market value at 31 March 1982 for all assets (but not some only) held on that date. Where such an election is made any distortions in the gain or loss are ignored. The election must be submitted within a period of two years following the end of the first year of assessment, commencing on 6 April 1988, in which the first disposal of an asset held on 31 March 1982 is made.

CAPITAL LOSSES

Not all disposals will produce gains and inevitably some will give rise to capital losses. Any capital losses arising in a year of assessment must be set against chargeable gains, if any, realised in the same

93
USING CAPITAL LOSSES

At the end of 1994–95 Alan had unused capital losses of £11,800 carried forward to 1995–96.

He realised chargeable gains of £16,000 and capital losses of £7,300 from disposals taking place in 1995–96.

The losses must be dealt with as follows for 1995–96:

	£
Chargeable gains	16,000
Less Capital losses	7,300
	8,700
Less Losses brought forward (part)	2,700
	6,000
Less Exempt amount	6,000
Tax chargeable on	NIL

The capital losses of £7,300 arising in 1995–96 must be set against chargeable gains for that year. It then remains to reduce the net gains remaining by £2,700 to the exemption threshold of £6,000.

The balance of capital losses brought forward from 1994–95, namely £9,100 (£11,800 less £2,700), will be carried forward to 1996–97.

year. If a surplus of losses remain these may be carried forward to future years.

Capital losses brought forward from a previous year of assessment may be subtracted from the net gains arising in the subsequent year. However, the application of earlier losses in this manner is not to reduce the net gains for the subsequent year below the exempt amount for that year. Any surplus losses brought forward from earlier years which cannot be relieved against net gains in a subsequent year may be carried forward and utilised in future years.

The capital losses relieved in this manner must be distinguished from the special indexation losses available for relief in 1993–94 and 1994–95.

BUSINESS LOSSES

Before 6 April 1991, it was not possible to set unused losses from a trade, profession or vocation against chargeable gains for the purpose of calculating capital gains tax payable. However, this restriction is relaxed for business losses arising subsequently.

Where business losses arise in a year of assessment a claim can be made to set those losses against income chargeable to income tax in the same year. If surplus losses remain they can be included in a similar claim for the following year, or perhaps the previous year, only (see page 65). Certain losses

——94——
USING BUSINESSES LOSSES

Susan had unused capital losses of £15,000 being carried forward at the end of 1994–95. In 1995–96 she realised chargeable gains of £21,000 and capital losses of £4,500. During the same year Susan suffered a loss of £18,400 when carrying on a trade. A claim was made to offset part of this loss against income but £7,260 remained unrelieved. Susan then made a separate claim to set this unrelieved balance against her net capital gains for 1995–96.

The result of this claim for capital gains tax purposes is as follows:

	£
Chargeable gains	21,000
Less Capital losses	4,500
Net gains	16,500
Less Business losses	7,260
	9,240
Less Capital losses brought forward (part)	3,240
	6,000
Less Exempt amount	6,000
Tax chargeable on	NIL

The business loss of £18,400 has been fully relieved, partly against income and partly against chargeable gains. The balance of capital losses carried forward to 1996–97 will be £11,760 (£15,000 less £3,240).

from hobby farming and non-commercial activities cannot be relieved in this manner.

If business losses arising in a year of assessment and qualifying for income tax relief cannot be absorbed against income for the same year, those losses may be set against net gains (chargeable gains less capital losses) for that year. Should surplus business losses remain, these can be set against income for the following year or previous year only, but here also if, or to the extent that, income is not sufficiently substantial the balance can be set against net capital gains in the other year. Any remaining losses can only be carried forward and set against future profits from the same business.

Where a claim is made to set business losses against net capital gains those losses must be used in priority to any capital losses brought forward from an earlier year.

If relief cannot be given, or fully given, for the post cessation expenses mentioned on page 69 against income for the year of assessment in which payment takes place, a claim can be made to treat the unrelieved expenditure as an allowable loss in the same year. This will enable that part of the outlay which is not relieved for income tax purposes to be set against chargeable gains.

ANNUAL EXEMPTION
The initial slice of gains (chargeable gains less capital losses) arising in a year of assessment is exempt from capital gains tax. For 1995–96 the exempt amount is £6,000. The corresponding figure for the six earlier years is shown by the following table:

	£		£
1989–90	5,000	1992–93	5,800
1990–91	5,000	1993–94	5,800
1991–92	5,500	1994–95	5,800

If the exempt amount is not utilised, or fully utilised, any balance remaining cannot be carried forward to succeeding years. It is therefore advisable to use fully the exempt amount wherever possible.

In earlier years only one combined exempt amount was available to shelter chargeable gains accruing to a husband and wife 'living together'. However, from the introduction of independent taxation each spouse has his or her own exempt amount without reference to the gains, if any, realised by the other.

CALCULATION OF TAX PAYABLE
Where net gains remaining exceed the exempt amount for a year of assessment the excess is chargeable to capital gains tax. The first step when calculating liability is to establish:

a the amount of net gains arising in the year of assessment which exceed the exempt amount; and
b the taxable income of the individual chargeable to income tax for that year. This will determine the amount of income charged at the lower rate, the basic rate or the higher rate.

Liability to capital gains tax is then calculated by reference to the individual's marginal rate of income tax. This requires that the amount of the excess net gains must be added to income chargeable to income tax, with income tax rates being used to establish liability on the excess. The tax remains a capital

95
CALCULATION OF TAX PAYABLE

Martin derived the following chargeable gains and capital losses from the disposal of assets made in 1995–96:

Chargeable gains	.	.	.	.	£14,800
Capital losses	.	.	.	.	£2,900

The amount chargeable to capital gains tax becomes:

					£
Chargeable gains	.	.	.	.	14,800
Less Capital losses	.	.	.	.	2,900
					11,900
Less exempt amount	.	.	.	.	6,000
Tax chargeable on	.	.	.	.	£5,900

To establish the amount of capital gains tax payable for 1995–96, Martin's marginal rate of income tax must be determined. It was found that he incurred liability at the basic rate on £12,000. As a further £9,100 would produce liability at the basic rate only, capital gains tax will be due as follows:

On £5,900 at 25 per cent	.	.	£1,475.00

If the income of Martin for 1995–96 produced, say, £19,900 liable at the basic rate, capital gains tax due would be:

		£
On first £1,200 (£21,100 less £19,900) at 25 per cent	.	300.00
On balance of £4,700 at 40 per cent .	.	1,880.00
Capital gains tax payable 1995–96 .	.	£2,180.00

If the income of Martin for 1995–96 was already sufficient to produce income tax liability at the higher rate of 40 per cent, the capital gains tax payable becomes:

£5,900 at 40 per cent	.	.	£2,360.00

Finally, a finding that the income of Martin was only sufficient to produce income tax liability at the lower rate of 20 per cent on income of £950 would support the following liability:

		£
On first £2,250 (£3,200 less £950) at 20 per cent	.	450.00
On balance of £3,650 at 25 per cent .	.	912.50
Capital gains tax payable 1995–96 .	.	£1,362.50

96
TAX PAYABLE – HUSBAND AND WIFE

John and Carol are a husband and wife 'living together'. After agreeing capital gains tax computations for 1994–95, it was found that the following capital losses were being carried forward:

John	£2,000
Carol	£18,000

In 1995–96 John realised chargeable gains of £16,500 from the disposal of assets. Carol made no disposals at all. The losses of Carol cannot be set against the gains of her husband. The husband must suffer liability on the following:

				£
Chargeable gains	.	.	.	16,500
Less losses brought forward	.	.	.	2,000
				14,500
Less exempt amount	.	.	.	6,000
Tax chargeable on	.	.	.	£8,500

Assuming John incurs income tax liability at the higher rate of 40 per cent for 1995–96, the tax payable becomes:

On £8,500 at 40 per cent	.	.	£3,400.00

or partly assessed at 25 per cent with the balance taxable at 40 per cent. Where the 20 per cent lower rate band has not been fully used any balance may be applied to calculate the tax due before proceeding to the basic rate or higher rate.

Personal representatives administering the estate of a deceased person will be assessable to capital gains tax at a rate equivalent to the basic rate of 25 per cent.

TAX PAYABLE – HUSBAND AND WIFE
For 1989–90 and earlier years the chargeable gains of a married woman 'living with' her husband were assessed on the husband, other than in the year of marriage. Capital losses of one spouse were subtracted from the gains of the other spouse, unless the loss making spouse filed an election to retain the benefit of the losses. Only one combined annual exempt amount was available.

Capital gains tax liability was calculated by reference to the husband's marginal rate of tax. Where a wife's earnings election was in force the chargeable gains were effectively treated as 'investment income' and added to the husband's income when calculating the marginal rate of income tax.

With the introduction of independent taxation on 6 April 1990 this system ceased to apply. Husband

gains tax notwithstanding the use of income tax rates.

It will be recognised that where income already incurs liability to the higher rate of 40 per cent for 1995–96 net chargeable gains will be assessed at the rate of 40 per cent. If the individual has not fully utilised the basic rate 25 per cent band of £21,100, the net gains may be wholly assessed at 25 per cent and wife are independently taxed, with each entitled to his or her £6,000 exemption and marginal rate for 1995–96.

RETURNS

Details of disposals, and the resultant chargeable gains, must be entered on the tax return form, where a form is required for completion. However, where the chargeable gains accruing to an individual do not exceed £6,000 for 1995–96 and the gross proceeds from all disposals do not exceed £12,000, it is sufficient to state this on the return form without submitting calculations.

In the absence of a tax return requiring completion, liability to capital gains tax should be notified to the Inland Revenue independently to avoid incurring a liability to satisfy interest and perhaps penalties.

TRUSTS

Complex provisions apply to the taxation of chargeable gains accruing to trustees. Where the trustees are resident in the United Kingdom, they will usually suffer capital gains tax at the appropriate rate. Trustees residing overseas are unlikely to be taxed direct but gains accruing to those trustees may be assessed on United Kingdom beneficiaries, or perhaps on the settlor, namely the individual who created the trust.

18

Making the annual return

EVERY INDIVIDUAL who has profits, gains or income which is chargeable to income tax or capital gains tax must notify the Inspector of Taxes of that fact. If he or she fails to do so a liability to satisfy penalties may be incurred. Many taxpayers will receive tax return forms annually, or at less frequent intervals of time. Should a completed return be delivered late, or contain insufficient or incorrect information, with the result that the issue of assessments is delayed, a liability to interest may also arise. Details of any chargeable gains assessable to capital gains tax must also be recorded on the return, unless the limits mentioned on page 127 are not exceeded.

The first part of the return form should record the income and gains for the previous year of assessment ending on 5 April. The second part is primarily concerned with allowances for the following year.

When completing the 1995–96 return, containing claims for allowances relating to 1995–96, it should not be overlooked that this return requires the insertion of details of income and gains for the year ended 5 April 1995. Husband and wife 'living together' are independently assessed and a return completed by one spouse will not contain details of income and gains accruing to the other.

A new style of income tax return form has been issued recently. Most forms are somewhat more extensive than their predecessors. However, there are a number of different versions of the personal tax return for individuals in different circumstances. These versions are as follows:

a Form 11 – for the self-employed
b Form 11P – for those whose main source of income is from employment rather than self-employment
c Form P1 – a simplified version of Form 11P for those with relatively straightforward tax affairs
d Form 11 – for clergy
e Form 11K – for certain employees who work overseas
f Form 11 Lloyd's – for Lloyd's underwriters

The need to file a return promptly will assume even greater significance with the introduction of self-assessment for 1996–97 and future years (see page 140 for further details).

19

Companies

PROFITS AND INCOME accruing to individuals are subject to income tax and any chargeable gains arising to such persons are assessable to capital gains tax. In contrast, profits, income and chargeable gains accruing to companies resident in, or carrying on business in, the United Kingdom, are assessed to corporation tax.

Corporation tax is charged on the profits, gains and income of an accounting period and this will usually be the period for which accounts are made up annually. In arriving at assessable profits a deduction may be claimed for capital allowances where expenditure is incurred on the acquisition of plant, machinery, industrial buildings and similar assets.

RATES OF CORPORATION TAX
The rates at which corporation tax must be paid are fixed by reference to a financial year which commences on 1 April and ends on the following 31 March. In those cases where the company accounting year does not end on 31 March the results must be apportioned on a time basis. This apportionment will only assume significance where there is a change in the rate of corporation tax.

In recent years corporation tax has been charged, or is being charged, at the following rates:

	Per cent
1 April 1990 to 31 March 1991.	34
1 April 1991 to 31 March 1992.	33
1 April 1992 to 31 March 1993.	33
1 April 1993 to 31 March 1994.	33
1 April 1994 to 31 March 1995.	33
1 April 1995 to 31 March 1996.	33

SMALL COMPANIES' RATE
Where the profits of a United Kingdom resident company do not exceed stated limits, the full rate of corporation tax is reduced to the small companies' rate. The application of the reduced small companies' rate is governed by the amount of profits and not by the size of the company.

The small companies' rate has remained at 25 per cent throughout the period from 1 April 1988 to 31 March 1996.

Full small companies' rate relief is available where profits do not exceed a 'lower limit'. Marginal relief will be forthcoming where profits exceed this limit but do not exceed an 'upper limit'. This marginal relief is calculated by subtracting from the liability determined at the full corporation tax rate a fraction of the difference between profits and the upper limit. Marginal relief ceases to have any application where profits exceed the upper limit as all profits are then chargeable at the full companies' rate.

The effect of marginal relief is to steadily increase the average rate of corporation tax from the small companies' rate to the full rate as the amount of profit escalates. An alternative method of achieving the same result for the year ending on 31 March, 1996, is to calculate tax at the small companies' rate of 25 per cent on income up to the lower limit and to add tax at 35 per cent for that slice of profits falling within the margin.

The lower and upper limits which have been used in recent years are as follows:

Year Ending 31 March	Lower Limit	Upper Limit
	£	£
1991	200,000	1,000,000
1992, 1993 and 1994	250,000	1,250,000
1995 and 1996	300,000	1,500,000

The fraction to be used in the calculation becomes:

Year ending 31 March	
1991	9/400ths
1992, 1993, 1994, 1995 and 1996	1/50th

Some modification to the calculation is necessary where there are associated companies, namely companies under common control, or the accounting period is less than twelve months. Adjustments must also be made for accounting periods overlapping 31 March where a change in rate or rates arises. The small companies' rate is not available to close investment-holding companies. These are companies which neither carry on a trade nor derive income from most forms of property letting.

97
SMALL COMPANIES RATE

The trading profits, calculated after subtracting capital allowances, accruing to Y Ltd in the twelve-month period ending on 31 March 1996, were £160,000. These profits fall below the ceiling of £300,000 and the corporation tax payable becomes:

£160,000 at 25 per cent **£40,000**

CHARGEABLE GAINS

The calculation of chargeable gains and capital losses accruing to companies is made on a basis similar to that used for individuals. Here also the indexation allowance can be subtracted from gains but cannot be used to create or increase losses for disposals after 29 November 1993. The special relief of £10,000 for indexation losses which can be obtained by individuals is not available to companies. Where the disposal of assets acquired before 1 April 1982 occurs after 5 April 1988, the calculation may usually proceed by treating the assets as acquired at market value on 31 March 1982. Unlike individuals,

98
MARGINAL SMALL COMPANIES RATE RELIEF

X Ltd derived trading profits, calculated after deducting capital allowances, of £520,000 for the twelve-month period ending on 31 March 1996. Marginal small companies' rate relief applies and the corporation tax payable is as follows:

Trading profits	£520,000

	£
Tax on £520,000 at 33 per cent (full rate)	171,600
Less marginal relief:	
£1,500,000 less £520,000 = £980,000	
× 1/50th	19,600
Tax payable	£152,000

An alternative calculation which produces the same result is the following:

	£
Tax on first £300,000 at 25 per cent . .	75,000
Tax on margin of £220,000 (£520,000 less	
£300,000) at 35 per cent . . .	77,000
Tax payable	£152,000

however, the annual exemption of £6,000 has no application to companies.

Any chargeable gains, calculated after subtracting allowable losses, become assessable to corporation tax. Those gains, or net gains, are included in profits

99
CHARGEABLE GAINS

A Ltd prepares accounts to 31 March annually. Trading profits, suitably adjusted for tax purposes by subtracting capital allowances, amounted to £180,000 for the year ending 31 March 1996.

On 12 January 1996, the company derived a chargeable gain of £45,000, after deducting the indexation allowance, from the disposal of an asset.

Aggregate profits do not exceed £300,000 and the small companies' rate applies. Corporation tax payable will therefore be calculated as follows:

	£
Trading profits	180,000
Chargeable gain	45,000
Total profits	£225,000
Tax on £225,000 at the small companies'	
rate of 25 per cent	£56,250

and may benefit from the application of small companies' rate relief.

INTEREST PAYMENTS
When making payments of yearly interest and other annual sums (but not dividends), a company will deduct income tax at the basic rate of 25 per cent. Any tax must usually be paid over to the Inland Revenue and cannot be retained by the paying company. Some relief for the outlay is available, however, as the gross interest, or other payment, may usually be deducted from profits chargeable to corporation tax, unless the payment represents a 'distribution'.

CHARITABLE PAYMENTS
Annual payments made to a charity under a properly drawn deed of covenant are satisfied 'net' after deducting income tax at the basic rate of 25 per cent. This tax must be accounted for to the Inland Revenue but the gross sum may be relieved when calculating the paying company's liability to corporation tax. A similar procedure applies to single donations made by larger companies where the requirements outlined on page 101 are satisfied, and also to donations exceeding £250 made by all companies under the Gift Aid scheme.

DISTRIBUTIONS
Payments which are treated as distributions cannot be deducted in calculating company profits. The expression 'distribution' has a wide meaning and includes dividends paid on shares, benefits provided to shareholders and other advantages.

Dividends and other qualifying distributions are paid in full, without deduction of income tax. However, on making such a distribution the paying company is required to make a payment of advance corporation tax (ACT) to the Inland Revenue. The rates of ACT for recent years and those for the immediate future are shown below.

Distributions made:		Rate
6 April 1988 to 5 April 1993	.	. 1/3rd
6 April 1993 to 5 April 1994	.	. 9/31sts
6 April 1994 to 5 April 1996	.	. 1/4th

Any ACT paid may usually be offset by the paying company against its liability to corporation tax for the accounting period during which the distribution is made. Therefore, as the title suggests, ACT is really an advance payment of corporation tax, where

the company has sufficient profits chargeable to that tax. Should the corporation tax liability be insufficient to absorb payments of ACT, the surplus may be carried forward to future periods or perhaps carried back to earlier periods.

For many years the rate of ACT when added to the distribution produced an amount identical to income tax at the basic rate on the grossed-up equivalent. For example, a distribution of £75 made in the year to 5 April 1993 would produce £25 of ACT, which is 25 per cent when applied to the grossed-up sum of £100.

The tax credit attaching to dividends and other distributions paid after 5 April 1993 is reduced to one-quarter of the sum received. Therefore a dividend of £75 has attached to it a tax credit of £18.75. The rate of ACT has also been reduced, but in two stages. ACT attributable to dividends and other distributions paid in the year to 5 April 1994 was 22.5 per cent of the aggregate of the amount paid and the ACT. This was reduced to 20 per cent for dividends and other distributions made after 5 April 1994.

The treatment of dividends received by shareholders is discussed on page 87.

PAY AND FILE
A new system for administering the assessment and collection of corporation tax from companies applies to all accounting periods ending on and after 1 October 1993. The system is known as 'pay and file' and, as the title suggests, requires companies to discharge corporation tax on a self-assessment basis and to submit both accounts and tax returns at a later date.

All corporation tax now becomes due and payable nine months following the end of a company's accounting period. Failure to discharge the proper amount of tax on that date will incur a liability to interest, which commences to run from the end of the nine-month period. Supporting accounts and corporation tax returns must be filed within a period of twelve months commencing on the annual accounting date. Should a company fail to satisfy this obligation a liability to penalties will arise. The amount of these penalties increases as the period of failure lengthens.

When applying 'pay and file' it should not be overlooked that the word 'company' has an extended meaning for corporation tax purposes. In addition to the more familiar public and private company, it also extends to clubs, associations and similar bodies.

20

Value added tax

VALUE ADDED TAX is charged on the value of supplies made by a registered trader and extends both to the supply of goods and also to the supply of services. Special rules must be applied to determine the nature of the supply and also the time at which that supply is made.

For many years value added tax was charged on the value of most goods imported into the United Kingdom, unless the importation was of a temporary nature. However, with the commencement of the European Single Market on 1 January 1993, value added tax is no longer charged where goods are imported from a Member State of the European Community. Instead of a tax on importation, value added tax will be imposed on the person who 'acquires' goods, in substitution for liability at the point of importation. Goods from suppliers outside the Single Market continue to attract tax on importation.

A registered trader will both suffer tax (input tax) when obtaining or acquiring goods or services for the purposes of a business and charge that tax (output tax) when supplying goods or services to customers and others. It is necessary for the trader to calculate both the input tax suffered and the output tax charged, or chargeable, during a prescribed accounting period. Should the output tax exceed the input tax qualifying for relief, the difference must be paid over to Customs and Excise. However, if the input tax exceeds the output tax a repayment will usually be due.

Not all input tax may be included in the calculation as some outgoings, for example supplies involving business entertaining and supplies relating to domestic accommodation provided by a company for use by directors and their families, must be disregarded. Nor can tax suffered on the supply of a new motor car be relieved as input tax, unless the vehicle has been imported or supplied to car dealers for resale, is acquired by taxi, self-drive hire firms or driving schools for business use, is acquired solely for business use, perhaps a business of leasing, or falls within a limited range of special vehicles.

Value added tax returns are usually submitted for prescribed accounting periods of three months, although some repayment traders may submit returns on a monthly basis. Very large traders will also submit returns on a three-monthly basis, although they must account for tax due at more frequent intervals. An optional scheme is available for traders having an annual taxable turnover falling below £300,000. Such traders may, if they so wish, render returns on an annual basis. Nine equal payments of value added tax will then be made on account, with a final, tenth, balancing payment accompanying submission of the return.

REGISTRATION

The collection and repayment of value added tax is confined to registered traders, an expression which includes individuals, partnerships and companies carrying on a trade, profession or vocation and certain other activities. Mandatory registration is confined to those making taxable supplies exceeding certain thresholds. These thresholds are amended periodically and from 30 November 1994 an unregistered trader must register:

a at any time, if there are reasonable grounds for believing that the value of taxable supplies in the next thirty days will exceed £46,000; or

b at the end of any month if the value of taxable supplies in the last twelve months then ending has exceeded £46,000.

A person liable to be registered under **a** is required to notify liability, and will be registered with effect from the date he or she becomes so liable. If a person is liable to registration under **b**, he or she must notify liability within thirty days of the end of the month concerned and will be registered with effect from the end of the month in which the thirtieth day falls, unless registration from an earlier date is agreed.

These stringent time limits must be fully recognised when commencing a new business, or where the value of taxable supplies increases, as failure to notify Customs and Excise promptly may result in demands for value added tax which ought to have been paid on earlier occasions.

A trader whose taxable supplies do not reach the mandatory registration threshold may apply for voluntary registration. This may sometimes be thought advisable, as only registered traders can obtain relief for input tax suffered. Persons acquiring an existing registered business as a going concern must usually register immediately.

Racehorse owners obtaining sponsorship or appearance money may register from a date not earlier than 16 March 1993. This possibility has arisen following a change in the Rules of Racing which enables those owners to carry on a business.

Registered traders may seek cancellation of their registration where the value of taxable supplies does not exceed certain limits. From 30 November 1994, an application for de-registration can be made if the value of taxable supplies is not expected to exceed £44,000 in the year then beginning.

EXEMPT SUPPLIES

Supplies of certain goods and services which comprise 'exempt supplies' are not chargeable to value added tax. These include the provision of finance, insurance and education, together with burial and cremation facilities. The granting of a lease or licence to occupy land will usually represent an exempt supply not chargeable to value added tax, but there are numerous exceptions. In particular, transactions affecting new non-domestic buildings may represent standard rated supplies. It is also possible for the landlord of a non-domestic building to exercise an option to treat rents as standard rated supplies. The purpose of such an election will be to avoid, or to limit, restrictions otherwise affecting the ability to recover input of tax suffered.

In those cases where a trader makes exempt supplies, no value added tax will be added to the prices charged, and in the absence of sufficient taxable supplies it may not be mandatory to register. A trader who is registered but who makes exempt supplies may be unable to fully recover the input tax suffered when obtaining goods or services. However, where a trader makes some taxable supplies and the input tax attributable to exempt supplies does not exceed £7,200 in a twelve-month period, it may be possible to obtain relief for all input tax suffered. This possibility has been considerably reduced following the introduction of new rules on 29 November 1994.

BAD DEBTS

Tax is charged on the supply of goods or services and not on the amount actually received for the supply, unless the supplier is operating a special scheme. As special schemes only require receipts to be included, those operating these schemes effectively obtain relief for bad debts. The range of special schemes which provide effective relief for bad debts may also extend to registered traders having an annual turnover falling below £350,000. Such traders may, at their option, adopt a system of cash accounting which only recognises payments actually made and received. Since the amount of any bad debt will not be 'received' traders adopting this scheme are not required to account for tax on that debt.

For other traders not within these schemes relief may be available for the value added tax element of bad debts suffered. This relief is limited to a genuine debt more than six months old and which has been written off in the books of the trader.

RATES OF TAX

Value added tax is levied at three rates, namely:

a a zero, or nil, rate; and

b a standard rate of 17.5 per cent (increased from 15 per cent on 1 April 1991).

c a reduced rate of 8 per cent on supplies of domestic fuel (introduced on 1 April 1994).

ZERO RATING

Zero rating extends to many supplies, including the following:

a The supply of food and drink for human consumption. This does not include such items as ice cream, chocolates, sweets, crisps and alcoholic drinks. Nor does it include supplies made in the course of catering, for example, at a wedding reception or dinner, or supplies for consumption in a restaurant or cafe. Take-away supplies of 'cold' foods for consumption off the supplier's premises are zero rated but the supply of 'hot' food and drink, for example, fish and chips or a container of hot tea, are taxable at the standard rate.

b Sewerage and water services, unless supplies are made for non-domestic purposes.

c Books, booklets, brochures, pamphlets, leaflets, newspapers, journals and periodicals.

d Talking books for the blind and handicapped and wireless sets for the blind.

e Electricity, gas and other fuels supplied for domestic purposes before 1 April 1994. From this date domestic supplies suffer tax at the reduced rate of 8 per cent. It was proposed that this reduced rate should be increased to the full standard rate of 17.5 per cent from 1 April 1995 but this proposal has been abandoned.

f Supplies made in the construction of the following:

    i A dwelling, for example, a house or flat. This may include the construction of a garage if work is undertaken at the same time as the construction of the dwelling.

    ii New buildings used as children's homes, old people's homes and to provide student accommodation, but not hotels or prisons.

    iii New buildings to be used by a charity for non-business purposes, for example, churches.

    iv Substantial alterations to listed buildings used for a purpose within i, ii or iii.

    The construction of other buildings, for example, offices, shops and factories, is not zero rated.

g Transport of passengers in a vehicle, ship or aircraft designed or adapted to carry not less than twelve passengers.

h Exports, including those to Member States in the Single Market where the required documentation is forthcoming.

i Supply of drugs, medicines, medical and surgical appliances.

j Supply of clothing and footwear suitable for young children.

This list is not intended to be exhaustive but it provides some indication of those supplies which may, and those which may not, be zero rated for value added tax purposes. In addition, a number of supplies made to charities obtain the benefit of zero rating and incur no liability to value added tax.

FARMERS

A special agricultural flat rate scheme was introduced on 1 January 1993. This scheme is optional and may be used by farmers engaged in crop production, stock farming, forestry, fisheries and processing. It cannot be used by individuals whose primary activity is to buy and sell animals, nor can animal trainers qualify. Persons who purchase dairy products from farmers and those operating sawmills are excluded from the scheme.

Where a farmer uses the flat rate scheme he will not be registered for value added tax purposes. In the absence of registration there will be no right to recover input tax. However, the farmer may make a special addition of 4 per cent to sale prices and retain that addition in lieu of relief for input tax. Non-farming activities undertaken by a farmer and which cannot be brought within the flat rate scheme must be dealt with separately. It will not be possible to add the flat rate addition to non-farming supplies of this nature. Where the value of taxable supplies attributable to non-farming activities is sufficiently substantial to require registration, or the farmer registers on a voluntary basis, he can no longer use the flat rate scheme.

Persons to whom supplies are made by a farmer can treat the 4 per cent addition as input tax and obtain relief for that tax in the normal manner.

ADMINISTRATION

Value added tax is administered by HM Customs and Excise and not by the Board of Inland Revenue. The tax performs no role whatsoever in the United Kingdom income tax system.

Registered traders should recognise that the application and administration of value added tax involves the satisfaction of many compliance requirements. Failure to submit value added tax returns, or to account for the proper amount of tax due promptly, may involve liability to penalties and interest.

21

Inheritance tax

INTRODUCED to replace estate duty, capital transfer tax imposed a wide-ranging liability to tax on lifetime gifts and also on the value of an individual's estate immediately before the time of death. Complex rules were included to deal with settled property held in trust. The potential scope of capital transfer tax was substantially redrafted for events taking place after 1 March 1986. Whilst much of the former administrative framework remained, the tax was re-named inheritance tax. The following comments outline the nature and scope of inheritance tax but apply only to events occurring on and after 19 March 1986.

When examining these comments it must be emphasised that the new system of independent taxation, which was introduced on 6 April 1990, has absolutely no effect on inheritance tax. Independent taxation of husband and wife is limited to income tax and capital gains tax. There was no need for this system to be extended to inheritance tax as husband and wife have been separately taxed since the introduction of capital transfer tax in 1974.

Liability to inheritance tax extends to assets located in the United Kingdom. The tax also applies to assets located overseas if the person concerned was domiciled in the United Kingdom at the time of the transfer or other event. There are two main occasions of charge, one affecting a limited range of lifetime transfers and the other of much wider application to the value of an estate immediately before death.

LIFETIME TRANSFERS
Lifetime gifts and other transfers which deplete the value of an individual's estate may fall into four broad categories, namely transactions to be disregarded, exempt transfers, potentially exempt transfers and chargeable transfers.

Transactions disregarded
Some lifetime gifts and dispositions are entirely disregarded and incur no liability to inheritance tax, notwithstanding the value of the transferor's estate is reduced. These include dispositions not intended to confer any gratuitous benefit, the provision of family maintenance, the waiver of the right to receive remuneration and dividends, and the grant of agricultural tenancies made for full consideration.

Exempt transfers
Transfers of value which can be treated as 'exempt transfers' also avoid liability to inheritance tax. These include the following:

a A transfer by an individual to his or her spouse. This is subject to modification if the transferee is not domiciled in the United Kingdom.
b The first £3,000 of transfers made in a year ending on 5 April. If the total value of transfers taking place in any year falls below £3,000 the excess may be carried forward for one year only and utilised in that year.
c Transfers of value made by a transferor to any person in a year ending on 5 April if the value transferred does not exceed £250.
d A transfer made as part of the transferor's normal expenditure and satisfied out of income.

e Outright gifts in consideration of marriage to the extent that the value transferred by any one transferor in respect of a single marriage does not exceed:

  i £5,000 if the transferor is the parent of either party to the marriage;

  ii £2,500 if the transferor is a party to the marriage or a grandparent or remoter ancestor of either party;

  iii £1,000 if the transferor is any other person.

f Transfers made to a charity where the assets transferred become the property of a charity or are held in trust for charitable purposes only.

g The transfer of property to a political party. If this exemption is to apply it must be shown that at the most recent General Election at least two members of the party were elected to the House of Commons. Alternatively, the requirement will be satisfied if a single member is elected with not less than 150,000 votes being cast for members of that party.

h Transfers made to an extensive list of institutions, including the National Museum, the National Trust for Places of Historic Interest or Natural Beauty, a local authority, and many others.

i Transfers of heritage property and other assets of value to the nation made to an approved body not established or conducted for profit.

Potentially exempt transfers

If a transfer is neither to be disregarded nor an exempt transfer it may comprise a potentially exempt transfer. This represents a transfer made by an individual to:

a a second individual;

b trustees administering an accumulation and maintenance trust; or

c trustees administering funds for a disabled or handicapped person.

The range of potentially exempt transfers also includes certain transactions affecting settled property in which an individual or individuals retain a life interest in possession. Most transfers made by an individual to such a trust may be treated as potentially exempt transfers and the termination of an interest in possession during lifetime may usually receive similar treatment.

As the title suggests, potentially exempt transfers are potentially exempt from liability to inheritance tax and no tax will become payable at the time of the transfer. The absence of liability will be confirmed should the transferor survive throughout a period of seven years from the date of the gift or other disposition. However, if the transferor dies within the seven-year inter vivos period tax becomes payable at the full rate or rates in force at the time of death. The amount of tax due may then be reduced to the following percentages by applying a form of tapering relief, which is governed by the length of the period between the date of the gift and the date of death:

Period of years before death	Percentage
Not more than 3.	100
More than 3 but not more than 4	80
More than 4 but not more than 5	60
More than 5 but not more than 6	40
More than 6 but not more than 7	20

Chargeable transfers

Finally, a limited range of lifetime transfers will incur liability to inheritance tax. These are restricted to transfers involving trusts, other than those falling within the exempt and potentially exempt transfer rules, transfers to non-individuals and transfers affecting close companies. Tax is payable at one-half the full rate or rates but should the transferor die within a period of seven years from the date of the lifetime chargeable transfer additional tax may become payable by substituting the full rates, less a deduction for tapering relief.

GIFTS WITH RESERVATION

Troublesome rules apply where a lifetime gift is made but the transferor continues to enjoy some benefit in the subject matter of the gift. This will frequently arise where parents transfer the matrimonial home to children but continue to reside in the property without payment of a commercial rent. Where a gift with reservation is made it becomes necessary to establish the period throughout which the transferor continued to enjoy a benefit. If the benefit ceased to be enjoyed more than seven years before the date of the transferor's death no additional liability to inheritance tax will arise. A finding that the benefit was enjoyed immediately before the time of death will require that the value of the asset must be included when calculating the value of the deceased's estate on which inheritance tax becomes payable. Finally, if the transferor ceased to enjoy the benefit within a period of seven years before death he or she is treated as having made a potentially exempt transfer equal to the value of the asset at the time of cessation.

DEATH

Immediately before the time of death an individual is deemed to make a transfer of value equal to the value of his or her estate, representing the value of assets less liabilities. However, exempt transfers involving transfers to a surviving spouse, charities, political organisations and national bodies will not incur inheritance tax liability, subject to limited exceptions. Inheritance tax payable is calculated by applying the full rates. In addition, death may trigger liability to tax on potentially exempt transfers, and also further liability for chargeable lifetime transfers made within a period of seven years before death.

VALUATION

The value transferred by lifetime transfers will usually reflect the fall in the value of the transferor's estate. Often this fall will be identical to the value of the asset transferred, but there are many exceptions, particularly where an individual transfers part only of his or her shareholding interest in a closely controlled company. Immediately before the time of death a person is treated as having transferred his or her entire estate for a consideration reflecting the value at that date. Therefore, the value transferred will represent the excess, if any, of the value attributable to assets, less liabilities.

BUSINESS ASSETS

In general, the value of property comprised in an individual's estate will reflect the price which that property might reasonably have been expected to fetch on a sale in the open market. However, where the transfer relates to certain assets the value transferred, both by lifetime transfers and on death, may be reduced by a percentage. When calculating this percentage a distinction must be drawn between dispositions, deaths and other events occurring:

a before 10 March 1992; and
b after 9 March 1992.

Events before 10 March 1992

The percentage deductions available for transfers and other events taking place shortly before 10 March 1992 are shown by the following table:

Asset	Percentage deduction
Business or interest in a business	50
Controlling shareholding interest in any company	50
More than 25 per cent interest in an unquoted company	50
Not more than 25 per cent interest in an unquoted company	30
Land, buildings, machinery or plant used by a controlled company or partnership	30

Where a controlling shareholding interest exists it is immaterial whether the underlying company is quoted or unquoted when determining the availability of the 50 per cent deduction. However, the percentage deduction for minority shareholding interests cannot apply to shares in a quoted company or a company dealt in on the Unlisted Securities Market.

Events after 9 March 1992

For transfers and events taking place after 9 March 1992, most percentage deductions have increased considerably to the levels shown by the following table:

Asset	Percentage deduction
Business or interest in a business	100
More than 25 per cent holding in an unquoted company	100
More than 25 per cent holding in a USM company	100
Controlling shareholding interest in a quoted company	50
Not more than 25 per cent holding in an unquoted company	50
Not more than 25 per cent holding in a USM company	50
Land, buildings, machinery or plant used by a controlled company or partnership	50

As a result of these changes, holdings in companies dealt in on the Unlisted Securities Market are now treated in the same manner as unquoted holdings. A more significant effect is that with the ability to obtain a 100 per cent deduction, many business assets may now be transferred without incurring any liability to inheritance tax whatsoever.

Generally

It remains a general requirement in all cases that assets must have been owned for a minimum period of two years before the date of the lifetime disposition or death if the percentage deduction is to be forthcoming.

Only part of the value may qualify for the percentage deduction if not all assets of a business are used for a qualifying purpose.

————— 100 —————
BUSINESS ASSETS RELIEF

The issued share capital of A Ltd comprised 100 ordinary shares of £1 each. Mr B retained 65 shares at the time of his death on 31 January 1992. It was agreed that these shares had a value of £150,000 and fully qualified for business assets relief.

The value to be included in the estate of Mr B for inheritance tax purposes is calculated as follows:

	£
Value of shares – as agreed . . .	150,000
Less 50 per cent business assets relief .	75,000
Value to be included . . .	£75,000

The maximum 50 per cent relief can be obtained in this case as, at the time of his death, the deceased retained a controlling shareholding interest in A Ltd.

If Mr B had died one year later on 31 January 1993, the value would be calculated in the following manner:

	£
Value of shares – as agreed . . .	150,000
Less 100 per cent business assets relief	150,000
Value to be included . . .	NIL

AGRICULTURAL PROPERTY

The value of agricultural property transferred may also qualify for a percentage deduction. This is limited to the agricultural value and where, for example, property retains an 'excessive' development value no deduction will be available for the excess. Agricultural property includes short rotation coppice farming for events after 5 April 1995.

To obtain this relief the property must either have been owned by the transferor for a period of seven years and used for agricultural purposes or occupied by the transferor for those purposes throughout a period of two years.

The percentage deductions for transfers and other events taking place before 10 March 1992 are:

Asset	Percentage deduction
Owner occupied farmland . .	50
Farm tenancies	50
Land subject to a tenancy not terminating within twelve months	30

For events and transfers taking place after 9 March 1992, the percentage deductions become:

Asset	Percentage deduction
Owner occupied farmland . .	100
Farm tenancies . . .	100
Land subject to a tenancy not terminating within twelve months	50

The deduction for land subject to a tenancy is increased to 100 per cent from 1 September 1995, but only for leases that commence on or after that date.

CALCULATION OF TAX PAYABLE

The value of each non-exempt lifetime gift or disposition is added to the value of previous dispositions, if any, to establish the rate of tax on the current transfer. On death the value of the estate, after excluding any exempt transfers, will be added to the cumulative total of lifetime dispositions, if any, and tax calculated on the additional slice. This cumulative procedure affects only dispositions taking place within a period of seven years before the current transfer. Any dispositions made before the commencement of the seven-year period are ignored. When constructing the cumulative total, lifetime dispositions taking place before 18 March 1986 and creating capital transfer tax liability must be included, if of course they fall within the seven-year period.

In those limited situations where inheritance tax becomes payable on a lifetime gift or disposition the value transferred must be 'grossed up' by including tax payable, unless the obligation is discharged by the transferee.

RATE OF TAX

For many years the rates of inheritance tax were usually amended annually, with revised rates being announced in the annual Budget Statement. However, no change was announced in the March 1993 Budget, nor was one introduced in the unified

——— 101 ———
CALCULATION OF TAX PAYABLE – GIFTS WITHIN SEVEN YEARS BEFORE DEATH

After making sufficient small gifts to exactly absorb the annual exemption, Mr R gifted freehold property to his son on 24 May 1994. The value of the property at this time was £250,000 and it did not qualify for business assets or agricultural property relief. Mr R died on 7 August 1998 without making any further gifts.

The gift was a potentially exempt transfer with no immediate liability to inheritance tax. However, as death occurred within the seven-year period, this will trigger liability. Assuming, for the purposes of illustration, that the rates of inheritance tax which apply from 6 April 1995 remain unchanged, the tax payable will be calculated as follows:

		Cumulative total £
Value of gift		250,000
Tax payable		
On first £154,000 . . .	NIL	
On balance of £96,000 at 40 per cent	38,400	
	£38,400	£250,000

As death occurred more than 4 years and less than 5 years from the date of the gift, the tapering relief shown on page 136 is available. The tax payable will therefore be reduced to:

£38,400 × 60% = £23,040

Budget of November in the same year. It was not until the Budget of November 1994 that a small increase on the nil rate band was announced for introduction on the following 6 April 1995.

Notwithstanding the virtual absence of any change in recent years, it is significant that when inheritance tax replaced capital transfer tax on 17 March 1986, an initial nil rate band of £71,000 was used, with six interim rate bands and a final 60 per cent top rate. Some nine years later the nil rate band has been increased to £154,000 with a single positive rate band of 40 per cent replacing all other bands.

Tables setting out the rates of inheritance tax which have applied since 17 March 1986 appear on

——— 102 ———
CALCULATION OF TAX PAYABLE ON DEATH

Using the facts in Example 101, let it be assumed that the value of Mr R's estate at the time of death on 7 August 1998 was £300,000, after subtracting all reliefs and exemptions.

The total inheritance tax then becoming due will be calculated as follows:

		Cumulative total £
Re gift within previous seven years . . .	£23,040	250,000
Re value on death		300,000
Tax payable		
On £300,000 at 40 per cent	£120,000	
		£550,000

Therefore the total inheritance tax payable, assuming rates which apply from 6 April 1995 remain unchanged, is £143,040 (£23,040 + £120,000).

page 160. These rates must be reduced by one-half when calculating tax on chargeable lifetime gifts.

SETTLED PROPERTY
Complex rules apply when establishing inheritance tax liability for settled property held by trustees. In general, where a beneficiary retains an interest in possession the settled property to which that interest relates will be effectively treated as being in the ownership of the beneficiary. Property held by discretionary trusts is subject to a ten-year periodic charge, with interim charges where property leaves the trust before the first ten-year anniversary or between anniversaries. An accumulation and maintenance trust for the benefit of individuals below the age of 25 years will not be subject to the ten-year periodic change, nor will liability to inheritance tax usually arise on the removal of property from such a trust.

These brief comments provide no more than a summary of the rules to be applied and in all cases consideration must be given to the trust deed or other document governing the administration of settled property.

22

Self-Assessment

The Future

THE MOST fundamental reform in personal taxation for more than fifty years will shortly take place with the introduction of self-assessment. This reform will affect all individuals required to complete tax returns, including the self-employed, members of a partnership, company directors, individuals having more than one source of income and those with investment income liable to higher rate income tax. Many individuals receive their only income from employment and suffer tax by deduction under the PAYE scheme. These individuals will not be directly affected by self-assessment but the situation may well alter if an individual ceases employment and becomes self-employed or perhaps receives investment income.

THE OLD SYSTEM

To recognise the significance of self-assessment a brief reference may be made to the pre-self-assessment system. As has been indicated, many individuals receive income after deduction of income under the PAYE scheme. Others may receive such income in addition to interest from deposits with banks or building societies which suffers deduction of income tax at the basic rate. Several other forms of income have tax deducted at source and dividends are received with the benefit of a tax credit which effectively represents a form of tax deduction. Where no tax has been suffered, for example, on business profits, or tax arises at the higher rate on investment

income, details must be supplied to the Inland Revenue by completing a tax return. This return also includes details of any capital gains.

It then remains for the Inland Revenue to issue a notice of assessment identifying the amount of taxable income or profits and showing the income tax and capital gains tax payable. There may well be more than one notice of assessment where an individual receives income from two or more different sources. Should the taxpayer challenge the accuracy of an assessment this will be made in the form of an appeal which is then settled by negotiation or determined on a hearing by appeal Commissioners. Both income tax and capital gains tax becomes payable on a variety of different dates.

This assessment procedure will continue for 1995–96. It will then be replaced by self-assessment.

SELF-ASSESSMENT

The general function of self-assessment is that taxpayers will calculate their own liability and remit both income and capital gains tax directly to the Inland Revenue without the need for any assessment. Income tax may become payable by three instalments with fixed interest and penalties arising for late compliance. Against this general background the application and administration of self-assessment is outlined below in greater detail.

For most taxpayers the self-assessment compliance requirements will commence shortly after the end of the tax year 1996–97 with the receipt of a tax return. This will require details of income, profits and gains chargeable to both income tax and capital gains tax for the year of assessment 1996–97 and ending on 5 April 1997.

FILING A TAX RETURN

On receipt of a tax return the taxpayer is provided with two options. The first of these requires that the return must be fully completed and filed not later than 31 January after the end of the year of assessment to which it relates or three months after the return was issued, if later. The completed return will show details of all profits, gains and income chargeable to income tax and capital gains tax. It will also provide calculations of both income tax and capital gains tax payable for the appropriate year of assessment.

The second option enables the taxpayer to file a completed return by 30 September after the end of the year of assessment or, if later, two months following the date on which the return is issued. The Inland Revenue will then calculate the amount of tax due and advise the individual accordingly.

Whichever option is exercised, the Inland Revenue are provided with the opportunity to correct any obvious errors or mistakes in the return. This may relate to such matters as errors in the arithmetic or perhaps errors of principle.

The taxpayer is given twelve months from the filing date to correct any errors in the return. However, at any time in this twelve-month period the Inland Revenue may notify the taxpayer that enquiries are being made. It is expected that notification will not be confined to cases where inaccuracies are likely to be found but may extend to other 'innocent' cases. Once notification has been received the taxpayer can no longer correct the return. When the Inland Revenue enquiry is complete the taxpayer will be advised of any adjustments which may be considered appropriate. This enables the taxpayer to amend the return or perhaps to enter into negotiations for the purpose of establishing an acceptable figure. Should the taxpayer be unable to reach agreement the Inland Revenue may amend figures, subject to the taxpayer's right of appeal.

None of these matters involves raising the familiar assessment but the Inland Revenue do retain the right to issue an assessment at a later date where, for example, profits have been omitted from the return or repayment claims have been incorrectly made.

Failure to file a return by the filing date, usually 31 January, will give rise to an automatic penalty of £100. This penalty increases to £200 if the return is more than six months late. In both cases the penalty cannot exceed the amount of tax due.

If no return is filed the Inland Revenue may make a determination of the tax due. The taxpayer can only replace this determination by including accurate figures in a future tax return.

Should no return be received the taxpayer is required to notify the Inland Revenue of liability within six months following the end of the year of assessment. This requirement commences for 1995–96 with the six-month period ending on 5 October 1996.

PAYMENT OF TAX

A feature of self-assessment is the date for payment of tax. In the case of income tax, there may be three payment dates for a year of assessment, namely:

a a first instalment falling due on 31 January in the year of assessment itself;

b a second instalment falling due on the following 31 July; and

c a balancing payment, or perhaps repayment, falling due on the following 31 January.

The first two instalments will be based on the net income tax paid for the previous year of assessment. This net sum will represent the full amount of income tax due for the previous year less that suffered by deduction, for example, under PAYE, by deduction of income tax at the basice rate or by the tax credit on dividends. One-half of the net income tax liability will then comprise the first instalment due for the following year and an identical sum will comprise the amount of the second instalment. A similar approach applies to instalment payments of Class 4 national insurance contributions by the self-employed.

Claims may be made to reduce the amount of each instalment on the grounds that a source of income has ceased to exist or income from a continuing source has fallen. Penalties will be imposed where it is shown that such a claim was without foundation.

The final balancing payment or repayment will gather together the total tax liability and the amounts discharged by instalments.

It may be possible to avoid paying the first two instalments where the amount due does not exceed a figure to be announced annually.

There is no instalment procedure for capital gains tax purposes as the full tax must be paid on 31 January following the end of the year of assessment in which the disposal took place.

—————— 103 ——————
PAYMENT OF TAX

Brian is self-employed and his only income arises from the business. Profits produced an income tax liability of £7,400 for 1997–98.

The business is continuing and the income tax liability for 1998–99 amounted to £9,250, again with no income from any other source.

The tax payable for the year of assessment 1998–99 will become payable on the following dates:

	£
31 January 1999	
First instalment – $\frac{1}{2}$ × £7,400 . .	3,700
31 July 1999	
Second instalment – $\frac{1}{2}$ × £7,400 . .	3,700
	7,400
31 January 2000	
Balancing figure	1,850
Total liability	£9,250

LATE PAYMENT OF TAX
Should tax be paid late interest will run from the date tax was due to the date of payment. The rate at which interest is imposed will be that ruling at the relevant time. In addition, if any tax is unpaid by 28 February following the end of the year of assessment a 5 per cent surcharge will be imposed. This surcharge is increased to 10 per cent if tax remains unpaid by the following 31 July.

PROVISION OF INFORMATION
It will be apparent that if individuals are to comply with the requirements of self-assessment those individuals must be in possession of all information needed to complete a tax return. Much of the information will be furnished in the form of dividend vouchers and certificates of tax deduction, which the individual must retain. There will, however, be some information which an individual can only secure from a third party, perhaps from his or her employer. To achieve this, and probably commencing during the calendar year 1996, an employer will be required to provide an employee with

a a certificate of PAYE deducted by 31 May following the end of the year of assessment to which it relates;

b copies of returns made to the Inland Revenue showing details of benefits in kind, expenses payments and tax liabilities by 6 July following the end of the year of assessment;

c copies of returns made to the Inland Revenue

—————— 104 ——————
PAYMENT OF TAX

The total income tax liability of Sharon for 1997–98 was £5,400. Of this sum £2,100 was suffered by deduction leaving the balance of £3,300 to be collected by direct assessment. Her total income tax liability for the following year, 1998–99, was £7,500, of which £1,900 was collected by deduction. In addition, Sharon had a capital gains tax liability of £980 for 1997–98 and a liability of £1,850 for 1998–99.

Tax payable for the year of assessment 1998–99 will be due as follows:

Income tax	£
31 January 1999	
First instalment – $\frac{1}{2}$ × (£5,400 less £2,100)	1,650
31 July 1999	
Second instalment – $\frac{1}{2}$ × (£5,400 less £2,100)	1,650
Suffered by deduction . . .	1,900
	5,200
31 January 2000	
Balancing figure	2,300
Total liability	£7,500
Capital gains tax	
31 January 2000	£1,850

showing details of benefits and payments made to employees by third parties which were undertaken by agreement with the employer. These also must be supplied by 6 July.

Failure on the part of the employer to provide this information may involve the payment of penalties.

These compliance requirements must be carefully reviewed in the run-up to the commencement of self-assessment. Although the first full tax return will not be lodged before 31 January 1998 it will include information for the period commencing on 6 April 1997. It is therefore of great importance that all information needed to complete a return is carefully preserved. Penalties may be imposed where there is a failure to preserve records.

PARTNERHIPS
The introduction of self-assessment significantly alters the assessment of partnership profits. A representative of each partnership is required to return details of profits earned by the partnership as a whole. This return will also disclose details of partnership capital gains. The Inland Revenue are then provided with powers to enquire into the contents of the partnership return in a manner similar to that

which applies to returns submitted by individuals. The partnership return will disclose the allocation of profits between the partners. In addition it is the responsibility of each partner to include his or her share of those profits on the personal income tax return. For this purpose there will no longer be any partnership income tax assessment as each partner must be assessed individually on his or her share.

CHANGES IN THE TAX SYSTEM

Although the completion of a tax return marks the cornerstone of self-assessment, numerous changes have been made in the tax system in an attempt to achieve some measure of simplification. These changes involve the withdrawal of the previous 'preceding year' basis of assessment and its replacement by a new 'current year' basis. The assessment of all sole proprietors and individuals carrying on business in partnership will at some stage be altered as a result. Other changes have included a re-drafting of the basis used to establish profits arising from letting property in the United Kingdom. These and other matters have received comment elsewhere in this publication.

23

Married couples

Some practical considerations

THE INDEPENDENT TAXATION of husband and wife is now a well-established feature of the United Kingdom taxation code. However, problem areas do sometimes arise and it may be of interest to readers if a number of matters which occasionally create difficulty are briefly examined. As this section affects only husband and wife 'living together' the following comments are limited to a married couple retaining such a status.

SCHEDULE D – BASIS OF ASSESSMENT
Pending the full introduction of the new current year basis, many items of income assessable under Schedule D are chargeable on a preceding year basis, with special adjustments inserted where a new source is commenced or an existing source discontinued. The application of independent taxation does not, by itself, affect this principle but merely governs the identity of the spouse who must suffer tax on profits or income.

In those cases where a married woman commenced a new business in her capacity of a sole proprietor during 1988–89, any election for the 1989–90 and 1990–91 assessments to be based on the actual profits of the business for each year must be made by the wife and not by the husband. There is a time limit of seven years from the end of 1989–90 within which an election can be made or withdrawn.

SCHEDULE A – BASIS OF ASSESSMENT
The preceding year basis of assessment does not apply to income from land and buildings chargeable under Schedule A. However, where the income for a year of assessment is insufficient to discharge the costs of maintenance and other eligible outgoings, any surplus expenditure may be carried forward and offset against similar income in future years. Where a surplus of unused expenditure remained on 5 April 1990, or indeed on any later date, it must be carefully allocated between husband and wife in the proper proportions to ensure that only the spouse who incurred the expenditure can benefit by offsetting that surplus against his or her future income.

DEEDS OF COVENANT
When making payments under a properly drawn charitable deed of covenant the payer will deduct income tax at the basic rate. Where the payments are made out of income chargeable to income tax the amount of tax deducted may be retained. It is also possible to offset the covenanted payments against income generally for the purpose of obtaining relief at the higher rate where income is sufficiently substantial. In those cases where the payer does not have sufficient taxable income to provide cover for the payment the tax deducted must be paid over to the Inland Revenue.

Husbands and wives 'living together' are advised to carefully consider which spouse should be making covenanted payments. If payments are made by a wife who has little or no income she may be required to account to the Inland Revenue for basic rate income tax deducted. In addition, there will be no relief at the higher rate. Where her husband is liable at this rate there will be a substantial advantage if the husband, rather than the wife, makes covenanted payments. In some situations, and with the consent of the charity concerned, it may be thought advisable for a wife to discontinue future payments due under an existing covenant, with these payments being replaced by a new deed of covenant entered into by her husband. If the gross amount of the covenant remains unaltered this will not affect income reaching the charity but will provide the 'household' with increased tax relief.

In the case of joint covenants the Inland Revenue will usually maintain that payments should be treated as made equally by husband and wife, unless there is evidence to support a different conclusion.

ENTERPRISE INVESTMENT SCHEMES
Both a husband and his wife may independently obtain relief at the reduced rate of 20 per cent on investments up to £100,000 made under enterprise investment scheme arrangements. As 20 per cent is equal to the lower rate it is largely immaterial which spouse invests, although the investor must have sufficient taxable income to provide cover for the relief.

However, where one spouse has and the other does not have capital gains capable of being rolled-over, the availability of roll-over relief may be an important factor when reaching a decision.

VENTURE CAPITAL TRUSTS
The identity of the spouse who should subscribe for shares under the venture capital trust scheme raises considerations similar to those offering investment in enterprise investment schemes.

MORTGAGE INTEREST
Only interest on qualifying loans not exceeding £30,000 and applied to acquire an individual's residence can obtain tax relief, usually under the MIRAS deduction scheme. In the case of husband and wife 'living together' £30,000 is the maximum amount of aggregate loans made to the couple on which relief will be forthcoming.

It remains possible for the couple to submit an 'allocation of interest' election, which enables the interest paid to be apportioned between the couple in whatever proportions they consider advisable. The election must be submitted within a period of twelve months following the end of the year of assessment to which it relates. It will then continue in force until being revoked by either spouse.

The election would frequently be made for 1990–91 if only one spouse was liable to income tax at the higher rate. With the withdrawal of relief at that rate and the further restriction of relief to a reduced rate of 15 per cent the election has lost much of its former importance. However, there may occasionally be an advantage where interest is paid outside the MIRAS scheme or where one spouse is over the age of 64.

MARRIED COUPLE'S ALLOWANCE
Where a couple are 'living together' a married couple's allowance may be obtained. In the absence of any election this allowance must be used by the husband and only where he has insufficient income can any unused balance be transferred to his wife. The decision whether to transfer is that of the husband only.

However, the wife may elect, as of right, to obtain one-half of the basic married couple's allowance, leaving the husband with the balance of that allowance. Alternatively, the couple may jointly elect that the entire basic allowance should be allocated to the wife only. Notwithstanding any election, if the spouse entitled to any part of the married couple's allowance is unable to utilise that part against taxable income the unused portion may be transferred to the other spouse.

An election must be submitted before the commencement of the year of assessment to which it is first to apply. An exception arises in the year of marriage where the election may be submitted at any time in that year. Disregarding matters of 'fairness', an election could be beneficial for 1995–96 where the husband has little or no income liable to tax. However, with relief limited to 15 per cent the election is now of limited importance.

LIFE ASSURANCE RELIEF
Where substantial premiums are paid on life assurance and other policies taken out before 14 March 1984, tax relief may be restricted by reference to the payer's income. Following the introduction of independent taxation the income of husband and wife cannot be merged for this purpose. Consideration must be confined to the income of the spouse paying premiums.

JOINT CHEQUE ACCOUNTS

Many married couples maintain joint bank current or cheque accounts. Where a cheque is drawn on such an account to discharge a liability it may become doubtful whether the payment is being made by the husband or by his wife. Little difficulty emerges where the cheque is drawn to discharge a joint liability and in practice it is unlikely that the Inland Revenue would dispute the identity of the alleged drawer in other cases. However, for the avoidance of doubt, where a cheque is to be drawn to satisfy a payment attracting tax relief, perhaps a donation made under the Gift Aid scheme, it may be considered advisable to open a separate account in the sole name of the drawer. This should place beyond doubt the identity of the person involved.

PARTNERSHIPS

Where the income of one party to a marriage substantially exceeds that of the other there is an obvious advantage from the transfer of future income by that party. One possible method of achieving this where a business is carried on by, say, a husband in his capacity as a sole trader is to admit the wife as a partner. This will enable partnership profits to be shared between husband and wife. However, caution must be exercised to ensure that a 'genuine' partnership exists between the parties and not merely a 'paper' or 'sham' arrangement which will fail to withstand detailed scrutiny.

DIRECTORSHIPS

A further method of providing one spouse, usually a wife, with income is for the wife to be appointed a director or employee of a company controlled by her husband. If this results in the earnings of the husband being reduced the Inland Revenue may decline to accept that income really has been derived by the wife. This rejection should be successfully opposed by the ability to demonstrate that real services have been provided in return for the remuneration paid.

JOINT INCOME

Some income-producing assets may be held jointly by a husband and his wife. The general rule is that any income arising from such assets must be apportioned equally between the couple. However, it is possible to submit a joint declaration requiring the income to be apportioned by reference to the beneficial interests held by the husband and by the wife. The declaration must be forwarded to the Inland Revenue within a period of 60 days from the date on which it has been made and will only apply to income arising subsequently.

Where husband and wife jointly retain income-producing assets the ability to submit an election, or indeed the ability to refrain from making any such election, is important. The election applies separately to each asset, and in some situations it will be advisable to submit an election for a number of assets only and to refrain from making any election for the remainder. Numerous cases will undoubtedly arise where wisdom indicates the inadvisability of submitting any election whatsoever.

TRANSFER OF ASSETS

Where a wife has little, if any, income and her spouse retains a range of income-producing assets, consideration may well be given to the transfer of an asset for the purpose of establishing future income accruing to the wife. If such a transfer is to be effective for income tax purposes it must comprise an 'outright gift'. Should any 'strings' be attached to the gift, or the transferor be entitled to enjoy any benefit whatsoever from the asset transferred, the transaction is likely to be ineffective. All future income from an ineffective transfer will remain that of the transferor for income tax purposes.

LOSSES CARRIED FORWARD

Losses incurred by a husband of wife from the carrying on of a trade, profession or vocation may be carried forward and offset against future profits. Losses incurred by a spouse may only be carried forward and offset against future profits from the same business carried on by this same spouse. It is not possible for those losses to be carried forward and used by the other spouse.

In some situations business losses incurred in 1989–90 could be offset against any income for the following year. As independent taxation applies to the following year, 1990–91, it is only the spouse incurring the loss who can benefit from this arrangement. For 1989–90 and earlier years business losses of one spouse could be set against income of the other without restriction.

Finally, losses arising in the first four years of a new business may be carried back and set against profits, gains and income of earlier years. A married woman who incurs losses which are carried back to a date falling before 6 April 1990 should be aware that the benefit of any loss relief will be enjoyed by her husband.

CAPITAL GAINS TAX

For capital gains tax purposes a husband and his wife each have an annual exemption of £6,000 for 1995–96. Any unused part of the annual exemption cannot be carried forward and will be lost. This may suggest a transfer of assets from one spouse to another before those assets are sold to a third party, thereby enabling the gain to be realised in the most tax efficient manner.

Problems may arise where gains or losses accrue from the disposal of a jointly owned asset. It will be necessary to allocate the gains or losses between the joint owners. No election is possible to determine the basis of allocation, which will probably proceed by an equal apportionment unless there is clear evidence that the beneficial interests support a different allocation. In some cases a husband and his wife may consider it advisable to adjust their interests to obtain the most tax efficient basis of apportionment.

24

Hints on saving tax

ALL TAXPAYERS are understandably anxious to reduce their tax commitments. This can be achieved by:

a taking advantage of all available allowances and reliefs.

b carefully planning the dates on which transactions or events take place;

c taking steps to increase the reliefs which can be obtained; or

d refraining from action which will increase the amount of tax payable.

The requirements of one individual will differ from those of another, and there are often personal or business considerations which will outweigh possible tax savings. For example, ready access to savings may be more important than the amount of tax incurred on income arising. But few financial transactions can be safely carried out without considering the effect on tax liabilities. The following notes outline some areas where tax savings can be achieved, or additional obligations avoided. Other matters have been reviewed in the previous chapter dealing with the independent taxation of married couples.

PERSONAL MATTERS

Allowances
All individuals are entitled to a personal allowance and should make sure that this is being claimed and used. Those approaching the age of 65 or 75 must advise the Tax Office if the increased personal allowances are to be forthcoming, and most other allowances will only be given where they are claimed.

Married Couple's Allowance
It is possible for a married woman 'living with' her husband to obtain one-half, or perhaps all, of the married couple's allowance. This requires the submission of a claim before the commencement of a year of assessment and may be advantageous where the husband suffers little or no liability to income tax. With relief restricted to the reduced rate of 15 per cent for 1995–96 any advantage will be small.

Marriage
In the year of marriage the married couple's allowance reduces by £143 (at 1995–96 rates) for each complete month from 5 May to the date of the ceremony. For example, by postponing the wedding from, say, 30 April to 15 May, the allowance will fall by £143, which represents some £21.45 if relief is available at the reduced rate of 15 per cent. This amount is small but may justify advancing the ceremony by days, weeks, or even months.

Marriage breakdown
On the breakdown of a marriage leading to separation or divorce a great many tax considerations will arise. Where maintenance payments are made under a 'new' Court order or agreement, the recipient will not suffer liability to taxation, nor can the payer obtain any significant relief. Thus in many situations payments must be financed in whole or in part out of taxed income. This obligation must be recognised when the order or agreement is being discussed

and it may be considered advisable to transfer the ownership of income-producing assets, rather than enter into a commitment for the payment of maintenance. Where there are children of the marriage the possible obligation of a parent to make child maintenance payments to the Child Support Agency is a further factor requiring detailed review.

Payments made under 'old' orders or agreements may continue to obtain some relief, but this must be limited to the amount payable in 1988–89. It follows that where such an agreement or order is subsequently increased, the payer will obtain no tax relief for the amount of the increase.

Although the transfer of assets between husband and wife 'living together' incurs no liability to capital gains tax, this exemption no longer applies once they are separated, or indeed divorced. Where the value of assets is substantial, this often creates considerable liability to capital gains tax. It is essential that parties to a marriage breakdown take professional advice on their potential tax commitments at an early stage.

Interest

Unless payments of interest can be deducted in calculating business profits, or profits of a Schedule of business, stringent requirements must be satisfied before the outgoing will qualify for relief in calculating income chargeable to tax. No relief is available for interest payable on a bank overdraft, and whenever possible a more permanent form of borrowing should be used.

Interest on a loan applied to acquire an individual's only or main residence will usually qualify for relief, subject to a maximum ceiling of £30,000 and with relief limited to the reduced rate of 15 per cent for 1995–96. Some individuals may obtain a loan on the security of an existing dwelling but no relief can be obtained for the subsequent payment of interest, unless the loan is applied for a qualifying purpose. If the need to obtain additional finance can be anticipated, it may be advisable to await the need for funds to ensure that any borrowings are applied to a purpose which enables tax relief to be obtained.

Relief may continue for interest paid on loans applied before 6 April 1988 on the acquisition of a private residence for occupation by a separated spouse, divorced former spouse or a dependent relative. Relief may also be forthcoming where the loan was applied to improve the residence. However, if qualifying occupation is discontinued, or the old loan replaced by a new loan, future relief for interest paid will be lost.

Interest on funds borrowed by an individual to refinance a partnership of which that individual is a member may only obtain partial relief if refinancing takes place on or after 31 March 1994.

MIRAS

Income tax relief is obtained by deduction where MIRAS applies to interest payments. A number of conditions must be satisfactorily discharged before MIRAS can apply, and failure to observe those conditions may later have serious consequences. As a general rule, MIRAS is limited to interest paid on a loan applied to acquire a qualifying home. It cannot be obtained on property used for some other purpose or on property merely provided as security. Particular difficulties arise where two single individuals each have loans under MIRAS and subsequently marry. In the case of a husband and wife 'living together' there can be only one recognised 'only or main residence'. Relief is limited to interest paid on a loan applied to acquire that residence and cannot extend to a loan on some other property. Nor can the couple obtain relief for interest on aggregate loans in excess of £30,000.

It is of great importance that when completing the initial MIRAS documents, or where some future change in circumstances takes place, the lender is made fully aware of the position. Subsequent detection that MIRAS has been applied to a non-qualifying loan may not only lead to a demand for the recovery of excessive relief but can result in demands for interest and penalties also.

Children

Minor children are entitled to the basic personal allowance of £3,525 for 1995–96. Many children have little, if any, income, unless they leave school or undertake a part-time job. This means that the personal allowance will be lost. To utilise that allowance, a grandparent, uncle or aunt would sometimes enter into a deed of covenant providing the child with income. Similar arrangements were used by parents having children over the age of 18 years and attending university or some other form of higher education establishment. On making payments under a deed of covenant the payer would usually deduct and retain income tax at the basic rate. The child could often obtain a repayment of the tax deducted from the Inland Revenue.

No payments made under such deeds of covenant entered into after 14 March 1988 will be recognised for taxation purposes. Nor is it possible to backdate a deed executed on some later date.

Covenants executed before 15 March 1988 and inspected by HM Inspector of Taxes not later than 30 June in the same year remained valid but any payments made after 5 April 1995 must now be disregarded for tax purposes.

Grandparents may contemplate placing funds in a building society account, bank deposit account or other income-producing investment in the name of a child as this can provide income absorbed by the annual allowance. Parents may undertake similar arrangements for their minor children but where income exceeds £100 it may be treated as that of the parent for income tax purposes. It is as well to take professional advice before parents transfer assets to, or for the benefit of, their minor children.

Charitable covenants

No income tax relief is available to individuals making modest voluntary gifts to charity unless those payments are made under an approved payroll deduction scheme. However, regular donors should contemplate using deeds of covenant. Payments made under charitable covenants enable the payer to obtain tax relief at the highest rate of tax suffered, without any limitation on the amount paid for 1995–96.

Single donations of £250 or more under the Gift Aid scheme will provide relief on a basis similar to that for payments under deed of covenant. Those contemplating substantial donations of an irregular amount may prefer the flexibility of Gift Aid to a formal deed of covenant.

DIRECTORS AND EMPLOYEES

Living accommodation

An additional taxable benefit arises where a director or employee is provided with expensive living accommodation. This benefit applies if the cost of the accommodation, together with the cost of carrying out improvements, exceeds £75,000. Those occupying property acquired at a cost falling below the £75,000 threshold should carefully consider the wisdom of moving to more expensive property where the threshold is to be exceeded. The move may create a taxable benefit which would not otherwise arise.

Car benefits

Directors and higher-paid employees provided with motor cars for private motoring suffer tax on the car benefit. This benefit must usually be calculated by reference to the list price of a vehicle, perhaps increased by the list price of accessories. The basic benefit arising from the availability of vehicle less than four years old is 35 per cent of the list price, or aggregate of list prices where accessories are involved. This is reduced by one-third where there are 2,500 miles of business motoring in a year or reduced by two-thirds where business motoring exceeds 18,000 miles annually. Wherever possible attempts should be made to exceed these thresholds and reduce the amount of the taxable benefit.

Those making little use of a motor vehicle may wish to consider whether the arrangement should continue. It may be cost efficient for an individual to provide his or her own motor vehicle for business travel and to receive a 'tax-free' mileage allowance under the Fixed Profit Car Scheme.

Particular consideration should be given to the proposed purchase by an employer of a 'classic' or 'veteran' motor car. Vehicles of this nature will usually be more than fifteen years of age and may well have a market value exceeding £15,000. It is the market value and not the original list price which governs the calculation of the taxable benefit for such vehicles. The magnitude of this benefit should always be considered before arranging for the purchase of an expensive or valuable motor car by an employer where that vehicle is to be used for private motoring.

Loss of office

The first £30,000 received as compensation for the loss of an office or employment is usually tax-free. Where dismissal or redundancy is likely and negotiations are taking place between the parties, there may be an advantage in accepting a tax-free lump sum, rather than an extended period of notice with taxable earnings.

BUSINESS CONSIDERATIONS

Accounting date

When a new business was commenced special rules previously applied to determine the amount of profits chargeable to income tax in the opening years. Once the business had become established profits assessable to tax were usually based on profits earned for a twelve-month period ending in the previous year. For example, if accounts were prepared annually to 31 March, profits for the year ending on 31 March 1993 were assessable in 1993–94 with tax becoming payable by equal instalments on 1 January and 1 July 1994. In contrast, where accounts were prepared to 30 April the results for the year ending on 30 April 1993 would be assessed for 1994–95 with tax becoming payable on 1 January and 1 July 1995. Some deferment in the payment of tax could therefore be achieved by adopting an annual accounting date ending shortly after 5 April.

This strategy generally remains available for established businesses until the introduction of a new current year basis of assessment. However, new businesses commenced on and after 6 April 1994 will not become involved in the preceding year basis of assessment. Different considerations will therefore apply when establishing an annual accounting date.

Of particular concern to the proprietors of all businesses commenced before 6 April 1994 is the selection of a future accounting date. In many situations an accounting date falling towards the end of a year of assessment, perhaps on 31 March, will secure many advantages. The main advantage is the duration of the final period used to measure liability in the year of assessment during which a business comes to an end. However, generalisation can be dangerous and accountancy advice should be obtained by all individuals continuing a business commenced before 5 April 1994. This advice will not only concern the advisability or otherwise of changing an established annual accounting date. It will also review the complex legislation which has been introduced to frustrate potential tax avoidance. This avoidance largely falls under two main headings, namely, the basis of assessment used for 1996–97, which will result in some profits not becoming assessable to tax, and the special overlap relief which can be obtained for profits arising in a period of account overlapping 5 April 1997.

Capital allowances

Attractive first-year and initial allowances were available for expenditure incurred, or contracts entered into, between 1 November 1992 and 31 October 1993. These allowances have no application subsequently. However, annual writing-down allowances remain available for many assets used for business purposes. It is sometimes considered that by advancing the date of payment allowances may fall into an earlier year of assessment or company accounting period. This possibility must be approached with considerable caution. For example, in the case of plant and machinery not only must expenditure be incurred but an asset must usually 'belong to' the person incurring that expenditure before an allowance will become available. An invoice or other document backdated before the time on which ownership changes hands will not be sufficient.

National insurance contributions

Class 1 national insurance contributions are based on the level of 'earnings' paid to an employed individual. Primary contributions suffered by an employee are subject to a threshold. Once this threshold has been reached, contributions are not payable on the excess. No similar threshold applies to secondary contributions payable by the employer who must satisfy contributions on all earnings of higher paid employees. Some employers may consider whether employees should be offered 'perks' or 'benefits', rather than an increase in salary. Certain advantages of this nature, whilst creating taxable benefits in the hands of employees, are disregarded when determining the level of earnings on which contributions must be paid, although recent changes have substantially reduced this advantage. The availability of a car for private motoring and the provision of fuel for a similar purpose will involve the employer, but not the employee, in a further liability to discharge contributions.

In the case of closely controlled family companies advantages may arise from the payment of dividends, or possibly rent for the use of assets, rather than remuneration. Before any steps of this nature are taken detailed consideration must be given to the possible effect on other forms of taxation. In particular it will not be overlooked that with the reduction in the rate of advance corporation tax to 20 per cent, many of the advantages from paying dividends have been eroded.

Transfer of business

Individuals carrying on business on their own account, or as members of a partnership, may contemplate the transfer of that business to a newly incorporated company. A transfer of this nature will be treated as the discontinuance of the old business and require the application of special rules for determining liability to income tax in the closing years. Before deciding on the proposed date of transfer consideration must be given to the impending introduction of a current year basis of assessment. This change may affect the date on which a business should be transferred as there may be either savings to be achieved or additional tax to be avoided.

INVESTMENT OPPORTUNITIES

Life assurance

No tax relief is available for premiums paid on new life assurance policies made after 13 March 1984.

However, relief continues for qualifying policies made on or before this date, unless the terms of the policy are altered. Relief reduces the cost of premiums by 12.5 per cent and this should be recognised before contemplating the surrender of older policies, or taking any steps which may terminate future relief.

Pensions for the employed

Employees who are members of a company, or other, occupational pension scheme obtain relief for contributions paid to secure benefits. The maximum relief is broadly limited to contributions not exceeding 15 per cent of earnings. Few schemes require contributions at this level but the employee may utilise the shortfall by paying additional voluntary contributions. The aggregate contributions paid must not result in the 15 per cent limit being exceeded, but subject to this the additional contributions may be paid to trustees administering the employer's scheme or to a 'free-standing' approved financial institution. These contributions produce relief at the employee's highest rate of income tax. For example, an individual paying additional voluntary contributions of £1,000 and suffering tax at the higher rate of 40 per cent for 1995–96 will reduce his or her tax bill by £400, so that the true net outlay is only £600. Membership of an employer's pension scheme is no longer compulsory but before ceasing to participate in such a scheme employees should carefully review the available alternatives. It may be found that these alternatives do not justify removal from the scheme.

Pensions for the self-employed and others

Self-employed individuals and employees not covered by a pension scheme may contribute up to 17.5 per cent, or perhaps more for those aged over 35, of their earnings to a personal pension scheme or a retirement annuity scheme. Premiums paid may be set against taxable income. Where insufficient premiums have been paid in any year the balance of unused relief may be carried forward for a maximum six-year period. Any unused relief remaining at the end of this six-year period is lost. Those able to contribute should consider the advisability of paying maximum contributions, particularly where they are approaching retirement age. Although the purpose of paying contributions is to provide a pension or annuity in retirement, it is possible to obtain a tax-free lump sum, with reduced periodic payments in the future.

Enterprise investment schemes

Tax relief can be obtained for the costs of subscribing for shares in a qualifying company where the enterprise investment scheme requirements are satisfied. Maximum relief is available on share subscriptions up to £100,000 in each year of assessment, although relief is limited to the lower rate of 20 per cent only. If any part of the £100,000 relief available for 1995–96 remains unused, it may be possible to utilise all or part of the balance by making investments in the first six months of 1996–97 which are related back to the previous year. Subject to this, any unused relief cannot be carried forward and will be lost.

Venture capital trusts

The subscription for shares in venture capital trusts will enable tax relief to be obtained at the rate of 20 per cent. This relief is limited to subscriptions not exceeding in aggregate £100,000 in 1995–96. Like subscriptions under the enterprise investment scheme, this effectively reduces the subscription cost by one-fifth. In addition, distributions from holdings in venture capital trusts incur no liability to income tax.

Enterprise zones

Capital allowances up to a maximum of 100 per cent are available for the cost of constructing buildings, including commercial buildings, in an enterprise zone. It is possible for these allowances to be set against income generally and the year in which relief is to be obtained should be carefully selected.

Investment generally

A modest tax efficient investment is the purchase of National Savings certificates, as interest arising to the eventual date of realisation is not liable to income tax. An identical yield will be received by those who suffer tax at the higher rate and those who are not chargeable. This may prove a particular attraction for higher rate taxpayers as the tax free annual compound yield of 5.85 per cent which, for example, is available on the 42nd issue held throughout the full five-year period, is equal to a gross yield of 9.75 per cent on which tax is suffered at 40 per cent.

A further tax efficient investment is a deposit in a TESSA account where interest is free of tax if the deposit remains undisturbed throughout a five-year period. This five-year period will terminate in January 1996 for those who made deposits at the inception of the TESSA scheme. It is possible to reinvest the entire capital proceeds on the maturity of a TESSA in a second TESSA. This overcomes the limitation on the amount which can be lodged in the first year of a deposit account.

Holdings of personal equity plans where both dividends and capital gains avoid the inroads of taxation are also tax efficient.

Interest received from building societies, banks and some other financial institutions suffers income tax by deduction at the basic rate. Investors not liable, or not fully liable, may obtain a repayment of any excessive tax deducted. Those of small means and not liable to tax may arrange for interest to be paid or credited gross. Interest on some government securities, with the addition of securities on the National Savings Stock Register and National Savings Income Bonds, is paid gross without deduction of income tax. Holdings of this nature also avoid the need to claim any repayment of tax, although where the investor is liable any tax must be paid.

A note of caution

Newspaper advertisements sometimes list attractive opportunities for investment designed to secure tax advantages or to provide an excessive income yield. Before taking advantage of the opportunities offered, potential investors should fully understand the working of the scheme and establish that it is not vulnerable to attack by the Inland Revenue. If substantial sums are involved, it may be worthwhile taking independent professional advice.

CAPITAL GAINS TAX

Annual exemption

The first £6,000 of gains, less losses, realised by an individual from the disposal of assets in the year ended 5 April 1996 are exempt from capital gains tax. If the exemption is not fully used the excess cannot be carried forward to the following year. Attempts should therefore be made to fully utilise the exemption, perhaps by bringing forward disposals to a date falling before 6 April 1996. In cases where the exemption limit has already been exceeded, disposals may possibly be deferred until the following year.

Losses

Where gains exceed the annual exemption of £6,000, it may be advisable to consider whether the excess gains can be reduced by creating losses. In some cases this may be achieved by bringing forward a disposal date which would otherwise fall after 5 April, or perhaps by arranging 'bed and breakfast'

transactions whereby shares are sold to produce a loss and subsequently reacquired.

Government securities

No capital gains tax will be payable on the disposal of Government securities and many securities (but not shares) issued by quoted and unquoted companies. Those retaining substantial holdings of securities should not overlook the accrued income scheme for calculating liability to income tax.

Deferment of tax

Liability to capital gains tax for disposals taking place in the year ended 5 April 1996 requires satisfaction on 1 December 1996. In some cases where the exemption of £6,000 has been used, it may be thought advisable to defer the contemplated disposal of assets until a date falling after 5 April 1996. This will delay payment of tax until 31 January 1998.

Roll-over relief

There are now several different forms of roll-over relief which can be applied to avoid or defer immediate liability to capital gains tax. Of particular interest to many investors will be subscriptions in enterprise investment scheme shares, subscriptions in venture capital trusts and direct investments in shares issued by many unquoted trading companies. In some situations roll-over relief will merely postpone the date on which capital gains tax becomes payable. In others it will reduce the cost of acquiring replacement assets. Several requirements must be satisfied and time limits adhered to before relief can be obtained. These matters must receive speedy attention where a gain is likely to arise or there is some possibility that previous relief may be withdrawn due to failure to satisfy some ongoing requirement.

Rate of tax

The rate of capital gains tax due on chargeable gains will reflect an individual's marginal rate of income tax. Where income is expected to fluctuate considerably as between one year and another, this could become a factor governing the year in which a planned disposal should be made.

INHERITANCE TAX

Annual exemption

Few lifetime gifts and dispositions now incur liability to inheritance tax. If a lifetime transaction within the limited range producing liability is contemplated, the annual exemption of £3,000 should not be overlooked. This applies to gifts made in a year ending on 5 April, and if the exemption is not fully utilised in a particular year the excess can be carried forward and absorbed in the following year only. An aggregate exemption of £6,000 may therefore be obtained for 1995–96 if no part of the exemption has been used in the previous year. Failure to absorb the amount brought forward in the second year will result in the exemption being lost. Wherever possible the available exemption should be used.

Gifts with reservation

The making of a lifetime gift which reserves some benefit to the donor may create liability to inheritance tax on death, unless the reservation ceased to apply more than seven years before the time of death. Gifts made subject to reservation which do not fall within a list of exceptions are to be firmly avoided.

Potentially exempt transfers

Many lifetime gifts made by an individual to a second individual or to a limited range of trustees comprise potentially exempt transfers. No liability to inheritance tax will arise should the donor survive the seven year inter vivos period. There is an obvious attraction of making such gifts at the earliest possible date.

Gifts within seven years before death

Should the donor die within seven years of making a gift, liability to inheritance tax may arise on the value of the gift. Although this is mainly designed to frustrate 'deathbed gifts', it will apply equally to all gifts within the seven-year period. The subsequent date of a donor's death cannot usually be anticipated with any measure of accuracy, except in the case of terminal illness, and an unexpected death within the seven-year period may create substantial liability to inheritance tax. In some situations it may be thought advisable to secure funds for the possible satisfaction of tax payable on gifts by means of a term assurance policy.

Reliefs

Certain reliefs, notably business asset relief and agricultural property relief, will only be available if assets have been owned throughout a required period of time ending on the date of a lifetime disposition or death. The need to establish a qualifying period should be recognised before transferring assets, particularly between members of a family, where ownership must inevitably change. Other requirements must be satisfied between the date of a gift comprising a potentially exempt transfer and the time of death if reliefs are to be preserved.

The need to satisfy these requirements is of particular importance where relief is available at the rate of 100 per cent for many business assets and a range of agricultural property.

Other considerations

Savings in inheritance tax and other tax considerations must never reflect the sole reason for making gifts. Once the ownership of assets has been transferred those assets will cease to be available to the donor, if the transaction is to secure the required tax advantages. Those contemplating substantial gifts must recognise the depletion in their available assets and perhaps a reduction in future income which the transfer will create.

GENERAL MATTERS

Claims and elections

Many tax advantages are only available if a written claim or election is lodged with the Inland Revenue. There is a very long list of time limits governing different elections and claims and it is essential that these limits are fully observed. If they are not, unexpected tax liabilities may arise.

Disclosure of information

The law requires that taxpayers should disclose details of income, profits or gains to the Inland Revenue, although this is of limited significance to those whose only income is derived from an employment and the PAYE deduction scheme applies. Failure to disclose details of a part-time job, the existence of a business, or details of chargeable gains assessable to capital gains tax, may have serious consequences. Not only will tax become payable but the individual may incur additional liabilities to interest and penalties.

Self-assessment

The impending introduction of self-assessment is a matter which many taxpayers cannot afford to overlook. Those required to complete a tax return for 1996–97 should carefully review the comments made in the chapter commencing on page 140. Others who do not receive a tax return but have income, profits or gains on which tax has not been paid must be prepared to advise the Inland Revenue at an early date. If they do not a liability to interest, penalties and surcharges may arise.

25

Action before 6 April 1996

AS THE END of the tax year approaches on 5 April 1996, taxpayers should consider whether any action is needed to reduce tax payable. The Chancellor of the Exchequer is due to deliver his Budget Statement towards the end of November 1995. This should disclose details of any tax rate changes coming into operation on 6 April 1996 and enable a comparison to be made with those in operation for the previous year. In addition, the following matters may be significant, among many others:

☐ Claims for repayment of income tax must be made within a period of six years from the end of the year of assessment to which those claims relate. The time limit for submitting claims in respect of 1989–90 expires on 5 April 1996.

☐ Elections which may be of interest to a large number of taxpayers concern the married couple's allowance. A wife 'living with' her husband can elect to receive one-half of the basic allowance for 1996–97 if action is taken not later than 5 April 1996. It is also possible for the entire basic allowance to accrue for the benefit of the wife only, if a suitable claim is submitted by the same date. New elections will not be necessary if a suitable election has already been made, unless that election is to be varied. Those contemplating new elections will recognise that for 1995–96 the married couple's allowance produces relief at the reduced rate of 15 per cent only. Whether this reduced rate will apply for the following year remains to be seen.

☐ Many other claims and elections have time limits expiring on 5 April 1996. For example, claims to relieve losses must usually be made within a period of two years from the end of the year of assessment in which those losses arose. An 'interest allocation election', which apportions interest paid between husband and wife, must be submitted not later than 5 April 1996 if it is to apply for 1994–95.

☐ Any additional voluntary pension contributions paid by an employed person must be satisfied by 5 April 1996 if they are to reduce the tax bill for 1995–96.

☐ Personal pension scheme contributions and retirement annuity premiums paid during the year ending on 5 April 1996 may be treated as satisfied in 1994–95, or perhaps earlier, if an election is made. The election may be particularly advantageous if the 17.5 per cent, or higher, maximum has not been fully used in the earlier year. Unused relief for previous years can be carried forward for a maximum of six years. This enables unused relief for 1988–89 to be used in the year ended on 5 April 1995 and that for 1989–90 to be utilised in the year ending on 5 April 1996. These are matters which an individual should carefully consider when paying premiums not later than 5 April 1996 which can, at his or her option, be allocated to the year ending on that date or to some previous year.

☐ There may be an advantage in entering into a deed of covenant in favour of a charity before 6 April 1996 to establish tax relief for a payment made under that deed in 1995–96. Those able to make substantial donations under the Gift Aid scheme may consider action before 6 April 1996 if tax relief is to be obtained at the higher rate for 1995–96.

□ A maximum of £6,000 may be invested in a general PEP, or £3,000 in a single company PEP, during the year ending on 6 April 1996. Investors who have not taken advantage of these limits should consider their position as 5 April 1996 approaches.

□ Investments up to a maximum of £100,000 can be made in an enterprise investment scheme during a tax year and obtain the relief at the rate of 20 per cent. A similar maximum and rate of relief applies to investments in a venture enterprise trust. These are matters which should receive attention by potential investors who have not taken advantage of the investment possibilities as the end of 1995–96 looms.

□ Employees earning £8,500 or more and directors provided with cars for private motoring should attempt to achieve 2,500 or 18,000 miles of business motoring before midnight on 5 April 1996 is reached. The mileage travelled will govern the amount of taxable benefit.

These individuals will be aware that the cal-culation of taxable benefits arising from the avail-ability of motor cars is now based on the list price of the vehicle and any accessories. The use of this basis should not be overlooked when replacing a car or adding expensive accessories to an existing vehicle. The application of this system could support a decision to change an existing model for the purpose of avoiding excessive liability to taxation.

□ If the full exemption of £6,000 is to be used for capital gains tax purposes in 1995–96, it may be necessary to undertake the disposal of additional assets not later than 5 April 1995. Action may also be required to create losses which reduce that part of any gains which exceed the exemption limit.

□ Any part of the annual inheritance tax exemption amounting to £3,000 and which has not been used in the year ending on 5 April 1995 will be lost unless it is utilised not later than 5 April 1996.

□ There may be an advantage in making an uncon-ditional gift of an asset between husband and wife, for the purpose of establishing the person on whom future income will be assessed for 1996–97.

SOCIAL SECURITY BENEFITS

WHILST SOME social security benefits are taxable, many do not incur liability to income tax. The general rule is that benefits which replace lost earnings are subject to tax, whereas those intended to meet a specific need of the claimant are not. A list of the taxable and non-taxable benefits is shown below:

BENEFITS WHICH ARE TAXABLE
Incapacity benefit (see Note 3)
Income support paid to the unemployed (see Note 1)
Industrial death benefit pensions
Invalid care allowance (see Note 2)
Retirement pension (see Note 5)
Statutory maternity pay
Statutory sick pay
Unemployment benefit (see Note 2)
Widowed mother's allowance (see Note 2)
Widow's pension

BENEFITS WHICH ARE NOT TAXABLE
Attendance allowance
Child benefit
Child's special allowance
Disability living allowance
Disability working allowance
Family credit
Guardian's allowance
Housing benefit
Income support (see Note 1)
Industrial disablement benefit
Invalidity benefit (see Note 3)
Maternity allowance
One-parent benefit
Severe disablement allowance
Sickness benefit (see Note 3)
Social fund payments
War widow's pension
Widow's payments

Notes:

1 Income support is taxable when paid to unemployed people who have to sign on, or to strikers or those directly interested in a trade dispute.

2 Child dependent additions to those benefits are not taxable.

3 Both invalidity benefit and sickness benefit were previously exempt from income tax. However these two benefits were replaced by incapacity benefit from 6 April 1995. Unlike its predecessors incapacity benefit is chargeable to income tax but there are exceptions. No tax is due on that part of any increased incapacity benefit attributable to a child. Nor is tax due on that part of the benefit payable for the initial period of incapacity, namely the period for which short-term incapacity benefit is payable otherwise than at the higher rate for the first 28 weeks.

4 Payments of short-term sick pay made by the recipient's employer are taxable through the PAYE deduction scheme but the previous long-term sickness benefit which the employer was not required to pay remained exempt from liability. Statutory maternity pay is also discharged by employers, with PAYE being deducted where required.

5 A married woman's retirement pension paid on the basis of her husband's contributions is treated as income of the wife. Where the pension includes an adult dependency addition the entire pension will also be regarded as that of the recipient.

6 The method of collecting tax on unemployment benefit is discussed on page 41.

7 Unemployment benefits are to be replaced by a new job-seeker's allowance at a later date.

RATES OF INCOME TAX FOR EARLIER YEARS

FOR THE CONVENIENCE of those readers who may wish to know the rates of income tax for earlier years, the following tables show the rates for the past six years.

1989–90 Basic rate 25 per cent

Higher rate (*payable on taxable income exceeding £20,700*)
40%

1990–91 Basic rate 25 per cent

Higher rate (*payable on taxable income exceeding £20,700*)
40%

1991–92 Basic rate 25 per cent

Higher rate (*payable on taxable income exceeding £23,700*)
40%

1992–93 Basic rate 25 per cent

Lower rate (*payable on first £2,000 of taxable income*)
20%
Higher rate (*payable on taxable income exceeding £23,700*)
40%

1993–94 Basic rate 25 per cent

Lower rate (*payable on first £2,500 of taxable income*)
20%
Higher rate (*payable on taxable income exceeding £23,700*)
40%

1994–95 Basic rate 25 per cent

Lower rate (*payable on first £3,000 of taxable income*)
20%
Higher rate (*payable on taxable income exceeding £23,700*)
40%

RATES OF INHERITANCE TAX

Events after 17 March 1986
but before 17 March 1987

Portion of value	Rate per cent
£ £	
0– 71,000	Nil
71,001– 95,000	30
95,001–129,000	35
129,001–164,000	40
164,001–206,000	45
206,001–257,000	50
257,001–317,000	55
317,001 and above	60

Events after 16 March 1987
but before 15 March 1988

Portion of value	Rate per cent
£ £	
0– 90,000	Nil
90,001–140,000	30
140,001–220,000	40
220,001–330,000	50
330,001 and above	60

Events after 14 March 1988
but before 6 April 1989

Portion of value	Rate per cent
£ £	
0–110,000	Nil
110,001 and above	40

Events after 5 April 1989
but before 6 April 1990

Portion of value	Rate per cent
£ £	
0–118,000	Nil
118,001 and above	40

Events after 5 April 1990
but before 6 April 1991

Portion of value	Rate per cent
£ £	
0–128,000	Nil
128,001 and above	40

Events after 5 April 1991
but before 10 March 1992

Portion of value	Rate per cent
£ £	
0–140,000	Nil
140,001 and above	40

Events after 9 March 1992
but before 6 April 1995

Portion of value	Rate per cent
£ £	
0–150,000	Nil
150,001 and above	40

Events after 5 April 1995

Portion of value	Rate per cent
£ £	
0–154,000	Nil
154,001 and above	40

TAX PAYABLE ON SPECIMEN INCOMES – 1995–96

	SINGLE PERSON OR MARRIED WOMAN[4]			MARRIED MAN[4]	
On total income of	Persons under 65 years of age		Persons over 65[2]	Persons under 65 years of age[2]	Persons over 65[2]
	One person[2]	One parent family[3]			
£	£	£	£	£	£
4,000	95.00	—	—	—	—
4,500	195.00	—	—	—	—
5,000	295.00	37.00	74.00	37.00	—
5,500	395.00	137.00	174.00	137.00	—
6,000	495.00	237.00	274.00	237.00	—
6,500	595.00	337.00	374.00	337.00	—
7,000	708.75	450.75	474.00	450.75	24.75
8,000	958.75	700.75	682.50	700.75	233.25
9,000	1,208.75	950.75	932.50	950.75	483.25
10,000	1,458.75	1,200.75	1,182.50	1,200.75	733.25
12,000	1,958.75	1,700.75	1,682.50	1,700.75	1,233.25
14,000	2,458.75	2,200.75	2,182.50	2,200.75	1,733.25
16,000	2,958.75	2,700.75	2,857.50	2,700.75	2,408.25
18,000	3,458.75	3,160.75	3,458.75	3,160.75	3,098.75
20,000	3,958.75	3,700.75	3,958.75	3,700.75	3,700.75
25,000	5,208.75	4,950.75	5,208.75	4,950.75	4,950.75
30,000	6,785.00	6,527.00	6,785.00	6,527.00	6,527.00
35,000	8,785.00	8,527.00	8,785.00	8,527.00	8,527.00
40,000	10,785.00	10,527.00	10,785.00	10,527.00	10,527.00
45,000	12,785.00	12,527.00	12,785.00	12,527.00	12,527.00
50,000	14,785.00	14,527.00	14,785.00	14,527.00	14,527.00
75,000	24,785.00	24,527.00	24,785.00	24,527.00	24,527.00
100,000	34,785.00	34,527.00	34,785.00	34,527.00	34,527.00
150,000	54,785.00	54,527.00	54,785.00	54,527.00	54,527.00

NOTES [1] The same amount of tax becomes payable whether income is earned or unearned.

[2] The tax shown is that due where there are no allowances other than the personal allowance and the married couple's allowance, as appropriate. Rather less tax will be payable by elderly persons aged 75 or over.

[3] A single person with a qualifying child receives both the personal allowance and an additional personal allowance of £1,720.

[4] The entire married couple's allowance has been allocated to the husband only.

READY RECKONER

Based on tax at 25 per cent

1p to 99p (to the nearest whole penny)

Amount	Tax	Amount	Tax	Amount	Tax
£	£	£	£	£	£
0.01	—	0.34	0.09	0.67	0.17
0.02	0.01	0.35	0.09	0.68	0.17
0.03	0.01	0.36	0.09	0.69	0.17
0.04	0.01	0.37	0.09	0.70	0.18
0.05	0.01	0.38	0.10	0.71	0.18
0.06	0.02	0.39	0.10	0.72	0.18
0.07	0.02	0.40	0.10	0.73	0.18
0.08	0.02	0.41	0.10	0.74	0.19
0.09	0.02	0.42	0.11	0.75	0.19
0.10	0.03	0.43	0.11	0.76	0.19
0.11	0.03	0.44	0.11	0.77	0.19
0.12	0.03	0.45	0.11	0.78	0.20
0.13	0.03	0.46	0.12	0.79	0.20
0.14	0.04	0.47	0.12	0.80	0.20
0.15	0.04	0.48	0.12	0.81	0.20
0.16	0.04	0.49	0.12	0.82	0.21
0.17	0.04	0.50	0.13	0.83	0.21
0.18	0.05	0.51	0.13	0.84	0.21
0.19	0.05	0.52	0.13	0.85	0.21
0.20	0.05	0.53	0.13	0.86	0.22
0.21	0.05	0.54	0.14	0.87	0.22
0.22	0.06	0.55	0.14	0.88	0.22
0.23	0.06	0.56	0.14	0.89	0.22
0.24	0.06	0.57	0.14	0.90	0.23
0.25	0.06	0.58	0.15	0.91	0.23
0.26	0.07	0.59	0.15	0.92	0.23
0.27	0.07	0.60	0.15	0.93	0.23
0.28	0.07	0.61	0.15	0.94	0.24
0.29	0.07	0.62	0.16	0.95	0.24
0.30	0.08	0.63	0.16	0.96	0.24
0.31	0.08	0.64	0.16	0.97	0.24
0.32	0.08	0.65	0.16	0.98	0.25
0.33	0.08	0.66	0.17	0.99	0.25

£1 to £50,000

Amount	Tax	Amount	Tax	Amount	Tax	Amount	Tax
£	£	£	£	£	£	£	£
1	0.25	46	11.50	91	22.75	136	34.00
2	0.50	47	11.75	92	23.00	137	34.25
3	0.75	48	12.00	93	23.25	138	34.50
4	1.00	49	12.25	94	23.50	139	34.75
5	1.25	50	12.50	95	23.75	140	35.00
6	1.50	51	12.75	96	24.00	141	35.25
7	1.75	52	13.00	97	24.25	142	35.50
8	2.00	53	13.25	98	24.50	143	35.75
9	2.25	54	13.50	99	24.75	144	36.00
10	2.50	55	13.75	100	25.00	145	36.25
11	2.75	56	14.00	101	25.25	146	36.50
12	3.00	57	14.25	102	25.50	147	36.75
13	3.25	58	14.50	103	25.75	148	37.00
14	3.50	59	14.75	104	26.00	149	37.25
15	3.75	60	15.00	105	26.25	150	37.50
16	4.00	61	15.25	106	26.50	200	50.00
17	4.25	62	15.50	107	26.75	250	62.50
18	4.50	63	15.75	108	27.00	300	75.00
19	4.75	64	16.00	109	27.25	350	87.50
20	5.00	65	16.25	110	27.50	400	100.00
21	5.25	66	16.50	111	27.75	450	112.50
22	5.50	67	16.75	112	28.00	500	125.00
23	5.75	68	17.00	113	28.25	550	137.50
24	6.00	69	17.25	114	28.50	500	150.00
25	6.25	70	17.50	115	28.75	650	162.50
26	6.50	71	17.75	116	29.00	700	175.00
27	6.75	72	18.00	117	29.25	750	187.50
28	7.00	73	18.25	118	29.50	800	200.00
29	7.25	74	18.50	119	29.75	850	212.50
30	7.50	75	18.75	120	30.00	900	225.00
31	7.75	76	19.00	121	30.25	950	237.50
32	8.00	77	19.25	122	30.50	1,000	250.00
33	8.25	78	19.50	123	30.75	1,500	375.00
34	8.50	79	19.75	124	31.00	2,000	500.00
35	8.75	80	20.00	125	31.25	2,500	625.00
36	9.00	81	20.25	126	31.50	3,000	750.00
37	9.25	82	20.50	127	31.75	3,500	875.00
38	9.50	83	20.75	128	32.00	4,000	1,000.00
39	9.75	84	21.00	129	32.25	4,500	1,125.00
40	10.00	85	21.25	130	32.50	5,000	1,250.00
41	10.25	86	21.50	131	32.75	7,500	1,875.00
42	10.50	87	21.75	132	33.00	10,000	2,500.00
43	10.75	88	22.00	133	33.25	21,100	5,275.00
44	11.00	89	22.25	134	33.50	25,000	6,250.00
45	11.25	90	22.50	135	33.75	50,000	12,500.00

READY RECKONER

Based on tax at 20 per cent

Amount £	Tax £	Amount £	Tax £	Amount £	Tax £	Amount £	Tax £
1	0.20	46	9.20	91	18.20	136	27.20
2	0.40	47	9.40	92	18.40	137	27.40
3	0.60	48	9.60	93	18.60	138	27.60
4	0.80	49	9.80	94	18.80	139	27.80
5	1.00	50	10.00	95	19.00	140	28.00
6	1.20	51	10.20	96	19.20	141	28.20
7	1.40	52	10.40	97	19.40	142	28.40
8	1.60	53	10.60	98	19.60	143	28.60
9	1.80	54	10.80	99	19.80	144	28.80
10	2.00	55	11.00	100	20.00	145	29.00
11	2.20	56	11.20	101	20.20	146	29.20
12	2.40	57	11.40	102	20.40	147	29.40
13	2.60	58	11.60	103	20.60	148	29.60
14	2.80	59	11.80	104	20.80	149	29.80
15	3.00	60	12.00	105	21.00	150	30.00
16	3.20	61	12.20	106	21.20	200	40.00
17	3.40	62	12.40	107	21.40	250	50.00
18	3.60	63	12.60	108	21.60	300	60.00
19	3.80	64	12.80	109	21.80	350	70.00
20	4.00	65	13.00	110	22.00	400	80.00
21	4.20	66	13.20	111	22.20	450	90.00
22	4.40	67	13.40	112	22.40	500	100.00
23	4.60	68	13.60	113	22.60	550	110.00
24	4.80	69	13.80	114	22.80	600	120.00
25	5.00	70	14.00	115	23.00	650	130.00
26	5.20	71	14.20	116	23.20	700	140.00
27	5.40	72	14.40	117	23.40	750	150.00
28	5.60	73	14.60	118	23.60	800	160.00
29	5.80	74	14.80	119	23.80	850	170.00
30	6.00	75	15.00	120	24.00	900	180.00
31	6.20	76	15.20	121	24.20	950	190.00
32	6.40	77	15.40	122	24.40	1,000	200.00
33	6.60	78	15.60	123	24.60	1,100	220.00
34	6.80	79	15.80	124	24.80	1,200	240.00
35	7.00	80	16.00	125	25.00	1,300	260.00
36	7.20	81	16.20	126	25.20	1,400	280.00
37	7.40	82	16.40	127	25.40	1,500	300.00
38	7.60	83	16.60	128	25.60	1,600	320.00
39	7.80	84	16.80	129	25.80	1,700	340.00
40	8.00	85	17.00	130	26.00	1,800	360.00
41	8.20	86	17.20	131	26.20	1,900	380.00
42	8.40	87	17.40	132	26.40	2,000	400.00
43	8.60	88	17.60	133	26.60	2,500	500.00
44	8.80	89	17.80	134	26.80	3,000	600.00
45	9.00	90	18.00	135	27.00	3,200	640.00

READY RECKONER

Based on tax at 40 per cent

Amount	Tax	Amount	Tax	Amount	Tax	Amount	Tax
£	£	£	£	£	£	£	£
1	0.40	46	18.40	91	36.40	136	54.40
2	0.80	47	18.80	92	36.80	137	54.80
3	1.20	48	19.20	93	37.20	138	55.20
4	1.60	49	19.60	94	37.60	139	55.60
5	2.00	50	20.00	95	38.00	140	56.00
6	2.40	51	20.40	96	38.40	141	56.40
7	2.80	52	20.80	97	38.80	142	56.80
8	3.20	53	21.20	98	39.20	143	57.20
9	3.60	54	21.60	99	39.60	144	57.60
10	4.00	55	22.00	100	40.00	145	58.00
11	4.40	56	22.40	101	40.40	146	58.40
12	4.80	57	22.80	102	40.80	147	58.80
13	5.20	58	23.20	103	41.20	148	59.20
14	5.60	59	23.60	104	41.60	149	59.60
15	6.00	60	24.00	105	42.00	150	60.00
16	6.40	61	24.40	106	42.40	200	80.00
17	6.80	62	24.80	107	42.80	250	100.00
18	7.20	63	25.20	108	43.20	300	120.00
19	7.60	64	25.60	109	43.60	350	140.00
20	8.00	65	26.00	110	44.00	400	160.00
21	8.40	66	26.40	111	44.40	450	180.00
22	8.80	67	26.80	112	44.80	500	200.00
23	9.20	68	27.20	113	45.20	550	220.00
24	9.60	69	27.60	114	45.60	600	240.00
25	10.00	70	28.00	115	46.00	650	260.00
26	10.40	71	28.40	116	46.40	700	280.00
27	10.80	72	28.80	117	46.80	750	300.00
28	11.20	73	29.20	118	47.20	800	320.00
29	11.60	74	29.60	119	47.60	850	340.00
30	12.00	75	30.00	120	48.00	900	360.00
31	12.40	76	30.40	121	48.40	950	380.00
32	12.80	77	30.80	122	48.80	1,000	400.00
33	13.20	78	31.20	123	49.20	1,500	600.00
34	13.60	79	31.60	124	49.60	2,000	800.00
35	14.00	80	32.00	125	50.00	2,500	1,000.00
36	14.40	81	32.40	126	50.40	3,000	1,200.00
37	14.80	82	32.80	127	50.80	3,500	1,400.00
38	15.20	83	33.20	128	51.20	4,000	1,600.00
39	15.60	84	33.60	129	51.60	4,500	1,800.00
40	16.00	85	34.00	130	52.00	5,000	2,000.00
41	16.40	86	34.40	131	52.40	7,500	3,000.00
42	16.80	87	34.80	132	52.80	10,000	4,000.00
43	17.20	88	35.20	133	53.20	25,000	10,000.00
44	17.60	89	35.60	134	53.60	50,000	20,000.00
45	18.00	90	36.00	135	54.00	100,000	40,000.00

GROSSING-UP TABLES

At 20 per cent

1p to 99p (to the nearest whole penny)

Net £	Tax Credit £	Gross £	Net £	Tax Credit £	Gross £	Net £	Tax Credit £	Gross £
0.01	—	0.01	0.34	0.09	0.43	0.67	0.17	0.84
0.02	0.01	0.03	0.35	0.09	0.44	0.68	0.17	0.85
0.03	0.01	0.04	0.36	0.09	0.45	0.69	0.17	0.86
0.04	0.01	0.05	0.37	0.09	0.46	0.70	0.18	0.88
0.05	0.01	0.06	0.38	0.10	0.48	0.71	0.18	0.89
0.06	0.02	0.08	0.39	0.10	0.49	0.72	0.18	0.90
0.07	0.02	0.09	0.40	0.10	0.50	0.73	0.18	0.91
0.08	0.02	0.10	0.41	0.10	0.51	0.74	0.19	0.93
0.09	0.02	0.11	0.42	0.11	0.53	0.75	0.19	0.94
0.10	0.03	0.13	0.43	0.11	0.54	0.76	0.19	0.95
0.11	0.03	0.14	0.44	0.11	0.55	0.77	0.19	0.96
0.12	0.03	0.15	0.45	0.11	0.56	0.78	0.20	0.98
0.13	0.03	0.16	0.46	0.12	0.58	0.79	0.20	0.99
0.14	0.04	0.18	0.47	0.12	0.59	0.80	0.20	1.00
0.15	0.04	0.19	0.48	0.12	0.60	0.81	0.20	1.01
0.16	0.04	0.20	0.49	0.12	0.61	0.82	0.21	1.03
0.17	0.04	0.21	0.50	0.13	0.63	0.83	0.21	1.04
0.18	0.05	0.23	0.51	0.13	0.64	0.84	0.21	1.05
0.19	0.05	0.24	0.52	0.13	0.65	0.85	0.21	1.06
0.20	0.05	0.25	0.53	0.13	0.66	0.86	0.22	1.08
0.21	0.05	0.26	0.54	0.14	0.68	0.87	0.22	1.09
0.22	0.06	0.28	0.55	0.14	0.69	0.88	0.22	1.10
0.23	0.06	0.29	0.56	0.14	0.70	0.89	0.22	1.11
0.24	0.06	0.30	0.57	0.14	0.71	0.90	0.23	1.13
0.25	0.06	0.31	0.58	0.15	0.73	0.91	0.23	1.14
0.26	0.07	0.33	0.59	0.15	0.74	0.92	0.23	1.15
0.27	0.07	0.34	0.60	0.15	0.75	0.93	0.23	1.16
0.28	0.07	0.35	0.61	0.15	0.76	0.94	0.24	1.18
0.29	0.07	0.36	0.62	0.16	0.78	0.95	0.24	1.19
0.30	0.08	0.38	0.63	0.16	0.79	0.96	0.24	1.20
0.31	0.08	0.39	0.64	0.16	0.80	0.97	0.24	1.21
0.32	0.08	0.40	0.65	0.16	0.81	0.98	0.25	1.23
0.33	0.08	0.41	0.66	0.17	0.83	0.99	0.25	1.24

Net column shows the actual dividend received.

Tax credit column shows the amount of the tax credit calculated at the rate of one quarter.

Gross column shows the total income for tax purposes.

£1 to £5,000

Net	Tax Credit	Gross	Net	Tax Credit	Gross	Net	Tax Credit	Gross
£	£	£	£	£	£	£	£	£
1	0.25	1.25	34	8.50	42.50	130	32.50	162.50
2	0.50	2.50	35	8.75	43.75	140	35.00	175.00
3	0.75	3.75	36	9.00	45.00	150	37.50	187.50
4	1.00	5.00	37	9.25	46.25	160	40.00	200.00
5	1.25	6.25	38	9.50	47.50	170	42.50	212.50
6	1.50	7.50	39	9.75	48.75	180	45.00	225.00
7	1.75	8.75	40	10.00	50.00	190	47.50	237.50
8	2.00	10.00	41	10.25	51.25	200	50.00	250.00
9	2.25	11.25	42	10.50	52.50	210	52.50	262.50
10	2.50	12.50	43	10.75	53.75	220	55.00	275.00
11	2.75	13.75	44	11.00	55.00	230	57.50	287.50
12	3.00	15.00	45	11.25	56.25	240	60.00	300.00
13	3.25	16.25	46	11.50	57.50	250	62.50	312.50
14	3.50	17.50	47	11.75	58.75	260	65.00	325.00
15	3.75	18.75	48	12.00	60.00	270	67.50	337.50
16	4.00	20.00	49	12.25	61.25	280	70.00	350.00
17	4.25	21.25	50	12.50	62.50	290	72.50	362.50
18	4.50	22.50	51	12.75	63.75	300	75.00	375.00
19	4.75	23.75	52	13.00	65.00	350	87.50	437.50
20	5.00	25.00	53	13.25	66.25	400	100.00	500.00
21	5.25	26.25	54	13.50	67.50	450	112.50	562.50
22	5.50	27.50	55	13.75	68.75	500	125.00	625.00
23	5.75	28.75	60	15.00	75.00	550	137.50	687.50
24	6.00	30.00	65	16.25	81.25	600	150.00	750.00
25	6.25	31.25	70	17.50	87.50	650	162.50	812.50
26	6.50	32.50	75	18.75	93.75	700	175.00	875.00
27	6.75	33.75	80	20.00	100.00	750	187.50	937.50
28	7.00	35.00	85	21.25	106.25	800	200.00	1,000.00
29	7.25	36.25	90	22.50	112.50	850	212.50	1,062.50
30	7.50	37.50	95	23.75	118.75	900	225.00	1,125.00
31	7.75	38.75	100	25.00	125.00	950	257.50	1,187.50
32	8.00	40.00	110	27.50	137.50	1,000	250.00	1,250.00
33	8.25	41.25	120	30.00	150.00	5,000	1,250.00	6,250.00

GROSSING-UP TABLES

at 25 per cent

1p to 99p (to the nearest whole penny)

Net	Tax	Gross	Net	Tax	Gross	Net	Tax	Gross
£	£	£	£	£	£	£	£	£
0.01	—	0.01	0.34	0.11	0.45	0.67	0.22	0.89
0.02	0.01	0.03	0.35	0.12	0.47	0.68	0.23	0.91
0.03	0.01	0.04	0.36	0.12	0.48	0.69	0.23	0.92
0.04	0.01	0.05	0.37	0.12	0.49	0.70	0.23	0.93
0.05	0.02	0.07	0.38	0.13	0.51	0.71	0.24	0.95
0.06	0.02	0.08	0.39	0.13	0.52	0.72	0.24	0.96
0.07	0.02	0.09	0.40	0.13	0.53	0.73	0.24	0.97
0.08	0.03	0.11	0.41	0.14	0.55	0.74	0.25	0.99
0.09	0.03	0.12	0.42	0.14	0.56	0.75	0.25	1.00
0.10	0.03	0.13	0.43	0.14	0.57	0.76	0.25	1.01
0.11	0.04	0.15	0.44	0.15	0.59	0.77	0.26	1.03
0.12	0.04	0.16	0.45	0.15	0.60	0.78	0.26	1.04
0.13	0.04	0.17	0.46	0.15	0.61	0.79	0.26	1.05
0.14	0.05	0.19	0.47	0.16	0.63	0.80	0.27	1.07
0.15	0.05	0.20	0.48	0.16	0.64	0.81	0.27	1.08
0.16	0.05	0.21	0.49	0.16	0.65	0.82	0.27	1.09
0.17	0.06	0.23	0.50	0.17	0.67	0.83	0.28	1.11
0.18	0.06	0.24	0.51	0.17	0.68	0.84	0.28	1.12
0.19	0.06	0.25	0.52	0.17	0.69	0.85	0.28	1.13
0.20	0.07	0.27	0.53	0.18	0.71	0.86	0.29	1.15
0.21	0.07	0.28	0.54	0.18	0.72	0.87	0.29	1.16
0.22	0.07	0.29	0.55	0.18	0.73	0.88	0.29	1.17
0.23	0.08	0.31	0.56	0.19	0.75	0.89	0.30	1.19
0.24	0.08	0.32	0.57	0.19	0.76	0.90	0.30	1.20
0.25	0.08	0.33	0.58	0.19	0.77	0.91	0.30	1.21
0.26	0.09	0.35	0.59	0.20	0.79	0.92	0.31	1.23
0.27	0.09	0.36	0.60	0.20	0.80	0.93	0.31	1.24
0.28	0.09	0.37	0.61	0.20	0.81	0.94	0.31	1.25
0.29	0.10	0.39	0.62	0.21	0.83	0.95	0.32	1.27
0.30	0.10	0.40	0.63	0.21	0.84	0.96	0.32	1.28
0.31	0.10	0.41	0.64	0.21	0.85	0.97	0.32	1.29
0.32	0.11	0.43	0.65	0.22	0.87	0.98	0.33	1.31
0.33	0.11	0.44	0.66	0.22	0.88	0.99	0.33	1.32

Net column shows the actual income received less tax.

Tax column shows the amount of the tax deducted from income.

Gross column shows the total income for tax purposes.

£1 to £5,000

Net £	Tax £	Gross £	Net £	Tax £	Gross £	Net £	Tax £	Gross £
1	0.33	1.33	34	11.33	45.33	130	43.33	173.33
2	0.67	2.67	35	11.67	46.67	140	46.67	186.67
3	1.00	4.00	36	12.00	48.00	150	50.00	200.00
4	1.33	5.33	37	12.33	49.33	160	53.33	213.33
5	1.67	6.67	38	12.67	50.67	170	53.67	226.67
6	2.00	8.00	39	13.00	52.00	180	60.00	240.00
7	2.33	9.33	40	13.33	53.33	190	63.33	253.33
8	2.67	10.67	41	13.67	54.67	200	66.67	266.67
9	3.00	12.00	42	14.00	56.00	210	70.00	280.00
10	3.33	13.33	43	14.33	57.33	220	73.33	293.33
11	3.67	14.67	44	14.67	58.67	230	76.67	306.67
12	4.00	16.00	45	15.00	60.00	240	80.00	320.00
13	4.33	17.33	46	15.33	61.33	250	83.33	333.33
14	4.67	18.67	47	15.67	62.67	260	86.67	346.67
15	5.00	20.00	48	16.00	64.00	270	90.00	360.00
16	5.33	21.33	49	16.33	65.33	280	93.33	373.33
17	5.67	22.67	50	16.67	66.67	290	96.67	386.67
18	6.00	24.00	51	17.00	68.00	300	100.00	400.00
19	6.33	25.33	52	17.33	69.33	350	116.67	466.67
20	6.67	26.67	53	17.67	70.67	400	133.33	533.33
21	7.00	28.00	54	18.00	72.00	450	150.00	600.00
22	7.33	29.33	55	18.33	73.33	500	166.67	666.67
23	7.67	30.67	60	20.00	80.00	550	183.33	733.33
24	8.00	32.00	65	21.67	86.67	600	200.00	800.00
25	8.33	33.33	70	23.33	93.33	650	216.67	866.67
26	8.67	34.67	75	25.00	100.00	700	233.33	933.33
27	9.00	36.00	80	26.67	106.67	750	250.00	1,000.00
28	9.33	37.33	85	28.33	113.33	800	266.67	1,066.67
29	9.67	38.67	90	30.00	120.00	850	283.33	1,133.33
30	10.00	40.00	95	31.67	126.67	900	300.00	1,200.00
31	10.33	41.33	100	33.33	133.33	950	316.67	1,266.67
32	10.67	42.67	110	36.67	146.67	1,000	333.33	1,333.33
33	11.00	44.00	120	40.00	160.00	5,000	1,666.67	6,666.67

Note: These grossing-up tables do not apply to dividends received as a tax credit of one-quarter must be used (see separate table). They do, however, apply where tax at the basic rate is appropriate on other income.

Index